WARTIME IMAGES, PEACETIME WOUNDS
THE MEDIA AND THE GUSTAFSEN LAKE STANDOFF

What does the media coverage of a crisis situation reveal about the nature of relationships between dominant and minority groups at the local, regional, and national level? In *Wartime Images, Peacetime Wounds*, Sandra Lambertus asks this question of the media coverage of the largest RCMP operation in Canadian history – the 1995 Gustafsen Lake standoff.

Drawing from extensive newspaper, television, and radio news coverage, legal and law enforcement documents, and ethnographic interviews with journalists, RCMP officers, and Native leaders, Lambertus examines the construction and dissemination of vilifying stereotyped portrayals of Native people. Employing a variety of methodologies including discourse analysis, the investigation shows how the values and perspectives of local communities, media, and law enforcement became overshadowed by those of 'outsiders' during the course of the event. The study culminates with an assessment of the structural elements that contributed to the damaging media portrayals. Provocative and convincingly argued, *Wartime Images, Peacetime Wounds* opens new avenues for the study of the representation of minorities in the news and for the study of news media in general.

SANDRA LAMBERTUS teaches Anthropology at Grant MacEwan College.

Sandra Lambertus

Wartime Images, Peacetime Wounds

The Media and the Gustafsen Lake Standoff

UNIVERSITY OF TORONTO PRESS
Toronto Buffalo London

© University of Toronto Press Incorporated 2004
Toronto Buffalo London
Printed in Canada

ISBN 0-8020-8745-0 (cloth)
ISBN 0-8020-8551-2 (paper)

Printed on acid-free paper

National Library of Canada Cataloguing in Publication

Lambertus, Sandra
  Wartime images, peacetime wounds : the media and the
  Gustafsen Lake standoff / Sandra Lambertus.

  Includes bibliographical references and index.
  ISBN 0-8020-8745-0 (bound).   ISBN 0-8020-8551-2 (pbk.)

  1. Gustafsen Lake Standoff, B.C., 1995 – Press coverage.   2. Shuswap
  Indians – Press coverage.   3. Native peoples in mass media.   4. Law
  enforcement – British Columbia.   5. Royal Canadian Mounted Police.   I. Title.

  E92.L33 2003   302.23′089′979071175   C2003-902981-6

This book has been published with the help of a grant from the Humanities
and Social Sciences Federation of Canada, using funds provided by the
Social Sciences and Humanities Research Council of Canada.

University of Toronto Press acknowledges the financial assistance to its
publishing program of the Canada Council for the Arts and the Ontario
Arts Council.

University of Toronto Press acknowledges the financial support for its
publishing activities of the Government of Canada through the Book
Publishing Industry Development Program (BPIDP).

All photographs appearing in this book are reproduced with the permission
of *100 Mile House Free Press*.

Contents

viii   Contents

Tables

Preface

Ever since I heard my professor in an undergraduate race and racism class explain that systemic discrimination of minorities is too difficult for anyone to research because it is so embedded within institutions, the seed was planted for me to prove otherwise. If academics believed that such research was impossible, or (as I suspected) too contentious to risk, institutions would continue their practices indefinitely, the status quo would prevail, and a vast amount of knowledge about the interplay between institutions and minorities would remain hidden. Everyone talks about how wrong institutional discrimination of minorities is, but what can anyone do? I believed then, as I do now, that such research is *essential* for the advancement of pluralist democratic societies.

As a researcher and an educator, I found evidence of systemic discrimination at a variety of institutions. At a co-educational prison that offered life-skills and training programs to inmates, the women complained to me that, in contrast to the men, they were seldom allowed to take these programs. Most of the male inmates regarded the women with disdain; the women were more violent, and their numerous infractions prompted the administration to regularly suspend all inmate privileges. The inmates and the administrators did not comprehend that the intake procedures and prison mandates for labour needs steered disproportionate numbers of women away from educational programs. At a hospital, immigrant staff in the housekeeping and sterilization departments felt disconnected from other hospital employees. They did not read (and certainly did not contribute to) the staff's newsletters because the language level was pitched too high. This, in turn, explained their absence at social gatherings that were advertised in the newsletters. Administration had not noticed the lack of representation of immigrant staff in social contexts that promote collegiality and team building, confirming the degree to which they had indeed become invisible in the hospital. At a middle-class elementary school, several grade-five students repeatedly teased a classmate from Tahiti during recesses, calling him a 'burnt sausage.' Despite the young boy's complaints, the teacher, who did not critically interpret that the name-calling was, in effect, a racial taunt, said nothing to her students – they were just being kids. In all of these cases, the 'victims' knew that something was wrong. However, the people in leadership roles did not fully understand the consequences of their decisions on the functioning of their operations or the dynamics of the social relationships within. In the big picture, they had no idea that they were inadvertently promoting systemic mechanisms that reinforce inequalities and a social hierarchy. Awareness is the first step towards change.

This case study of the 1995 Gustafsen Lake standoff is the culmination of four years of research, and three years of writing and publishing. It is first and foremost an anthropological research that raises questions about the fundamental relationships between media and law enforcement institutions in a pluralist democratic society. I consider anthropology the most suitable approach for this investigation and the most compatible with my own eclectic academic background and personal interests. Anthropology is the most broadly based and interdisciplinary of the social sciences. It examines the human condition from the lived experience, and seeks out patterns of learned human behaviour and social interactions by incorporating a wide range of systematic analytical methods. As a tool for policy studies, anthropology can get to root causes with greater ease than other disciplines; in so doing, it can contribute to the knowledge base of several of them.

My introduction to the Gustafsen Lake standoff was from the perspective of the media audience. I was immediately struck by the volatility of the situation, the drama of the media coverage, and the potential for the conflict to converge with that summer's standoff at Ipperwash, Ontario, as well as smaller pockets of Native protests throughout the country. During the early part of the research, when I was going through the news stories across Canada, I was amazed at the audience reach of Canadian Press's near-identical reports. Overall, I found little variation in the news accounts, even from newspapers in British Columbia that sent their own reporters to cover the conflict. There were no 'other sides to the story' until the trial, nearly a year later. My interviews with the news media and their sources took me to newspaper newsrooms, television and radio stations, police headquarters, a trial, a cattle ranch, Native communities, and numerous coffee shops throughout British Columbia. The patterns that emerged pointed to the extent that systemic factors contributed to damaging media characterizations. Without extensive interviews, the adverse effects on people beyond the Gustafsen Lake defendants would not have been apparent. In my final analysis, the coverage *was* damaging to the relations between Native and non-Native people *and* to Canadian society in general. I think that it is an important story with many lessons.

I have written this book to contribute to the historic record, to model innovative ways to research media characterizations of Native people and other minorities, and to be an instrument of social change. My intention is that this research will inspire others to conduct more studies of institutions and race relations. In the wake of increasing intolerance of minorities since the 11 September 2001 attacks, they are needed more than ever.

Acknowledgments

Several people in the media, the RCMP, Native communities, and at 100 Mile House made significant contributions to this research. I am indebted to the journalists who took time from their hectic work schedules at the *Vancouver Sun*, *Vancouver Province*, *Victoria Times Colonist*, the *Globe and Mail*, Canadian Press, Broadcast News, CKNW Radio, CBC Radio, Cariboo Radio, CBC Television, BCTV, and CTV. Special thanks to George Garrett, now retired from CKNW Radio in Vancouver, for his participation in the research and for reading parts of this work. I want to acknowledge especially Steven Frasher, former editor of the *100 Mile House Free Press*, for his participation in the research, hospitality during my fieldwork at 100 Mile House, and comments on earlier drafts.

I am appreciative of the cooperation and information provided by the RCMP for this research, specifically former District Superintendent Len Olfert, Staff Sergeant Peter Montague, Dr Mike Webster, and Staff Sergeant Martin Sarich.

Many thanks to Chief Antoine Archie, who generously provided essential background information on the events leading up to and during the standoff, and for his feedback on excerpts of this work. I would also like to thank Chief Nathan Matthew, Lyle and Mary James, John Hill, William Lightbown, George Wool, Paul Corns, as well as the local citizens from 100 Mile House for their contributions.

Several people and institutions helped me to gather a vast data collection. Thanks to the Edmonton Public Library for the boxes and boxes of newspapers! In addition, I am appreciative of the generosity of the *Vancouver Sun*, *Victoria Times Colonist*, and CBC for copyright permission for assorted media materials. I owe a special thanks to individuals at 100 Mile House for their assistance in providing other materials: Heather Colpitts, editor, and Chris Nickless, publisher, of the *100 Mile House Free Press*, for copyright permission for newspaper photographs; Peter Lunn, from Lunn Enterprises for copyright permission for the regional and town maps; Nigel Hemingway, from Kidston and Hemingway, for supplying me with survey maps of Gustafsen Lake; and Allan Forcier, from the British Columbia Ministry of Forests, for a forest cover map of Gustafsen Lake.

I sincerely thank several mentors from my doctoral program: Michael Asch, Rod Wilson, Carl Urion, Tony Fisher, Anne Marie Decore, and the late Bruce Bain. Their respective scholarship in anthropology, sociolinguistics, sociology, and cognitive psychology influenced my approach to this study. In addition, I appreciate the encouragement and support that I received from Gurston Dacks, from the Department of Political Science at the University of Alberta, and Catherine Murray, from the School of Communications at Simon Fraser University. Doctoral Fellowship 752-98-1227 from the Social Sciences and Humanities Research Council of Canada assisted in the funding of the research on which this book is based. I received additional funding from a Province of Alberta Graduate Fellowship, as well as a two-year University of Alberta PhD Scholarship.

I have benefited from comments made on this research by colleagues who heard my paper presentations in 1996 at the Sociolinguistics Symposium 11, University of Wales, at Cardiff; in 1999 at the Annual Meeting of the American Anthropological Association, Chicago, Illinois; also in 1999 at the 25th Congress of the Canadian Anthropological Society / Société canadienne d'anthropologie, at Université Laval, Quebec City, Quebec; and in 2000 at the 26th Congress of the Canadian Anthropological Society / Société canadienne d'anthropologie, University of Calgary, Calgary, Alberta.

My warm appreciation goes to Dianne Smyth, whose editing skills helped me to transform the dissertation into a book and whose enthusiasm for this project was unwavering.

I want to thank Virgil Duff, executive editor of University of Toronto Press, Catherine Frost for the final edits, and the University of Toronto Press Manuscript Review Committee for supporting the publication of this book.

I could not have completed the research or the book without the patience and humour of my husband Marc and our daughters Shannon and Heather, who begged me to finish this project, wash off the newspaper ink, and finally get a life.

Prologue

The following is a vignette taken from the recollections of one journalist who covered several Native blockades in British Columbia. This particular narrative concerned the Douglas Lake blockade, which occurred a few months before the Gustafsen Lake standoff.

There was an incident up in Douglas Lake ... So, we get up to Douglas Lake ... and all the media was lined up on the road outside the church – And of course, where the Natives had blocked this road. And – it was kind of the D-day before the potential riot the next morning, where the RCMP were going to go in and clear the area. And so we attempted to talk to their chief, and they said, 'In good time, [Chief] Scotty Holmes will come out – Scotty Holmes will come out and talk to you.' In the meantime, all the rest of the media had left – gone back to Merritt – it was 'Miller time' – it was time for a beer ...

And [our crew] stayed on the road there for about two and one-half hours – played cards, and just stayed there. And sure enough, the chief came out, and walked out to the road with a small group of warriors, as they called themselves. We talked and explained to him our concerns about what could happen tomorrow – and no record of it. He – the chief said – 'we've got our own people here with cameras,' but [a colleague] indicated to him that – 'a professional, independent [witness] – if history was going to happen, or change to take place, that this was a recognized, public witness' ... So he said, 'Wait.' And we waited another two hours on this road, and he came back out. It was about midnight, and he said that he believed that we were sincere and honest and that we'd showed good patience, which they liked. And that if we came back at two in the morning, we would be welcomed past the line, and to park by the tent, the big teepee ...

[The crew] was allowed access under three conditions – that we didn't take pictures of a Native if he asked us not to – didn't interview any Natives (they

could certainly talk to us, but only go to the spokespeople) – and if asked to leave, we would respect that and leave ... 'So, we went back – raced back to Merritt about 30 minutes away, to get some food. We went into the pub to drop off some walkie-talkies, and didn't tell our other crew what was happening. Because what was happening the next morning was, the media was going in on the bus – with the RCMP in the media tour. Well, we knew that they were going to be twenty miles away. If any shot rang out – nobody would hear it. We know that. And then once again, it would be our word against theirs – the RCMP against the Natives, and of course they'd fly over a helicopter and tell us what happened ... So, we drove back out again. The Natives searched our vehicle and we went back in. But the next morning, [Sgt] Montague showed up. Adamant – [questioning] what we were doing across the line, through the line, by the teepee and [he] ordered us out. And we looked at each other and said 'ahh ...' He ordered us out because the other stations couldn't get in.'

The journalist described how some of the Aboriginal people had been at other blockades, and he recognized them. A few removed their bandannas from their faces to talk to the journalist, whom they now recognized from the night before.

The one thing that got the blockade down was a meeting face to face with the federal minister and the provincial minister. And it happened in the church. It was all fenced off and no media were allowed in. And we were all like cattle on the outside of this fence looking in. And Chief Scotty Holmes said [to me], 'Please, come.' And he said, 'You must come for the blessing, and then you can come and go.' And he said to the warriors that 'he can come and go' and [the other media outlets were] stuck outside this fence – and I came in. And we did the eagle feather and the ashes and cleansed ourselves. And he said to keep respect when an elder speaks, that the time to interrupt is when she or he is finished – not in the middle. And they realized that having me there – while the ministers spoke – was a bit of insurance. And both ministers and the minister's aide asked if I was supposed to be there. And the chief said, 'Concern yourselves with the elders – not with him.' And they [the minister and the minister's aide] weren't happy I was there. They were very unhappy that I was there.

Why do you think they were unhappy? *Well, my opinion is that they could say, 'We smoothed everything over with the Natives,' and the Natives could say, 'Hey, but nothing happens, and we're not getting any better,' and I was an intermediary ... I mean, I was a bit of insurance. Now, if what you were going to say in these meetings – this politician was going to say was – 'I promise you better roads' and I'm not pressuring the politician to say that – but if he says that,* *he's more apt to keep his word 'cause he's on camera. And I know – because they* [the minister and the assistant] *drew the attention to me right away, that they said, 'There's no media allowed in here.' And the chief said, 'But he's a guest of ours.' And the chief stood up and ... it took probably an hour to bless everybody – everybody was blessed ... And there was no bullshit. There was no bullshit. Because the politicians had nowhere to go. And I remember they interrupted a couple of the other Natives a couple of times. And the chief got up and ordered them to listen to the elder – her seventy years on this land has got to account to more than some months in the legislature in Victoria. And so, that night I was the only one ... that got any clips, the only one that got anything – everybody else had to wait for the scrums after. And it didn't fare well. It didn't fare well with the competition. Anyways, so Douglas Lake was huge for* [our crew]. *And it was honest.* (Interview with journalist)

The above narrative makes it evident that all of the players – media, police, government officials, and Native leaders – had varying degrees of power and ability to negotiate and compete for control over the definition of the situation. The narrative supports the contention that, generally, the police and the government have the most power over the media to control access and hence the characterization of the situation. On this particular occasion, the Native leaders and the media crew with whom they aligned successfully challenged this typical outcome. By asserting their support for the presence of a mainstream media outlet, the Native leaders were now in a strategic position to correct their disadvantage. This account demonstrates that the negotiations between media and their sources are not necessarily predictable, and it challenges the simplistic stereotype perceptions of how the media cover Native protests.

The Douglas Lake vignette also provides a perspective of an event that seldom, if ever, becomes part of the news. This is because revelations of the underlying dimensions of media competition and the negotiation of information between media and their sources would situate the journalists as part of the news story and hence break with journalistic conventions. At the same time, these details would have provided vital insights about the people and the event as they were portrayed by the news media. Public awareness of such details could have contributed to the debate about the relationships of Native people with the police and the media, and ultimately about their place in Canadian society.

The Douglas Lake blockade is not entirely representative of the circumstances at the Gustafsen Lake standoff. At Gustafsen Lake, the people in the camp were heavily armed and had a more direct and complex set of relations with the media. However, the RCMP's attempts to limit media access, the competition between journalists, and the media's omission of news-gathering contexts in the Douglas Lake blockade coverage foreshadow what transpired during the Gustafsen Lake standoff.

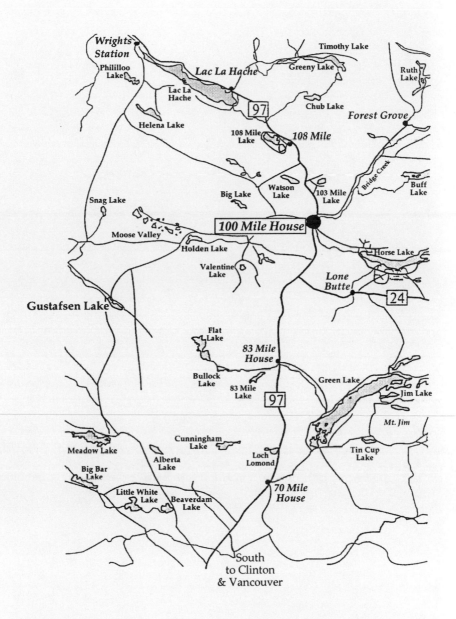

Map of Gustafsen Lake, British Columbia, and Surrounding Area
(Courtesy of Lunn Enterprises, 100 Mile House)

WARTIME IMAGES, PEACETIME WOUNDS: THE MEDIA AND THE GUSTAFSEN LAKE STANDOFF

Introduction

The 1995 Gustafsen Lake standoff was the largest and most expensive Royal Canadian Mounted Police (RCMP) operation in Canadian history. The standoff involved Natives and non-Native supporters camped on a small parcel of ranch land, which they defended as unceded Aboriginal territory. They refused to leave the location, and the RCMP were called in to assist in mediation. After a series of shooting incidents and a seizure of weapons associated with the camp, however, the RCMP declared the situation a criminal investigation. Over the next month, more than 400 RCMP from across Canada were called in, and with them came a large contingent of media. There were more incidents of violence between members of the camp and the police, and two individuals sustained injuries.[1] At the conclusion of the standoff, the RCMP arrested and charged 18 individuals with various offences, ranging from attempted murder to mischief. During the pre-trial phase of the court case, the lawyers for the defendants submitted to the court that the RCMP had jeopardized a fair trial because of the pre-trial media coverage.[2] Evidence from media products, statements by witnesses for the defence, and testimony from the RCMP media liaison supported this allegation. The senior defence lawyer identified one journalist as contributing to a police strategy that allegedly transgressed journalistic ethics. The media reported some of the trial revelations concerning the media coverage of the Gustafsen Lake standoff. However, most of the circumstances of the news event were never brought to light.

This book is about the media coverage of the Gustafsen Lake standoff. It is, more profoundly, a story of manipulation of media. As it turns out, it is also about the underlying relations between Canadian Aboriginal peoples, the media, and the RCMP, which emerged during a serious conflict. Because of the shortcomings in the news coverage at the time, this book provides a historical record of the standoff. This case study asks, how *did* the media characterize the 1995 Gustafsen Lake standoff, and what contextual factors underpinned the media coverage? A subsidiary question is, how did the media characterizations affect the principal players,[3] audiences involved in the standoff, and, ultimately, Canadian society?

Media images at the time of the Gustafsen Lake standoff were similar to those found during war. Screaming headlines announced violent clashes. News photographs and videos captured angry-looking protesters in camouflage clothing, their faces hidden by bandannas. Grim-looking Emergency Response Team (ERT) personnel in flak-jackets were shown carrying high-powered weapons. The most striking image was of a convoy of armoured personnel carriers barrelling down a dusty forestry road at dawn. The news stories alluded to frequent helicopter patrols, reminiscent of the Vietnam War, and constant references were made to the presence of AK–47 automatic weapons in the camp. Stories of police searches of civilians and their vehicles and police blockades to prevent public access to the region reinforced the seriousness and tension of the time. There was a profusion of labelling from various sides to vilify the people in the camp, the police, and the government. Specific incidents in the news stories cast the participants in the event as war enemies and war heroes.

Early in the standoff, the *Vancouver Sun* news stories began openly challenging the police perspective of the event. There was greater contextual information about the dynamics between the police and the media and the interactions between police and various sources. The *Sun* printed a story describing a closed-door meeting with the journalists in which the RCMP media liaison criticized them. In a few of the news stories the writers explained the lack of journalistic witnessing after the first week of the standoff was because the RCMP was denying journalists access to the camp. The *Vancouver Sun* also included information not found in the other sample newspapers – on one occasion, a heated conversation between the people in the camp and the RCMP.

The Media, Law Enforcement, and Aboriginal Peoples

The media are central in defining the position of Canada's Aboriginal peoples in the social hierarchy and in disseminating stereotypes of this group to the Canadian public. The issue of media representation is a topic examined in the 1996 *Report of the Royal Commission on Aboriginal*

Peoples (RCAP), which, ironically, was convening during the Gustafsen Lake standoff. In the report the commissioners discuss the harm done by negative media representation through stereotyping Aboriginal people across Canada. They identify the proclivity of the media to create images of Native people that invoke fear and hostility among the public during serious disputes over land and resources. They assert that such displays distract from the actual issues of Aboriginal disputes and contribute to misperceptions about Native peoples (vol 3: 623). The Canadian Association of Journalists is quoted in the document, admitting that the mainstream media's representation of Natives 'often contains misinformation, sweeping generalizations, and galling stereotypes about natives and native affairs' (vol 3: 634). How do these assessments compare with the media characterizations of the Gustafsen Lake standoff?

Law enforcers, largely because of intense public and media scrutiny of their relations with Aboriginal peoples over the past few years, have also examined their policies and practices. Policy studies and reports for the RCMP regarding their dealings with Aboriginal peoples have been conducted in house, the most recent being the 2000 RCMP *Aboriginal Policing Review Final Report*. It is suggested in the report that, in order to improve service delivery at the community level, the RCMP need to enhance the 'quality of communication at the interpersonal and organizational level.' One means of accomplishing this is for the RCMP to work more collaboratively with Aboriginal communities; officers also need to become more informed about Aboriginal cultures, customs, and traditions. A further suggestion is that officers 'make an effort to know the people and not just the criminals who tend to occupy police time and resources' (iii). Can the experience of the Gustafsen Lake standoff offer other insights towards improving relations between law enforcers and Aboriginal peoples?

History of Aboriginal Disputes in Canada

It is helpful to understand the Gustafsen Lake standoff within the wider historical context of Aboriginal disputes in Canada. This is provided in appendix 3, History of Aboriginal Disputes in Canada.

The British Columbia Context

Between the time of the British Royal Proclamation in 1763 and the year 1921 government authorities and Aboriginal leaders negotiated several treaties in various parts of Canada. In British Columbia, however, treaties did not evolve in the same manner, which helps to explain why treaty settlements in the province have become so contentious in this era. A few treaties had been finalized for Vancouver Island between 1850 and 1854, at about the time that Europeans began settling in the province. On the mainland, Chief Factor of the Hudson's Bay Company James Douglas established a system of allocating meagre reserve acreages to Native communities in order to accommodate the influx of European settlers and their need for land. Yet, as individuals, Indians could acquire an even larger portion of homesteading land by formally relinquishing their ties to their traditional communities. In doing so, they could adopt livelihoods similar to those of European settlers on Vancouver Island and the mainland. Few Native people, however, took advantage of this opportunity (Tennant 1990:34–6).

There was a prevalent notion that Indians should be assimilated – be taught white ways – and live in urban areas. They were encouraged to leave the reserve and were advised that if they relinquished Aboriginal title, they would be rewarded with increased social status and political rights. There was no incentive to establish treaties (as provided in the Royal Proclamation of 1763). Under Chief Commissioner of Lands and Works Joseph Trutch, the size of the reserves was reduced when the reserves were surveyed for homesteading. A catastrophic smallpox epidemic that wiped out one-third of the Aboriginal population was yet another circumstance that justified the reductions.

At Confederation, the British North America Act gave the federal government responsibility for Indians and land reserved for Indians. Yet, when British Columbia joined Confederation in 1871, Ottawa had no authority to compel the province to acknowledge Indian title or to exceed the 10-acre per family formula (Tennant 1990:44).

Despite overtures from the federal government to British Columbia to clear title through treaty-making, little substantive progress was made. Other than Treaty 8 in the northeastern corner of British Columbia and the Douglas Treaties in the 1850s, there have been no agreements with the Indians of British Columbia to extinguish Aboriginal title.

Some Native communities in British Columbia became active in their response to the stalemate between the provincial and federal governments. In 1874 the Coast Salish protested, asking for 80 acres per family. Their attempts at reform were rebuffed. Between 1880 and 1899 Indians in British Columbia developed greater political awareness, making specific demands for Aboriginal title, treaties, and self-government. They mounted protests to call attention to their case. By 1886 overtures by British Columbia Native leaders were rejected in Ottawa. In 1887 a blockade was staged at Fort St John, where the Native community demanded a treaty. In the same year, Treaty 8 was extended from Alberta into British Columbia, which challenged the notion that Aboriginal title would not be recognized in the province. After 1927 Aboriginal political activity went underground in the interior of British Columbia, and the outlawing of land claims was quietly accepted (Tennant 1990:82). In 1958 the Native Brotherhood was formed and activism resurfaced. However, over the next 10 years this movement was unable to achieve solidarity among the various Native communities. The impetus for solidarity came from Native responses to the federal government's *White Paper on Indian Policy* (1969). The Aboriginal peoples' common rejection of the White Paper prompted them to create new organizations in British Columbia (as well as in other provinces) for the purpose of advocating reform. The Supreme Court's split decision regarding the 1973 Nisga'a case (discussed in greater detail in appendix 3) created openings for Native groups to push for a Supreme Court acknowledgment of pre-existing Aboriginal title. It also provided the impetus for development of the British Columbia treaty process. In addition, the Nisga'a ruling revitalized Native protests in the province.

Native communities in British Columbia have been using blockades to express discontent since the 1870s. A century later, blockades remain a frequently used political tool to draw attention to their frustrations over land allocation and resource extraction (Blomley 1996:10). Responses by Natives to the glacier-paced resolution of land and resource issues took two forms, which were not mutually exclusive. One approach was to seek mediation through legal and political processes. By the mid-1980s the majority of British Columbia Native communities had submitted formal statements of land claim to the federal government, in spite of the insistence of the provincial government that Aboriginal title did not exist. The second response, often taken by either those groups frustrated by the treaty process or those who declined this option, was to protest with a blockade. Over the past 15 years, blockades have been more prevalent in British Columbia than in any other province in Canada. The provincial government's refusal to recognize Aboriginal title, combined with the pressures of increasing resource extraction, resulted in renewed commitments by disgruntled Native communities to stage blockades, such as those at Lyell Island and Clayoquot Sound (Blomley 1996:9). In the summer of 1990 the most extensive round of protests took place, involving 20 different Native groups. In contrast to previous occasions, in 1990 these blockades involved shutting down public transportation routes on major roads and rail lines. Duffey Lake was the most protracted instance, lasting from July to November. Duffey Lake sparked counter-blockades by non-Natives (Blomley 1996:9).

Although many blockades were associated with the 1990 Oka standoff in Quebec, Nicholas Blomley considers that each one was rooted in local factors (1996:9–10). The tension of Native disputes in British Columbia seemed to abate with the 1991 election of the New Democratic Party (NDP) provincial government and the subsequent acknowledgment of Aboriginal title. The treaty process was supported by the majority of Native communities, and consequently blockades decreased in frequency, 'but the furore around them has not' (1996:10–11). In 1995 Native communities that refused to participate in the treaty process mounted several blockades, including those at Douglas Lake Ranch and at Adams Lake. Dissenting groups discounted the treaty process as a sell-out of Native sovereignty and as a strategy to stall resolution while valuable resources were being extracted. These groups also contended that some of the Native leaders who promoted the treaty process did not have the mandate from their communities to do so.

Over this past decade, the economic instability in the province and the mounting frustration of Aboriginal people over stalled land negotiations have been punctuated by an increase in the number of protests and blockades. Non-Native groups, outraged by the inconvenience, have sprung up in response. Members of one such group, One Right for All, regard any treaty settlement as an affront to democracy because they perceive it as a concession that privileges Native communities. Conversely, many Native people in British Columbia have strong feelings about their traditional rights to the land, and they are supported by legal precedents and settlements in other parts of Canada. Along with a general lack of awareness of the historical background of the treaty situation (Tennant 1990), this issue remains highly contentious, years after the Gustafsen Lake standoff. Most British Columbians have a stake in the resolution of issues of title and resource allocation. In the event that all Native communities in British Columbia are reimbursed and allocated property, non-Native citizens will relinquish provincial revenue sources and opportunities for private resource development.

The 1995 Gustafsen Lake standoff did not bring calm to the province. Indeed, Aboriginal communities continue to use blockades as a demonstration of political will during land and resource disputes in British

Columbia, as well as in almost every province in the country. Politicians and Native leaders in British Columbia and in other parts of Canada have expressed concern that the serious nature of some of the conflicts could easily escalate to the scale of the 1990 Oka crisis.

Media Representation of Aboriginal Peoples

In the literature regarding media representation of minorities, several issues resonate with Canadian Aboriginal peoples who become involved in serious conflicts that are in the news. Most media researchers concur that news stories about minorities are a major source of stereotyping. Daniel Parenti asserts that the press has the power to repeat untruths over and over again until the concepts become absorbed into the consciousness of the audience (1993:193–4). T.A. van Dijk suggests that we base our knowledge about ethnic groups and racial minorities largely on what we see, read, and hear from the news media. He considers that the everyday lives of ethnic minorities are unknown in mainstream society, but when they do become newsworthy, ethnic minorities are portrayed in stereotyped themes. Van Dijk dichotomizes the themes as passive roles (as society's dependants) or as active roles (as society's enemies) (1987:235). Both themes carry a negative social connotation. The press is a particularly compelling source when there are no personal experiences of relationships with members of minorities. In the media, minority voices are most often represented (if they are represented at all) as the model for the entire group. While this tendency has the potential to create positive as well as negative stereotypes, neither possibility acknowledges the complexity of the composition of any group. Events involving racial minorities in particular are reported through 'white eyes,' which is the primary reason for the alienation and distrust of news outlets by minority citizens (Wilson and Gutierrez 1985; van Dijk 1987).

The media may inadvertently rely on and perpetuate stereotypes without any regard for the impact of such portrayals on the larger group. This is especially the case when they are casting individual members of racial minorities who gain notoriety. Jack Lule's (1997) evaluation of the newspaper coverage of the 1992 rape trial of former heavyweight boxing champion Mike Tyson finds the portrayal of Tyson 'ugly and flawed by its reliance upon racist imagery' (1997:377). He acknowledges that Mike Tyson's attitudes and behaviours towards women were offensive, but he also contends that the media character-

izations abandoned restraint, casting Tyson as a powerful, dichoto-
mized, symbolic type. For Lule, journalism that produces such thematic
portrayals of an individual member of a racial minority has no control
over the ensuing process of stereotyping of the whole group. He calls
for the confrontation of racism in society and journalism through the
examination of the language and images in the press.

The media also have a track record of promoting a deficit or *threatening image* of minorities to mainstream society. According to Clint Wilson
and Felix Gutierrez, 'minority coverage in mainstream news reporting
provides insight into the status of minorities' (1985:134). Exclusion and
misrepresentation of racial minorities foster an *us against them* syn-
drome in the mainstream (1985:139–41). Wilson and Gutierrez explain
that when a minority group offers resistance to hegemonic forces, the
media characterize the actions of the minority as a threat and bring this
to society's attention. Then the media proceed to cover society's response, which is often violent in nature (135–6). One of the primary
ways to legitimize violence in response to minority resistance is to
criminalize minority behaviour without examining the history and the
context of the issues from the minority perspective.

The media have a tendency to agitate rather than conciliate when
there is a conflict between dominant and minority groups. Van Dijk
(1987), Fairclough (1989), and Parenti (1993) reason that the press is an
unsatisfactory conciliator between dominant and minority groups because the media act as both the recipient and the transmitter of pressures to conform to the dominant ideology. The pressures to conform
diminish the possibilities of fair representation of racial and ethnic
minorities, particularly representation that enhances reciprocated positive value for their differences. Instead, these differences are most likely
portrayed as stereotyped images and, more often than not, presented as
inferior or threatening to dominant values. If the representation concerns the political activity of a minority, it is most likely cast as a threat
to the stability of the society (van Dijk 1987:363–4). Wilson and Gutierrez
conclude that during confrontations between minority groups and the
dominant society, 'the news media have the opportunity to exhibit
leadership in race relations, unfortunately, their historical track record
has been poor' (1985:137).

The above theories and concepts regarding the media representation
of minorities are based on analyses of diverse media in the United
States, Great Britain, and the Netherlands. These assessments of media
representation of minorities take a generalized view of how the press

depicts minorities. A major flaw in these assessments is the assumption that the media contexts are either irrelevant or all the same. Michael Pickering (1995) points out that the problem with most research of media stereotyping is that the research contradicts itself, by taking a stereotypical attitude towards media. This case study challenges these preconceptions by incorporating the lived experiences of the journalists, their primary sources, and select media audiences.

Canadian Studies of Media and Aboriginal Resistance

There are relatively few studies of Canadian Aboriginal resistance and the media, and most were generated by the 1990 Oka crisis. Rick Ponting (1990) discusses how the Mohawks of Quebec benefited from the media coverage of the Oka conflict because of the international attention they received. As a result, we should expect continued international involvement in Aboriginal disputes. He warns that stakes may be raised in Aboriginal affairs with the threat of international loss of reputation, Canada's response to Quebec's sovereignty aspirations, and the radicalization of Indian protest tactics. In his content analysis of the *Montreal Gazette* prior to and during the 1990 Oka standoff Marc Grenier finds that substantial media attention did not occur until the introduction of the Quebec Provincial Police in riot gear (1994:317). He argues that the newspaper was 'literally obsessed with conflict-based Indian issues during the sample period, with conflict orientations present in 80% of all Native Indian straight news stories' (1994:320). For instance, after the blockade was established at Oka, 'Native Indians [were presented] as unreasonable, bent on hostility, and a threat to established order.' The news stories expressed the general theme: 'Indians versus us' (1994:328). Grenier outlines various media theses to account for the portrayals, but none of these is based on the actual accounts of the journalists or their editors. Bud White Eye (1996), a First Nations journalist employed in mainstream media during the Oka crisis, describes how a managerial decision ensured that the story plan concerning local Aboriginal perceptions of the Oka conflict was projected through the non-Native lens. Media management did not trust First Nations perspectives of conflicts involving their group, and were hesitant to allow him to write stories about Aboriginal disputes. In his estimation the issue at hand was that his stories might offend a mainstream audience.

There are even fewer studies of media representations of Aboriginal peoples during conflict situations in British Columbia. The examples cited here did not have media as a focus of study. Paul Tennant (1990) relates how, during the mid-1970s and 1980s, Native people in British Columbia established blockades as a show of resistance to resource and land allocations. On these occasions, a senior RCMP police officer would act as a media spokesperson (Tennant 1990:207–8). Subsequent demonstrations in the 1980s reveal greater sophistication and assertiveness as 'protest leaders actively sought the understanding of the non-Indian editors and journalists in order to influence white public opinion' (1990:209). Beginning in the 1980s, the media became instrumental in bringing Native land claims to the public forum. David Long notes that Aboriginal activists have learned the importance of media and media coverage of a dispute. Media brought issues to the level of consciousness and fostered a broad support base (1992:129). In his article concerning the Native Indian blockades in British Columbia between 1984 and 1995 Blomley identifies a distinct pattern: roadblocks followed by 'the predictable round of condemnation and fulmination on editorial pages and in the provincial legislature' (1996:5). He states that the press under-reports conciliation during Native disputes, 'perhaps because they detract from the media tendency to seek confrontation' (1996:27).

Although these studies offer important insights into the media representations of Native protests in Canada, none of them provides a comprehensive treatment of the media coverage that includes media contexts, products, and audiences.

Methodology

Originally, I designed this research as a discourse analysis of 529 news stories taken from a cross-Canada sample of newspapers at the time of the Gustafsen Lake standoff. The large size of the sample should have yielded many possibilities for understanding national and regional media portrayals of Native resistance, and the story content indicated that the media and their sources had developed complex relations. However, text analysis alone could not explain why the media portrayed the event and the players in a particular way. Nor could a textual approach confirm audience reactions to the portrayals and the degree to which the portrayals affected them. As an anthropological problem, what was required was a means to explore the lived experiences of those closest to the media event.

In order to understand the underlying context, I extended the data collection beyond the news stories to include the journalists who covered the event, their principal sources of information, and audiences (directly or indirectly) affected by the media coverage. These sources in turn led me to non-media textual sources of information about the standoff. As my data became more diverse, the potential for appreciating the news context that underpinned the news stories expanded exponentially.

The data on which this book is based are composed of media products, legal and law enforcement documents, interviews with journalists, RCMP officials, as well as Native and non-Native civilians. The data include 561 newspaper stories from 18 newspapers across Canada in either hardcopy or CD ROM versions from the *Victoria Times Colonist, Vancouver Sun, Vancouver Province, Calgary Herald, Edmonton Journal, Saskatoon Star Phoenix, Regina Leader Post, Winnipeg Free Press, London Free Press, Toronto Star, Globe and Mail, Montreal Gazette, Le Devoir, Halifax-Chronicle Herald, New Brunswick Telegraph Journal, Charlottetown Guardian, St. John's Evening Telegram,* and *100 Mile House Free Press.* In addition, I cite news stories published before and after the standoff and news stories of the trial.

Additional media products include: select news clips from BCTV (1995); the CBC documentary, 'Standoff at Gustafsen Lake,' from the news program, *The National* (1995); the videotape, 'Gustafsen Lake,' from the Vancouver East Community 4 television program *Nitewatch* (1997); the CBC Radio program, 'The Cops, the Natives and the CBC' from *Now the Details* (1995); the CBC Radio program, *Sunday Morning,* broadcast on 10 September 1995; and select radio news clips from the Vancouver radio station, CKNW (1995).

I also acquired legal and procedural archival documents discussed during the trial that were relevant to the media coverage of the event. These are composed of a copy of the *Direct Indictment*; a copy of the *Petition for the Release from Custody of Defendant Joseph Adam Ignace*; excerpts of court transcripts of the pre-trial *Challenge for Cause Application*; excerpts of the transcripts from the trial; and a copy of the *Reasons for Judgment.* Two articles that appeared in the *RCMP Gazette*, written by Dr Mike Webster, an RCMP psychologist at the Gustafsen Lake standoff, provided insights into the RCMP negotiation strategies employed during the standoff. I also obtained a copy of the *RCMP Operational Manual* regarding media relations, a copy of the handbook, *The RCMP and the Media: A Spokesperson's Guide*, a copy of the RCMP's *Report to Crown Counsel*, and, courtesy of the RCMP, some memoranda from their files regarding their operational plan at Gustafsen Lake.

Interviews with 26 journalists from the *Victoria Times Colonist,*

Vancouver Province, Vancouver Sun, Globe and Mail, Canadian Press, *Broadcast News,* CBC Television (national and provincial), CBC Radio, CTV, BCTV, CKNW Radio from Vancouver, Cariboo Radio (based in Kamloops), and *100 Mile House Free Press* offered candid perspectives. These journalists represented (by conservative estimate) about 75% of the major media outlets that covered the standoff. In addition, 17 non-media sources included RCMP and government officials, Native leaders and spokespersons, the ranch owners, and local people from the town of 100 Mile House. The RCMP officials furnished details and experiences of the event that they did not release to the media during or after the standoff.

A few people of whom I requested an interview declined, including the former British Columbia attorney general and premier, Ujjal Dosanjh, and Ovide Mercredi, the former grand chief of the Assembly of First Nations. To compensate for these omissions, I collected interviews from news products at the time of the standoff.

Aboriginal media sources would have provided a valuable perspective for this work, but they were not available. Only one of the journalists working for a mainstream media outlet mentioned that he had Native ancestry, but he did not disclose this fact to his colleagues at the time of the standoff. Several Native media outlets covered all or part of the standoff. In order to include this aspect in the data, I contacted the editor of *Wolf Howls,* a Native newspaper in the interior of British Columbia. Unfortunately, no one returned my calls. Perhaps this work will create the impetus for further research of Native media coverage of conflicts involving Native and non-Native people.

I conducted most of the interviews in coffee shops or private offices, and a few took place over the telephone. Interviews with journalists were structured around pre-set questions (raised from the news discourse analysis and from the news content) intended to elicit information regarding news production practices and experiences of covering the event. Interviews with non-media were less structured and hinged on the frames of reference of the non-media interviewees and their connections to the media event.

I transcribed the interviews and interview notes and coded the transcripts according to the topic themes. I cross-referenced the interview data according to the chronological account of the event. This chronology allowed me to organize news reports, chronological narratives, and court documents, into an integrated framework that provided details about specific incidents. Because it unified most of the data, the chronology became the central organizational feature, which I carried over to the book.

The anthropological approach is based on Claude Lévi-Strauss's (1963) *structural analysis*. Structural analysis connects the media products (*surface structures*) with the media contexts (*deep structures*). The distinction between surface and deep structures replicates how we understand media. What we hear, see, and read in the news is a distillation of struggles between media and sources to define the situation, logistical contexts, production processes, and editorial policies that usually remain hidden from the public. This framework establishes triangulation with its suitability to multiple sources of data, theoretical constructs, and analytical techniques. Another strength is the validity offered in the dialectic between surface and deep structures that link the analysis of media products to the experiences of the journalists and their sources. Causal relationships, relations of power, processes that are passed between elements in the deep and surface structures, and temporal change within and between media texts and contexts may be viewed as a complex and dynamic whole. The unification of media texts and contexts makes it possible to discern patterns that otherwise may remain unnoticed. It provides a snapshot of the ranking order of cultural values and the social hierarchy. Structural analysis, although in itself a theoretical construct, promotes theory-building specific to the social phenomena being studied. It is a mode for discovery, rather than a formulaic guide. For example, in the examination of media, rather than applying a priori media theory to interpret the data, the patterns within the data are used to build on or challenge existing theory or to introduce new conceptualizations.

As will be demonstrated in this case study, a structural approach to media research has several advantages. It is useful for investigating media representations of members of minorities. It is suited to questions related to accuracy and bias of media content, such as the cases cited by Edward Herman and Noam Chomsky (1988), where there were contradictions between media representations and reality. In applied research, it can be used to identify specific areas for public policy recommendations. In sum, structural analysis is an open-ended, inductive approach that is connected to the real world, making it a powerful heuristic tool. (We will return to the advantages of using a structural approach to study media in chapter 7.)

However, Lévi-Strauss's structural theory has inherent weaknesses, because it does not anticipate assessing news discourse, media speech events, or audience responses. In order to compensate for these short-comings, I turned to additional modes of analysis from contemporary media studies as well as from cultural and linguistic anthropology.

In this work I also incorporated discourse analysis, more specifically, media discourse analysis. Discourse refers to 'an analytical unit of communicative behavior, widely varying in length, form and content' (Salzmann 1993:272). Discourse may be oral or may be written. In an anthropological approach to discourse analysis, naturally occurring discourses are examined in their social contexts. The media discourse analysis in this book invokes van Dijk's (1987, 1988, 1989) *discourse analysis* of newspaper stories. I incorporated his categories for patterns of representation and thematic structures,[4] which include the layout of the news story, journalistic style, syntax structures, and placement of clauses. Semantics, lexical choice, and the evocative meanings conveyed are also examined. The content is assessed in terms of reported speech, particularly how journalists signal approval or disapproval of sources and topics, and of rhetorical strategies that consider techniques used to increase the impressions of authenticity and precision of information. More specific to studying ethnic minorities in the press, van Dijk employs the study of *relevance structures* in the news discourse, in which the hierarchical ordering of information and sources are seen as indicative of their placement in terms of news worthiness and credibility as well as of their social status. Van Dijk identifies the fact that headlines and leads summarize what media outlets consider most important, according to the production standards and the functions of the media outlet. Headlines and leads are also the most likely aspect to be recalled by the audience to define the situation at a later time (1987:257).

A *quantitative analysis* of the news stories of the 1995 Gustafsen Lake standoff documents the frequency of stereotype labelling that reinforced the creation and dissemination of a stereotyped theme of the people inside the Gustafsen Lake camp. The incorporation of this quantitative component is also found in van Dijk's (1987) quantification of headline themes. Quantitative aspects of news discourse have been recognized as a superior means of identifying patterns of representation for large databases of discourse (Roberts 1997). I have added a *qualitative* component to the quantitative analysis, drawing from interviews with the journalists to explain the media processes and contexts that promoted the media's reliance on stereotype labels during the standoff.

J. van Velsen's (1964, 1967) *situational analysis* of strategic events was employed to analyse the data at macro and micro levels of the research. Van Velsen considers strategic events, such as disputes, the most fertile source of data – because it is then that social positioning and processes between individuals, groups, and institutions become most discernable. The 1995 Gustafsen Lake standoff was such an occasion, and during the standoff there were several crisis points. At the micro level, I examined specific episodes of the standoff, checking for patterns and developments that I then extrapolated to the macro level for further study. Connections between the micro and macro levels were made possible through a feedback process between news texts, institutional documents, interviews with the players, the context of the unfolding event, and the context of the news production.

The analysis of relations between the players that may have influenced the media portrayals covered several aspects. Of primary importance are the roles and statuses of the actual players in the event with respect both to Canadian society and to group affiliation. The roles and statuses are also distinguished in terms of agency and adaptive strategies to particular developments. Relational aspects between players consist of interpretive frames, power, competition (for resources and control of frames of interpretation), conflict, resistance, compliance, presentation strategies, information control, and negotiation of information. These components allow for an appreciation of the complexity of the situation and the dynamics between institutions, groups, and individual players. The chronological reconstruction of the media event reveals changes in the relations over time.

Frame analysis (Goffman 1974; Fairclough 1989; Hackett 1991; Tannen 1993; Robinson 1998) accounted for the divergent perspectives found in the media texts and interviews. Frame analysis is recognized as a tool for information processing and is a methodology that successfully transfers between textual and contextual modes. It entails discovery of the underlying bases for interpretations of reality. In this research, frame analysis centred on the assessment of the dominant frame of the news discourse, which involved seeking the dominant meanings and themes through lexical and grammatical features in news headlines and lead-ins, as well as the way in which information and sources were represented in the media. The interpretive frames of interview sources (or the RCMP media and operational plans) required an examination of the subject positions of the players (considering roles, status, and connections to the event). Next, it involved seeking evidence of this frame in behaviours (individual as well as group) or material products (including institutional documents and media products). Frame analysis was another means that integrated textual (news products and documents) and contextual (interview) data.

I incorporated elements from *The Ethnography of Communication* (Gumperz and Hymes 1964) to assess news-gathering contexts (for example, press conferences) and to provide a model for appreciating audience evaluations of the media coverage. I borrowed Hymes's (1974) speech event criteria for studying the environments where news gathering took place. Generally, this approach considers the communicative setting, the participants, the emotional tone of the communication, the mode of communication (visual, oral, or written), and norms of interpretation (such as media conventions for press conferences).

Anthropological studies of *performance* and *audience* (Bauman 1977; Hymes 1981; Tedlock 1983) were useful in the assessment of audience evaluations of the media coverage. Within the realm of the media event, the concept of performance can be found in the interactions between journalists and their sources during news-gathering opportunities, as well as in the news products. During the media coverage of the Gustafsen Lake standoff, local audiences were often witnesses to situations of news-gathering, and occasionally they were media sources. During this investigation I also appreciated that certain audiences have different resources and abilities with which to judge the media coverage and to judge the abilities of the journalists and their sources to convey the news. Audience evaluations provided an important validity check on the analysis of the news coverage.

A culminating step in the research was the re-evaluation of the news text, in light of the information regarding news production practices, context of news gathering, and the unfolding event. I have situated the findings of the discourse analysis in specific episodes of the narrative of the standoff and in a final assessment of the media coverage. The contextual details enriched the process of conducting the discourse analysis and provided testable conclusions.

Validity Checks

Although I argue that the media coverage did not represent the event fully or accurately, on occasion I still relied on media products as historical referents for this research. I compensated for possible weaknesses by testing the news data against court and law enforcement documents and interviews with journalists, the RCMP, Native leaders, and Native and non-Native people. In addition, this study has benefited from hindsight understanding of the Gustafsen Lake standoff trial, where many of the instances of media misrepresentations were pointed out in court. The media relayed some of this information to the public in their news stories. I have been cautious in ensuring that the news accounts that I use for information can be authenticated with other non-media sources.

Ethics Protocols

This case study involved an emotionally charged situation, and some people were reluctant to participate or were concerned that I might distort the information that they volunteered. Consequently, research ethics were critical.[5] Prospective research participants first read and signed an ethics and consent form before the interview began. I assured participants that their quotations in the study would be anonymous, except people who were public figures during the event and those who played unique roles in the media coverage. I requested that these individuals waive the protection of anonymity, which they did.[6] I provided all of the participants with interview transcripts or copies of tape recordings and opportunities to request changes or to drop out of the research. After the participants reviewed their interview data, I asked that they sign and return a release form that granted me permission to incorporate their interviews into the study.[7] In a few cases, participants requested minor changes, which I accommodated. Nobody withdrew from the research. Later, I asked some of the journalists, RCMP officials, Native chiefs, and non-media sources to review earlier drafts of the work in order to provide feedback and to test for validity.

Representation

I have dealt with my representation of people, communities, and the interview material in the following ways. The terms 'Indian,' 'Native,' 'Aboriginal,' and 'First Nations' are highly contested within academia as well as among Canada's Indigenous peoples (Coates 1999). In this book, I use the collective terms 'Native,' 'Aboriginal,' and 'First Nations' interchangeably, but I do not use these terms to distinguish status or non-status for eligibility under the Indian Act. My usage is consistent with Long and Dickason (2000), Canadian scholars of Aboriginal history and contemporary issues. I also employ anglicized names to identify Native communities because this is how they are commonly referred to by Native and non-Native people living in the region.

I am preserving the anonymity of interview sources, except people who hold a public office or (with their permission) those who were central participants in the event or the media coverage. I cite quotations from anonymous sources as members of a generic class, such as 'journalist.' Although I interviewed several women journalists, I refer to all of the journalists as if they are men, in order to ensure their anonymity.

Direct quotations from sources I have interviewed appear in italics, and my own questions or comments during the interviews are in bold type.

Organization of the Book

The first five chapters of the book constitute a chronological narrative of the standoff. Each of these chapters examines specific aspects of the media coverage. The final two chapters deal with larger themes of the media coverage and address the research questions.

In chapter 1, I reconstruct the events that led to the local dispute becoming a serious criminal investigation and a national news story, from the perspectives of the rancher, the Sundance leader, a local chief, various RCMP personnel, and the local newspaper editor. The chapter concludes with the identification of the emergent struggle between insider and outsider perspectives of the conflict.

In chapter 2, I explore the developing relationships between the journalists, the protesters, the RCMP media personnel, and the affects of these relationships on the media characterizations from the time of the initiating RCMP press conference. This investigation includes a study of the impression management strategies employed by various sources in order to influence the dominant frame in news accounts. Next, the journalists explain their coverage of Grand Chief Mercredi's mediations at the camp and the limiting effects of the protesters who restricted journalists' access to the camp and later the RCMP prevention of media access when they set up barricades. This is followed by the RCMP's, the camp's, and the media's interpretations of the barricades and the effects on their respective groups. These differing frameworks demonstrate the incongruity between the RCMP operational strategy and the reality of the situation for the camp and the media. The chapter concludes with an analysis of how the barricades altered the impression management and information control strategies of various media sources as well as the news-gathering practices for the duration of the conflict.

In chapter 3, the gathering of news is conceptualized as a negotiation of information that includes barter, coercion, and appropriation. Examples of how information was negotiated include: RCMP press conferences, the media's use of police radio-telecommunications; the RCMP's engagement of a journalist in a police initiative; the media outcomes of the shooting episode of 4 September; and the RCMP's confiscation of CBC videotapes of the camp. In conclusion, I assess the power relations between the media and the RCMP that underpinned the various modes of negotiation of information.

In chapter 4, I look at the heightened importance of information control during crisis periods by examining the two last violent incidents of the standoff. The chapter begins with my interpretation of the firefight from the RCMP wescam[8] video recording and the ensuing press conference from the journalists' perspectives. A media discourse analysis contrasts a Canadian Press newspaper account with the rogue account from the *Vancouver Sun*. Next, I present an examination of how the RCMP relayed corrections to the media and a table that reveals the consistency of inaccurate details of the episode published in newspapers across Canada. This is followed by a discussion of the RCMP's strategy to announce the criminal records during the firefight press conference and the factors that compelled various media outlets to publish and broadcast this information. The second violent episode, which was not made known to the media (and hence the public), is described, based on my interpretation of an RCMP wescam videotape recording. The chapter concludes with a discussion of information control, media contexts at the time, and how these contributed to nation-wide media stereotyping and continued suppositions concerning the firefight.

Chapter 5 wraps up the narrative of the Gustafsen Lake standoff. Much of the chapter centres on the ways the media and their sources adapted to a reduction of the tension. The explication of the surrender message broadcast by CBC Radio on behalf of the RCMP shows how the broadcast was made possible and the ramifications for CBC Radio and several other groups and individuals. This is followed by an examination of a series of news-gathering opportunities arranged by the RCMP as the conflict was winding down. The chapter concludes with an evaluation of how the RCMP was able to continue its dominance of the media interpretation of the event and the people involved.

In chapter 6, I examine media stereotyping within television and print media and how the media coverage affected various groups and audiences. Journalists reveal the media processes and the conditions of covering the standoff that explain certain predilections for their stereotyped depictions of the conflict. A quantitative analysis follows, in which the extent of stereotype labelling in 18 newspapers across Canada is identified. These data are further refined with a second analysis in which the stereotype labels in Canadian Press news stories across Canada are distinguished. Next, various stakeholders and audience members contribute their views of the media coverage and its impact on their respective groups and communities. The effects of the media coverage were significant for local Native and non-Native communities, who responded with image-management strategies of their own. The chapter concludes with an evaluation of the variety and extent of harm brought on by the media characterizations.

In chapter 7, I draw together the case study by revisiting how a structural approach to the study of media representations creates openings for new understandings and policy evaluations compared with media studies that rely solely on textual materials. I demonstrate this with an examination of the structural elements that were found to have influenced the media coverage at the macro level. They include tension of the situation and media proximity to the police, media competition and cooperation, media bias, media resistance, media empowerment, eclipse of insider definitions by outsiders, and cultural misperceptions. A discussion follows of the larger social ramifications of the media coverage and a brief examination of public policy in Canadian media and RCMP media relations. The chapter concludes with an epilogue of developments since the Gustafsen Lake standoff.

CHAPTER ONE

Serious Red Alert

The truth about what? Truth from whose perspective?
Chief Antoine Archie, interview, 25 July 1997

The conflict at Gustafsen Lake was *not* an isolated event. Similarly, the media coverage was *not* a one-time phenomenon without precedent. Both the standoff and its media characterization connect in various ways to the history of Aboriginal people in Canada, previous instances of Native disputes, and the recent history of the relations between the media, the RCMP, and others who participated as media sources.

In this chapter, we will first examine the pre-existing contexts for the central players in the conflict. The RCMP Media Relations Program, which is guided by the national *Media/RCMP Operational Manual* (in effect in 1995), provides a baseline for comparison with what transpired during the Gustafsen Lake standoff. The relations between the media and the RCMP at 100 Mile House and at Vancouver offer a backdrop to understanding differing motivations for media practice at these two locales. In the latter part of the chapter the early stage of the standoff, before the large contingent of media and police arrived on the scene, is described. Because there were disagreements regarding several circumstances that contributed to the escalation of the conflict, I have enlisted a variety of perspectives to tell this part of the story.

RCMP Media Relations Program

Since the early 1990s the RCMP have developed a media relations program, which is a component of community policing. According to

Sergeant Peter Montague, RCMP media liaison for British Columbia, *'We had always been a silent force and suffered from a fortress mentality when it came to dealing with media issues.'* To address this problem, the RCMP designed a media relations program, based on marketing principles. The goal of the program is to keep the public apprised of what the police force is about and what they are doing. The emphasis is on accessibility and accountability, and the RCMP teaches its members how to interact with the media.

In the earlier stages of the program, the RCMP went to the media to learn how to communicate with the public. Sergeant Montague explains, *'We put together a program and a policy which we reduced from say, ten pages of – which said nothing – to basically five paragraphs – which captures our – the essence and spirit of our program – still leaving a lot of artistic freedom to the members to deal with the media.'* The media program is considered open to public scrutiny, which is important for the RCMP public image. Sergeant Montague states, *'Everything that we do we try to enhance our confidence level – the public's confidence level – in us as a police force ... If we ever lost our credibility with the public then, we really wouldn't exist very, very long.'* Media relations also entails correcting misinformation, making sure that the media have the facts, and that they have *'our point of view accurately reflected, and reported.'* He states, *'Leading up to a charge, we can discuss the matter in a more generic sense, and advise the public what we're doing,'* but *'We can't discuss anything before the courts that could be deemed to be contemptuous.'* The relationship between the police force and the public is important: *'It's not a secret police force, and it's not an ominous place to come – it's a friendly place – it's a place where we want to share the information – always keeping the integrity of evidence in mind – we have to protect the integrity of evidence, and protect the privacy of individuals – make sure that we do not say anything inappropriate about a person. We could never name a suspect, for instance. You know, we could only say that "we have a suspect in mind, and we're continuing an investigation of the bank robbery"'* (interview with Sergeant Montague, 27 May 1997).

The above depiction offered by Sergeant Montague needs to be framed as an idealized model. It was not the prototype for media and public relations that was employed during the standoff at Gustafsen Lake.[1] The decision made by the RCMP to alter the media plan for the Gustafsen Lake operation was shaped by a series of incidents associated with the Gustafsen Lake camp and its occupants and the police investigations into them. According to the RCMP assessment, those inside the camp were capable of violence, and there was substantive evidence of people preparing for an armed engagement with law enforcement personnel. I will examine the effects of these RCMP assessments on their operational plan, and ultimately their media strategy, throughout this book.

Media and RCMP Relations

The relations between the Vancouver media and RCMP media section and their local counterparts at 100 Mile House illustrate the differences in the dynamics between small-town and large-urban media and police. At 100 Mile House, the town newspaper is totally reliant on the somewhat limited police information from the local RCMP detachment, but the newspaper is not compelled to establish alternative networks for information. Any of the RCMP officers involved in investigations are called upon to provide information to journalists, and there is no formal media program. The newspaper staff considers the communications between them and the local police very satisfactory and amiable. Editor Steven Frasher commented that if the reporters find something that they think the RCMP has mishandled, *'they call them on it.'* However, he also found the detachment to be very cautious about releasing information. *'For example, if we have someone involved with – even quite a significant crime ... they won't release the name – even if there's 90% likelihood the person will be charged before the magistrate – before we hit the streets. They still won't release the name to us – prior to the formal charge being laid.'*[2] This policy is often in conflict with the editor's goal to *'explain the incident as thoroughly as we can – to effectively shut down the rumour mill ... get the correct story out there to start with, and have that story hold water and credibility'* (interview with Steven Frasher, 23 July 1997).

In the case of the *100 Mile House Free Press*, seeking informal sources of police information for the publication of stories does not offer a competitive or economic advantage. The accrued law enforcement news updates over the space of a week are sufficient to satisfy the appetites of the local audience. The editor contrasted his weekly newspaper with the larger outlets in Vancouver and stated that the newspaper is not likely to scoop a breaking-news story. But at the same time, the newspaper strives to provide complete and balanced reporting of events by attending to pertinent detail without being sensationalist.

The majority of journalists who covered the standoff, including those whom I interviewed, were from Vancouver. All had had previous experiences in dealing with each other and with the RCMP at various news events. As a group of journalists, they talked of respecting each other, but they understood that competition between news outlets was a driving force and could take place at several levels: scooping a story, landing choice interviews, being assigned to a big story, and working for the outlet with the most prestige and financial resources. Another area of competition was maintaining a positive rapport with important media sources. For the Vancouver media outlets, the RCMP are a crucial media source.

Although about half of the journalists interviewed for this case study either were complimentary towards the Vancouver RCMP media division or declined making any comments, these attitudes did not form the consensus. Those who were supportive of the RCMP media personnel appreciated the efforts taken by the force to provide information and access to news stories and described the RCMP media liaison as fair and reasonable. Nonetheless, journalists from several outlets believed that the relationship between the media and the RCMP media liaison had become strained before the standoff at Gustafsen Lake. They contended that the RCMP media relations personnel were manipulating the media's dependence on the police for information.

The journalists who were critical of the relationship between the media and the RCMP media division described a carrot-and-stick approach used by the media liaison in dealing with them. There was a sense that even before the Gustafsen Lake standoff, the RCMP media liaison was heavy-handed in the way that he attempted to control the Vancouver news media. When journalists sought out unofficial networks for news stories before an RCMP press release took place, (a typical strategy for large media outlets) the RCMP media liaison was known to have retaliated against them. For example, after the Gustafsen Lake standoff (in an unrelated news story), journalists from a major Vancouver outlet scooped a breaking RCMP story. Shortly after, the RCMP media liaison publicly stated that the RCMP media relations would exclude the offending outlet from future RCMP press conferences.[3] Journalists from several media outlets talked about being ostracized or humiliated in front of peers by comments made by the RCMP media liaison. The worst sanction was being excluded from breaking-news announcements and other news-gathering opportunities. Such snubs reflected poorly on a journalist's ability to maintain connections with an essential source, rendering the individual a liability to his employer. Several journalists also believed that the professional boundary between BCTV and the RCMP had become blurred, with the media liaison enlisting BCTV to assist the RCMP in becoming more 'media aware.' Related to this was the suspicion that BCTV was favoured with inside police information about stories that were about to break. Suffice it to say that the competition between the various outlets in Vancouver was stiff. According to interviews with many journalists, the RCMP media personnel, unwittingly or otherwise, had become part of this dynamic. Because of the need to maintain a positive working relationship with the media relations staff, resistance to the RCMP media relations program had to be carefully weighed, especially when sanctions could be professionally harmful.

Long before Gustafsen Lake, Native blockades in British Columbia (such as the one previously described at Douglas Lake) had become major news stories. The RCMP, who were often called to defuse these situations, established the practice of bringing many of the Vancouver-based journalists (and camera crews) to news events in jets, helicopters, or buses. The RCMP's media division considered complimentary transportation a cost-saving courtesy for the media. Once there, the media were kept at a distance from locations where conflict could occur between police and Native protesters, as well as from venues where conciliation talks took place. Interviews with journalists suggested that the majority of the media accepted these arrangements while covering Native blockades. The police restriction on access to mediation sites neutralized the media, preventing them from becoming independent witnesses, a pattern that began before the Gustafsen Lake standoff. A few journalists acknowledged that these logistical arrangements and professional associations had a limiting effect on their coverage of Native conflicts.

In this large urban context, the tensions between the media and the police regarding information are mostly over access to and competition for information. The aggressive competition between news outlets ensures that measures taken by the RCMP to control information will be met with some degree of media resistance.

Early Beginnings of the Conflict at Gustafsen Lake

100 Mile House is located in the rugged interior of the Province of British Columbia and had celebrated its thirtieth anniversary as an incorporated district municipality in July 1995. Historically, the town had been on the Cariboo Gold Rush Trail during the 1860s gold rush era. Several decades ago, the primary commercial activities included lumber, ranching, and tourism. Over the past few years, the population

in the town has dramatically increased, its citizenry primarily consisting of non-Native people. Some Native people work in the town, but
usually they commute from other places. Highway 97 is the main
thoroughfare in the town, linking 100 Mile House to Vancouver, 400
kilometres to the south, and to Williams Lake, 90 kilometres to the
north. 100 Mile House is about halfway between Vancouver, British
Columbia, and Jasper, Alberta, making it a regular stop-over location
for tour buses. Four Native Indian reserves are located in the region.
Canim Lake is located about 30 kilometres northeast of 100 Mile House,
Dog Creek is situated about 50 kilometres to the west and Canoe Creek
about 10 kilometres further west. Alkali Lake is approximately 130
kilometres west of 100 Mile House and is easier to access from Williams
Lake. These three reserves to the west are located off Highway 97,
accessible only by forestry roads.

The James Cattle Ranch incorporates Gustafsen Lake and is located
in the area between the Canim Lake and Dog Creek reserves. Gustafsen
Lake, the site of the standoff, is located about 35 kilometres away, on the
Exeter Station Road, which runs northwest from the town. The owners
of the James Cattle Ranch, Lyle and Mary James, are an elderly couple
who live in a modest home next to the Dog Creek and Canoe Creek
reserves. They had lived and ranched on the Flathead Indian Reserve in
Montana for 25 years, before they moved to the interior of British
Columbia in 1972. Lyle James purchased the ranch for $1.1 million. The
ranch property is extended by leases and a grazing permit issued by the
forestry department, which James purchased. His total property ex-
tends to about a half-million acres (182,000 hectares), on which he has
roughly 3,000 head of cattle and 70 horses. The James Cattle Ranch
Company is a family operation, and one of Lyle James's sons-in-law is
from one of the local reserves.[4] James has six or seven ranch hands (this
number fluctuates) and he employs people from the local reserve.

13 June 1995

A growing dispute between the sundancers and James comes to a head
after native Indians fence off the religious site, blocking cattle from the
area. James arrives at the camp bearing an eviction notice. He brings along
about a dozen ranch hands 'for support' and to witness the serving of the
notice. There is a wide disparity between the Indian and non-Indian
version of what occurs that day. Splitting the Sky says: 'About 15 of his
hands drove up in 4 x 4s and pickups. They pulled out rifles and threat-

ened to kill them. One of them pulled out a bull whip and said: "This is a good day to string up some red niggers.' James denies any of that happened. 'There was no confrontation. We went in and served them the notice,' James said. 'We didn't have any arms whatsoever.' (Chronology, *Vancouver Sun*, 12 September 1995, A3)

14 June 1995

Two members of the B.C. forest service are near the lake inspecting timber when they see people in the trees. Suddenly there's a loud gunshot and the forestry workers see dust fly from the road in front of them. They flee, unhurt. (Chronology, *Vancouver Sun*, 12 September 1995, A3)

In 1989 Percy Rosette, who was residing at the Alkali Lake Reserve No. 1 asked Lyle James if he could hold a Sundance at Gustafsen Lake.[5] Lyle James did not have any concerns when he gave his permission. The local Natives had already been camping in the location, and the area had always been open for the enjoyment of local people as well as visitors. But the rancher did not like it when Percy said, '"*If you don't let me, I'll pull the Indian Act on you*,"' he recalled, '*but – that didn't even concern me – I didn't know what he could do, but it still didn't concern me. And – so – [he had Percy promise] ... there were to be no structures or anything built there.*' There was no written agreement between Percy Rosette and Lyle James during those years leading up to the standoff.

In the first two years, there were complaints that people fishing in the lake had received minor threats from some of the participants of the Sundance. A more serious incident took place one night in 1992 when two couples vacationing at the public campground near the lake had shots fired through their tent while they were sleeping. One of the guests, accompanied by one of Lyle James's Native ranch hands, went to the Sundance camp and made a positive identification. The police conducted an investigation and identified two people from outside the area as suspects, but nothing further developed.[6] It was after this incident that Lyle James and Percy Rosette signed a formal written agreement, witnessed by a Native RCMP officer. There were to be no permanent structures built, and the agreement for the use of the area for the Sundance expired at the end of 1993. Lyle James was agreeable to allowing the Sundance to take place on the property, but he was increasingly concerned about the threats made to people who were also in the area. He stated, '*But the thing was, it wasn't really and never was really the ones that – of the Sundance – that caused the problem. It was always some others that came in'* (interview with Lyle James, 27 July 1997).

Although the four-year Sundance cycle and the agreement ended in 1993, another Sundance was held at the site in 1994. In the winter following the 1994 Sundance, Lyle James discovered that Percy Rosette and his wife were living in a cabin at Gustafsen Lake. Neither James nor the RCMP realized at the time that Percy Rosette and John Stevens had hired Native rights lawyer Bruce Clark in early January 1995 to represent their claim to the area used for the Sundance.[7] Without this knowledge, Lyle James considered Percy Rosette's continued occupancy on the property a private civil matter. He made enquiries at the local RCMP detachment to have the sundancers evicted, and he consulted with a lawyer.

Since the 1960s the Canim Lake reserve has been working towards a positive and accepting relationship with the town of 100 Mile House and the local RCMP detachment. During the 1960s, racist episodes occurred, and there was a sense that Native community members were subjected to unfair policing. In the early 1970s the Canim reserve formed an Integration Council with the members of the Emissaries of the Divine Light, a spiritual community at 100 Mile House.[8] Their main purpose was to deal with discrimination against Native people in the region. According to Chief Antoine Archie, *'Through that, we got a good relationship working with 100 Mile, and we maintained that for a number of years – maybe 20 years or so – and that's something we wish to hang on to!*

One element that Chief Archie felt might damage this relationship was the militancy associated with the Gustafsen Lake Sundance. Chief Archie had never heard about the Sundance before it was introduced at Gustafsen Lake. He recalled attending some of the meetings held to explain the ceremony to the local Native communities. He stated that, in 1992 *'a couple of particular meetings that I had gone to – [they] weren't just talking – they were mixing politics ... But I brought my son – and I told him to come and listen, so that later on he could say, "Well, I took part in that – I took part and I listened" ... So when I talked to the sundancers out here ... and I read up on other stuff ... I talked to a few other people who were involved in other Sundances, and they're not saying the same thing.'* It seemed to Chief Archie that the people who brought the Sundance to Gustafsen Lake *'developed some of their own kind of lines 'cause it really doesn't really fall in with traditional Sundance.'* He believed that the Sundance practised at Gustafsen Lake was different from the traditional Sundance of the Lakota, and he said that they brought this up with the sundancers: *'We challenged them out there. And we told them – the Sundance was supposed to only occur for four years, and you've got to give the land a rest, according to the real sundancers'* (interview with Chief Archie, 25 July 1997).

John Hill, also known as Splitting the Sky or Doc, had attended the Gustafsen Lake Sundance in the summer of 1994 and was invited to lead the Sundance in 1995. He is a Mohawk Aboriginal, who had been residing in Alberta for a few years before the standoff. William Ignace (Wolverine) introduced him to Percy Rosette, who asked Hill to lead the 1995 Sundance; they had a number of planning meetings throughout 1994 and 1995. The Sundance was significant to Hill, and he was committed to the exacting preparation of the grounds, the fasting, and the dance: *'And – of course, during Sundance times, we post signs up at – you know – on the grounds there that there'll be no guns, no booze – no alcohol – no negative attitudes – just a good code of conduct there. And anybody that comes there comes to pray, and comes to pray for the people.'* The previous year, Hill had learned about the conflict between Lyle James and Percy Rosette. According to Hill, Lyle James had *'started to call the Sundance a form of devil worshipping,'* as part of his argument that the Indians should get off the land, that the time had expired, and that too many people were coming. It seemed to Hill that Lyle James thought the Sundance was getting out of control and that he wanted the people removed.

In 1994 Hill remembered the hundreds of cattle that *'kept coming onto the grounds ... defecating all over our grounds.'* According to Hill, there could have been as many as 500 to 700 head of cattle grazing in the area of the Sundance grounds. In preparation for the 1995 Sundance, Hill and others saw the remnants of an old fence lying around, and with the help of the others, erected a fence to keep the cattle out. For the sundancers, putting up the fence prevented the animals from interfering with the Sundance, but it also took on a deeper significance. Hill maintained that the building of the fence was innocent, a way of eliminating the *'hassle of chasing cattle away while praying for the ancestral beings to come and visit us, because they won't visit when the cows are defecating on the site.'* They built the fence, but later felt the hostility from the rancher and his employees. This did not bother them *'because – it had become well established that the land wasn't theirs in the first place, and the fact that there was no real legal surveys done down there, the reality was that this Lyle James would never produce a deed.'* Hill mentioned that he participated in making the videotaped program, 'The Defenders of the Land.' One scene in the videotape shows him teaching people inside the camp techniques of defence, skills he thought they needed because there was already a sense that the camp would be attacked.

In Hill's estimation, tensions peaked when the rancher figured the sundancers were trying to establish a *'territorial imperative.'* Hill admitted that building a fence to ensure that there was no desecration upon the Sundance site was a form of staking out the territory. The sundancers complained to the RCMP about a number of gunshots into the camp that originated from behind the bush at Bottle Lake. **Were you firing back?** *'Ahh – initially no. We filed and lodged complaints that there was being shots fired into the camp. Initially no. And any shots that were fired in a future role – were warning shots – never direct shots – were only warning shots. Because we didn't want any physical confrontation – because as I say – it was against the rules of a Sundance time to have weapons – to have guns, while you're conducting the ceremony. So we couldn't violate that. It's a spiritual law.'* According to Hill, the RCMP did not get involved in the shooting incidents because they said it was outside their jurisdiction and that conflict between them would have to be settled in a civil court, in a civil fashion. Lyle James was advised by his lawyers that it would cost $25,000 to $30,000 (which he did not want to spend) to get a civil injunction. Hill said that it still would have cost James *'a couple of thousand dollars'* to have the land surveyed, and James was still adamant about not producing a deed.

Hill recalled, during the preparation time for the Sundance, that the cowhands came in with guns, and a bullwhip, and that *'the guy with the bullwhip said that "this was a good day to burn down a Goddamned cook house and to string up some red niggers."'*[9] This sounded like the Ku Klux Klan, *'and that's heavy Ku Klux Klan country up there.'* According to Hill, the rancher and his hands scared the young men in the camp when they saw the guns in the car: *'they didn't know what them guys were going to do!'* (interview with John Hill, 23 July 1996). Hill stated that if the rancher and his employees had not acted so aggressively, everyone would have left the camp after the Sundance. At the conclusion of the Sundance, the participants were asked if they were going to break their resolve and leave, but, Hill admitted, even before the Sundance, they were still very angry and upset from the hostilities shown to them. They felt that they were being watched and stalked, and they claimed that they could see people with weapons in the bushes. Sometimes these situations led to angry confrontations, but the RCMP did not become involved.

Lyle James tells a much different version of presenting the eviction notice. He learned early in June that the people at the Sundance camp had built a fence down to the lake and closed the gate into the area. They had posted someone to watch the gate. The fence prevented his cattle from moving freely in the area and from being able to follow the trail, which was part of their annual summer trek.[10] Consequently, Lyle James was even more anxious to have the people removed. The RCMP told him that they would not get involved to serve an eviction notice, and Lyle's lawyer advised him to bring several witnesses. On 13 June 1995 James and several of his ranch hands drove to the Gustafsen Lake camp and waited for Percy Rosette to return. While they were waiting, one of the ranch employees began playing with a bullwhip. According to Lyle James, this employee was not in the immediate vicinity of the camp and the people waiting for Rosette. James recalls, *'And they played that up so much! And − it wasn't that he had any intentions of threatening with it − he was just playing − foolin' around with it.'* **Was he within sight of the cabin?** *'He was within sight, yeah. Probably within sight.'*

While at the Sundance camp, the rancher and his employees re-moved the stove from the cabin because it had been taken from their cattle camp. According to Lyle James, they were particularly careful about the language they used when speaking with the people at the camp and denied that anyone used the phrase *'string up some red niggers.'* *'But what they wanted was a direct confrontation with us. And − there was no way. Where would we be? We'd be dead.'* He did concede that on a different occasion one of his employees had arrived at the camp one night after drinking, but James could not vouch for anything that might have been said by this individual; he had no prior knowledge of the visit, and he would not have given his consent to it.[11] Shortly after this late-night incident, the employee *'found a threatening note on a tree there, and ... he quit and left.'* According to the rancher, they gave the note to the RCMP (interview with Lyle James, 27 July 1997).

The *100 Mile House Free Press* had been covering stories about the Sundance ceremony held at Gustafsen Lake since 1993. First celebrated there in 1990, the Sundance had drawn 400 to 500 Native people to the remote location in the first two years. In 1992 there was a shooting incident involving tourists, and two Native men (both from the United States) were arrested, but no charges were laid. In 1993 the Sundance participants were mostly from the local Native communities. That year there were three incidents reported to the local RCMP detachment between sundancers and non-Native people who were in the vicinity, camping and fishing. The sundancers complained that the tourists did not respect their need for privacy, and they asked the tourists to stay away from the general area of their Sundance camp during the 10-day ceremony. None of the incidents that year involved weapons, nor were there any injuries. The 1994 Sundance ceremony was celebrated without reported incidents. In June 1995, while the Sundance preparations were being made, there were confrontations between the sundancers and rancher Lyle James as well as an alleged shooting incident involving forestry workers. At this time, news stories about various disagreements and incidents connected to the Sundance camp began appearing regularly in the local newspaper, and many were front-page stories.

Local newspaper editor Steven Frasher recalls that in the middle of June, someone allegedly fired at two forestry workers out *'timber cruising,'* but the people at the Gustafsen Lake camp denied any knowledge of such an incident. Locating physical evidence was nearly impossible because the area was thick with bush. A further impediment was that the forestry workers could not identify a shooter.

John Hill argued that *'someone had "architechted" some lie about some forestry worker being shot at.'* He stated that it was known that the only way that the RCMP would become involved was if there was a threat to the general community. Hill considered the forestry worker shooting incident *'as well as about five other incidents'* as constructed *'solely for the purpose of allowing the RCMP to get involved ... Nobody has ever been indicted, nobody has ever been brought up as a suspect, and none of the investigations are ongoing – they've all been completed.'* He was convinced that the alleged charges against the camp were part of a conspiracy to close down the camp (interview with John Hill, 23 July 1996).

On 17 June 1995 a meeting arranged by the local RCMP between the Cariboo Tribal Council, representatives of the ranch owner, Gustafsen Lake camp members, and the RCMP took place at the Gustafsen Lake camp.[12] The Cariboo Tribal Council representatives included Chief Agnes Snow of Canoe Creek and Chief Antoine Archie of Canim Lake. The various parties discussed their concerns, and they drew up an agreement. The negotiations included guidelines for the Sundance and a provision that after the Sundance everyone would leave the camp. The ceremony was to be held from 2 July to 12 July 1995. Chief Archie, as one of the local chiefs at this meeting, recalled telling the people at the camp, '"When you people are gone, we're going to be here, we're going to clean up the mess. We're going to pick up our lives and carry on. But you people are here, and you are going to be gone. And we told that to the people at Gustafsen Lake – is that you people are going to come here, cause a disturbance, and you're going to be gone, and we're going to have to be here to deal with that. And we have to start building up our relationships the way it was. The way we had it – because we're stuck – we have to live here. We can't have animosity. Nobody can live on when there are grievances. It's not good for our kids. We've got to think for our kids, not just of ourselves"' (interview with Chief Archie, 25 July 1997).

At the end of June, one of the people inside the camp invited Steven Frasher out to the Sundance site. This invitation was a surprise, because he knew that white people would not normally be allowed, since the presence of non-Natives was traditionally considered a defilement of the Sundance area. When Frasher arrived at the camp, he learned that the local television station, CFJC, had also been invited, although in previous years media attention had been declined. Splitting the Sky (also known as John Hill or Doc), Ernie Archie, and Percy Rosette were at the camp. Frasher recalled that Splitting the Sky 'was talking in terms entirely different than anything we'd associated with Gustafsen Lake up to that point.' According to Frasher, the discussion was about having to deal with Queen Elizabeth II to resolve the dispute. They also mentioned that at one time the land had been designated as part of the reserve.[13] 'And yet they couldn't show you anything to back it up ... And then – they walked us out past the Sundance site, and had earlier agreed that we could take some pictures out there – which again – according to the Sundance rules – just is not done.' During this visit, he surmised that there had been a shift in attitude at the camp. He believed that the central force behind the shift was John Hill, who was to be the Sundance leader that year.

In Frasher's opinion, the invitations to the media, the discussion of the politics, and the opening up of a sacred area was '*to create their spin on the situation, and that was all controlled by Hill – I think. Percy seemed to be very uncomfortable with the attention, because to him, it was a Native spiritual thing.*' Frasher observed Percy Rosette and Ernie Archie speaking in Shuswap, and Archie then came to Hill; Frasher recalled his comments to Hill: '"*No, they're not going to take pictures of the Sundance arbour. It's just not right.*"' By this time, Frasher had already snapped a picture with his camera, in the belief that it was permissible.[14] It appeared to Frasher that when Percy Rosette asserted his authority, the others respected him. He was also under the impression that Rosette may have been overwhelmed by these stronger personalities. Frasher was concerned that the vocal militant element '*would have to latch onto his cause to take whatever legitimacy they could from what Percy was doing ... And that's what we were contending – even before the standoff concluded – just based on what we knew of Percy Rosette*' (interview with Steven Frasher, *100 Mile House Free Press*).

Shooting Incident at Lac La Hache

5 July 1995

Elder sundancer denounces militancy of some of the people inside the camp. (100 Mile House Free Press, 5 July 1995)[15]

In the 5 July 1995 edition of the *100 Mile House Free Press*, a news story appeared, in which a Sundance elder[16] spoke of concerns over the militant nature of the 1995 Sundance. This media source mentioned that rifles were present 'right in the Sundance grounds,' and that people were wearing camouflage fatigues at the worship site. The elder did not agree that guns were necessary to defend the area and expressed concern that Percy Rosette, the Sundance faithkeeper, was being manipulated by people who had been shunned in their own communities. The elder stated that the militant attitude present at the 1995 Sundance was 'part and parcel of the Confederacy movement for sovereignty under the umbrella of the Sundance.' The Sundance participants quoted in the news story thanked and commended rancher Lyle James for 'his past kindness and understanding regarding the use of his land.' They also stated that John Stevens and other true sundancers were angry that the relationship with the rancher had been upset.[17] In the same issue, the *100 Mile House Free Press* ran a story in which Ernie Archie, Gustafsen Lake 'war chief,' admitted to Sundance elders that a gunshot was 'accidentally' fired weeks ago. This admission changed an earlier statement given by Ernie Archie and Splitting the Sky (John Hill) to the *100 Mile House Free Press* reporters the week before. The allegations of the elder and the subsequent story of a shooting incident at Lac La Hache[18] were not widely known outside the local communities. The incident is pivotal in demonstrating how the media had become part of the story, even at this early stage of the conflict.

Several weeks after the 5 July 1995 news stories, editor Steven Frasher received a cryptic press release from the RCMP, advising him that someone had shot a gun into a house at Lac La Hache. Canim Lake Chief Antoine Archie and Steven Frasher linked the Lac La Hache shooting incident with the elder's criticizing some of the people and activities at the Sundance.[19] By July, the local newspaper editor and other journalists in the interior had become aware of the changed tenor from previous Sundances: it had been transformed into a political vehicle. However, not everyone associated with the camp was considered part of this politicized element. Indeed, even Percy Rosette had told a friend in town that '"some of the young people in the Sundance were getting short-fused, and he was really worried"'; the source said that he believed that the shots fired did not come from 'true sundancers,' but from 'angry young men.'[20]

Disagreements between the Camp and the Local Native Communities

Despite the previous agreement to leave after the Sundance, some of the people remained at the camp. Hill explained that they had decided to complete the Sundance first, and then deal with the land issue by citing various international laws and by getting their *'day in court.'* He did not elaborate on how the group had made the decision or who was involved. He argued that the land was put up for sale and/or leased by the Canadian government illegally. Hill quoted from the Proclamation of 1763, saying *'that unless the Aboriginal peoples and their Aboriginal hunting grounds are unceded territories – unless they are willfully ceded to the crown – the land shall be left unmolested and undisturbed.'* He reasoned that, historically, this land had never been wilfully ceded by this Shuswap nation and that it was acquired illegally (interview with John Hill, 23 July 1996).

According to Chief Archie, when he and others who were concerned about the nature of the Gustafsen Lake Sundance named various people who supported them, *'Those people told us to mind our own business.'* He told the people at the Sundance camp that they had promised to leave after the Sundance cycle was over: *'And I pointed out to them – I told them – that Indians – that the Indian word is stronger than any written word. You give your word, and you don't break it – that's it. And he had broken the word out there. He had an agreement originally to practise for four years, and then they were going to leave.'* **And that agreement was with Lyle James.** *'Right. That agreement was* [makes facial/hand gestures] *it seems.'*

Chief Antoine Archie recalled how Percy Rosette had said that he had had a vision of some graves around the Sundance area. Chief Archie explained that because of the smallpox epidemic, which had killed so many Native people in the previous century, *'there are Indian graves all over the place,* [but that] *it's pretty hard to prove.'* He pointed out that the paradox of the situation was that it would be sacrilegious to dig up the area in order to prove the case:[21]

> They said it was their land, that it was Indian land, and they said that they were going to get it. And we told them – if they were going to claim the land, it would have to come through consensus ... We told them that we were in the treaty process ... and we told them that they couldn't speak for us; I told them that my people have chosen me to speak for them, and I spoke for over 500 people. And I told them that anything I said, I was accountable for. I told them that you people here can get away with anything – you people here can say anything you want and get away with it, because you're not accountable to anybody.
>
> And they said, 'Well, you're – you're under a government elected system,' and I told him that our people had developed their own electoral system – here at Canim Lake. We developed it, it's not the same as any other band, we're elected for four years, each and every council is elected for four years, but we have an election every two years – so that our members are staggered. We never, ever have a full new council ... and that's the way we designed it. And that's not the DIA [Department of Indian Affairs] system; that's our system. We designed that, and we put it forward to our band members, and the band members voted for it, and that's what we do.

In spite of Chief Archie's explanation, the people had in the camp insisted that Antoine Archie was still working for the DIA.

Some of the sundancers used the argument that they only acknowledged hereditary chiefs. Chief Archie explained that since so many Shuswap people had died during the smallpox epidemic more than a century ago, hereditary lines had all but vanished. On a rare occasion, someone might mention having a hereditary chief in the family, but nobody pursues this point to gain authority. Chief Archie said that the elected band council structure at Canim Lake had a system of checks and balances that his community appreciated. *'Because if you've got somebody in there that you're really not happy with, you can't change it. We needed something that we could change, and something that we could fix. Something that we can evaluate, measure, and work.'*

In the summer of 1995, when Lyle James and the people who stayed after the Sundance were at loggerheads, Chief Antoine Archie went to their camp on his own to talk to them a few times before anything more serious happened. As many as five local people were there at the time, including two of Chief Archie's nephews. Nobody would leave. He concluded that many of the young men in the camp were *'urban Indians'* with little, if any, knowledge of traditional languages and skills. They did not seem prepared to look after themselves by hunting and living off the land. He described one of his visits to the camp: *'I went in there, the first time we sat down – [with] Splitting the Sky [John Hill] ... and he asked us to bring in burgers. So I knew that – they're not used to this kind of lifestyle – they're from the streets – a lot of them. They're not used to living in the bush. Percy – he could live there forever. Wolverine – could live there forever. But the young guys would get sick – and they started to get sick.'* On one occasion, Chief Archie and his wife had been fishing at the lake, and he dropped by to visit. Only one of the people would talk to him: *'And at the time I was joking with him – I said, "This here is our traditional territory. What the hell are you doing – scaring all the game up here?!"'* (interview with Chief Antoine Archie, 25 July 1997).

Proclamations to the Media

19 July 1995

The sundancers issue a press release describing themselves as 'defenders of sovereign unceded Shuswap territory.' They announce that they are making preparations 'to resist an invasion by the RCMP.' The press release quotes their lawyer, Bruce Clark, as advising them that 'as a matter of strict law, you are acting within your existing legal rights by resisting the invasion.' (Chronology, *Vancouver Sun*, 12 September 1995, A3)

Another local journalist recalled receiving facsimiles from the camp in mid-July, one in particular signed '*the Defenders of the* [Shuswap Nation].' The information was similar to a mission statement. As the journalist remembered the message read something like '*We the Defenders ... will not tolerate use of our traditional land.*' The message alluded to the fact that they had not left the Gustasfen Lake camp and explained why their group was remaining.

The local Native response to the people remaining at Gustafsen Lake proclaiming themselves '*Defenders of the Shuswap Nation*' was to deny the group's identification and to distance themselves. According to Chief Antoine Archie, the local chiefs made public statements declaring '*These people don't represent us, we do not promote violence – we just kept saying that all the way through.*' Some of the local Native people became so irate that they threatened to confront the people inside the camp. Chief Archie said that he explained to the local Native people that '*These people* [in the camp] *had nothing to lose – they had nowhere to go back to, they didn't have anywhere to go back to – and the more publicity they got, the better help to them – you were just playing into their hands. And I pointed out to them that our constable, Bob, knew and told us that these people were heavily armed, they had automatic weapons ... Which, with stuff like that, and they told the media – 'we want a fight.' But, if the RCMP had stepped back, and we had taken them out – see the problem?*' (interview with Chief Antoine Archie, 25 July 1997).

On 20 July 1995 people inside the camp allegedly threatened two of Lyle James's Native ranch hands. The frightened employees rode all night to report the incident to James. They contacted the local RCMP, and the ranch hands described gunfire that may have come from semi-automatic weapons. At first, the police discounted the notion that semi-automatic weapons were involved and suggested that the shots were more likely from hunting rifles. According to James, the police revised this assumption after the weapons seizure at the Fraser River by two Native fisheries officers from two individuals who previously had been involved in the celebration of the Sundance.

Emergency Response Team Compromised

11 August 1995

A pivotal development takes place when two Native Indians from Gustafsen Lake – Dave Penna[22] and Ernest Archie – are arrested by fisheries officers for allegedly gillnetting salmon in the Fraser River during a closed period. Searching their truck the officers find a weapons cache – including an AK–47, a Soviet assault rifle that is popular with guerrilla organizations. The rifle has a magazine with 30 rounds of ammunition, which it can fire in three seconds. The two men are taken into custody along with their arsenal: a loaded AK–47, a Glock 9-mm semi-automatic pistol loaded with Black Talon bullets designed to inflict maximum damage on human tissue, knives, machetes, camouflage clothing and a garrote made of piano wire. (Chronology, *Vancouver Sun*, 12 September 1995, A3)

18 August 1995[23]

Shot narrowly misses Mountie. (Chronology, *Vancouver Sun*, 11 September, 1995 B8)

Both Staff Sergeant Marin Sarich and District Superintendent Len Olfert discussed the activities at the Gustafsen Lake camp that the police had been documenting for several months. Nobody believed that the Sundance could evolve into the flash-point of violence that it became. The ceremony had been held in the Cariboo for a number of years, and the incidents at Gustafsen Lake were considered minor (relative to other situations in the province). In the summer of 1995 three Native RCMP officers from the area had been assigned to help to negotiate a peaceful settlement with the sundancers; one of these officers attended the Sundance. The Native officers also frequently met with the people in the camp to discuss a resolution, and they were in the process of arranging another negotiation meeting later in August.[24]

After the confiscation of the cache of weapons at the Rudy Johnson Bridge on the Fraser River, Staff Sergeant Sarich discussed with his superiors the possibility of intensifying the investigation of the camp.[25] According to Staff Sergeant Sarich, he and District Superintendent Olfert disagreed on the extent to which the media should be notified of the developments. Staff Sergeant Sarich was not in favour of going to the media, and he debated this point with his superior for about a half hour. His concern was *'that we would create a media* [event] *and a standoff – we would give them the audience. I said that these are a group of radicals, they have seized some property, they're 40 kilometres out – and that's the other thing that I had to be able to justify to everyone.'* After the strategy meetings at Kamloops, a decision was made not to contact the media. Instead, the plan was to put in a reconnaissance team to assess the camp for artillery, foxholes, and booby traps and to estimate the number of people. Next, they would devise a strategy to contain and remove the occupants and then go to the media. *'Unfortunately, we were compromised.'*

The Emergency Response Team (ERT) reconnaissance mission, which included District Superintendent Olfert, began late in the afternoon on 17 August.[26] They spent the night a few kilometres away from Gustafsen Lake camp. In the early morning, while they were attempting to film defensive structures and the camp area, the camp horses started moving around, alerted to their presence. Shortly after, someone in the bush spotted the camouflaged officers and called out. When no one answered, the individual fired a shot in the direction of the ERT, narrowly missing one of the team.

Staff Sergeant Sarich assessed that the willingness of people inside the camp to shoot at anyone warranted a more serious approach from the police.[27] With the element of surprise gone, they could not proceed safely to the next phase of the plan. The RCMP senior officers asked that the three local Native RCMP constables not go into the camp for further discussions, because they thought that the situation was too dangerous.[28] The ERT reconnaissance team was called back, and District Superintendent Olfert wanted to inform the media. By this time, Sergeant Sarich was willing to concede on this point. District Superintendent Olfert contacted Sergeant Montague in Vancouver to set up a press conference for the following day (interview with Staff Sergeant Sarich, 24 July 1997).

Steven Frasher was contacted by a man calling from Lac La Hache on behalf of Percy Rosette. He reported that armed men were seen wandering around close to the camp, *'sneaking around in the bushes,'* and that these individuals were all camouflaged. The message relayed was that these individuals might be vigilantes. Frasher learned that Rosette had telephoned the RCMP detachment to report the sightings.[29] According to Frasher, the messenger described him as quite upset on the telephone with the RCMP, exclaiming to them, *'They're out to get us you know!'* (interview with Stephen Frasher, 23 July 1997).

However, the RCMP did not want to reveal that it was their ERT in the bush until the reconnaissance team was safely out of the area. It was at least eight hours before the RCMP contacted Rosette to tell him not to worry (by this time the ERT had long since retreated) and that the men in the bush were RCMP officers.

Shortly after Percy Rosette discovered armed men (ERT) lurking around their camp, John Hill, who was by this time at home in Hinton, Alberta, received a telephone call, advising him of a *'serious red alert.'* In Hill's opinion, the situation was life threatening, and Rosette and his wife, Toby, telephoned him an hour later to confirm threats of future confrontations. Hill called Jones (William Ignace, or Wolverine), as well as *'a bunch of people from down the area down there,'* and told them to *'go on red alert'* and *'to send up some men in there, man – and make a physical presence ... in case they come – at least we're ready to meet them head-on – you know what I mean?'* Thus began a series of networked telephone calls to Vancouver and other parts of the province to people who would come to Gustafsen Lake to support the dispute. These supporters were those involved with Native sovereignty, human rights activists, and environmentalists.

John Hill argued, *'If I hadn't have been on the outside – that threat assessment team* [ERT] *that they sent in there on August the 19th* [actually 18 August] *three days* [after] *that – that crucial meeting was to happen – and we assert that they sent that threat assessment in there to kill the occupants. To create an incident so that they would not have to deal with the larger question of jurisdiction, to paint us as terrorists, to paint us as cultists, to paint us as renegades, militants, criminals – the whole works – to demonize and discredit us – so that they could justify and they could wipe out – that they could wipe out the issue for jurisdictional arguments'* (interview with John Hill, 23 July 1996).

In Vancouver, CBC-TV broadcast a story that evening (18 August) about the Gustafsen Lake dispute, incorporating a film clip from a videotape produced by the camp, 'Defenders of the Land.' The CBC received the videotape from supporters who had recently been in the camp. The camp supporters believed that the videotape would present their side of the developing conflict. The newscast drew the immediate attention of the RCMP because the film clip showed people inside the camp preparing for (what seemed apparent to the police) an armed battle against the RCMP. John Hill, appearing as a spokesperson in the videotape, announced that any entry by police would be considered an 'act of war.' According to Sergeant Montague, the videotaped program went beyond expressing the goals and ideals of the camp. It featured a blatant display of weapons and an intention to harm police. Sergeant Montague recalls that [the videotape was] *'showing them with AK–47s, making statements like 'take the high ground here, if the RCMP arrive, this is the best way to shoot at them from here.' And this caught our attention – that they're openly telling the public through the CBC National News, that there's going to be big trouble, there's going to be a showdown. Now up until this point, the RCMP had been very passive and trying to deal with the situation.'* (interview with Sergeant Montague, 27 May 1997).

Insider versus Outsider Perspectives

One of the patterns that emerged from the case study of the media coverage of the Gustafsen Lake standoff is that of insider versus outsider perspectives. We find it in the contrasting relations between the RCMP and the media at 100 Mile House and at Vancouver (further explored in chapter 7). It is also evident in the adversarial positions taken by several of the other players. For example, Lyle James's and John Hill's differing frames are informed by their contrasting understandings of land ownership in British Columbia. Similarly, Chief Antoine Archie's and John Hill's perspectives disagree on many levels: over Sundance practices and interpretations, legitimate Native forms of governance, the British Columbia treaty process, and the right to act on behalf of Native people.

Although Chief Archie and John Hill were only two of the players in the conflict, their frames of reference are also representative of insider and outsider perspectives. Chief Archie's level of appreciation of the social relations that were most affected and resolutions of land and resource issues was informed by insider knowledge of the local Native communities and how they have struggled with racism and intolerance. His concern was the immediate and protracted impact of a serious conflict on local Native and non-Native community relations. John Hill's understanding of the social relations at play and of resolutions to land and resource issues centred on historical and legal precedents, with an eye towards wide-based reform for Aboriginal people at the provincial and national levels. The clash of perspectives between the sides that these two individuals represented was particularly evident over the issue of group identity. When the people at the camp began referring to themselves as 'Defenders of the Shuswap Nation,' signifying the group's implied legitimacy and wide support, there was a strong local disavowal. The local leadership and many of the local Natives contested this identity because they considered most of the people at Gustafsen Lake 'outsiders,' whose radicalized perspective and political goals did not represent those of the local Native communities.

The narrative also shows how the dispute developed into a volatile situation and, in the process, transformed the role of the RCMP. Originally, the RCMP had acted as mediators in the argument over the occupation of a 20-acre parcel of land. According to the information collected for this study, it appears that the escalation of the situation began when those remaining in the camp became embroiled in a series of shooting incidents and when the weapons were seized. These events provided the impetus for the RCMP to shift their interpretation of the situation from a civil dispute to a serious criminal offence. The police defined the shooting incidents and the possession of dangerous weapons as acts of terrorism. This label implied that the social order was under a serious threat. When we compare the frameworks of the local native communities, the camp, and the local and regional RCMP, it becomes apparent that the local interpretation of the conflict had become subsumed. The new definitions necessitated the raising of the stakes of the dispute, with each side claiming a moral justification and a need for public support. The escalation of the dispute and the revisions of the definition of the situation were also related to the introduction of people and agendas outside the local context.

The account of the early part of the dispute reveals the nature of the relationships between the local media, the camp, and the local RCMP. The local media were involved as participants in the event in addition to reporting the developments. A few of the sundancers (both the militant and the conservative sides) sought out the local media outlet to convey to a public audience their definitions of the situation of the camp. The militants dominated the local media coverage and engaged in what appeared to be a public relations campaign. By taking the initiative with the media early in the dispute, the camp enjoyed an unfettered media status and an audience that normally would not be presented with a group so vocal against law enforcement and government institutions. There was little or no challenge by law enforcement and government institutions through the local media. In contrast to this proactive bid for media attention in the camp was the reluctance of the local RCMP to involve the media, especially the large outlets. When the RCMP decided to invite in the large media outlets to introduce them to a breaking-news story, the camp's dominance over the media was contested. The people in the camp would now have competition from the RCMP and government officials for control of the news stories and the influence on public opinion.

CHAPTER TWO

Media Circus

'We know the weaponry is there and we also now know that they're prepared to use it,' Olfert said. 'We clearly associate this as an act of terrorism.'

District Superintendent Len Olfert[1]

The focus in chapters 2 through 7 is on the media coverage at the time of the 1995 Gustafsen Lake standoff, primarily from the perspectives of the journalists. The emphasis on the recollections of the journalists is not to suggest that they suffered any worse than the other groups (thereby trivializing the conditions endured by others). Indeed, some of the details of the adaptations and inconveniences for the reporters covering the event seem trivial compared with the living conditions of many of the other people involved. Nor is the choice of this dominant frame intended to imply that the journalists' experiences have the greatest legitimacy in this event. Nonetheless, it is through the journalists' recollections that we can more fully appreciate the unpublished context of the media coverage of the Gustafsen Lake standoff.

In order to appreciate how the media coverage became enmeshed with the escalation of the conflict it is helpful to understand that the RCMP operational plan for the most part took as its model a *barricaded situation*.' This model provides guidelines for engagement used by law enforcement personnel for hostage-takings and similar crises. A component of these guidelines is conflict management, a process approach to facilitate cooperative communication, with the goal of eventually reaching a resolution. Conflict management promotes initiatives that *'make it easy for them to say "yes" and make it tough for them to say "no."'* This technique is in contrast to *'that idea of amassing a significant amount of force and crushing the opposition,'* an approach more likely to result in casualties. A *'velvet-glove and an iron-fist'* characterized the method the RCMP employed during the Gustafsen Lake standoff, but it was not common knowledge at the time (interview with RCMP psychologist, Dr Mike Webster, 21 June 1997). The RCMP adoption of the barricaded situation model had a significant bearing on the media characterizations during the standoff.

Williams Lake Press Conference

19 August 1995

> The media are taken on an RCMP flight to Williams Lake where they are briefed on events at Gustafsen Lake. In a press conference reporters are shown the weapons cache and hear from James and a local native Indian leader, Chief Bill Chelsea of the Cariboo Tribal Council.[2] (Chronology, *Vancouver Sun*, 12 September 1995, A3)

The Williams Lake press conference set the media frame for the RCMP definition of the situation. The RCMP were the most authoritative source physically present at the conflict. Because of this, their perspective offered the most compelling frame for the media to promote in the news stories. It would also be the frame the media would use for contrast in their attempts to offer balance in their news accounts. The opportunity for the latter was greatest during the few days in which the RCMP allowed journalists access to the people at the camp.

Almost all of the journalists from Vancouver had covered previous Native protests in British Columbia, including those at Clayoquot Sound, Lyell Island, Duffy Lake, Adams Lake, Penticton, and Douglas Lake. Two of the journalists had covered the 1990 Oka crisis in Quebec, and a few had covered hostage-taking incidents. Few, if any, of the journalists interviewed for this study were surprised to get the call to travel to Williams Lake to cover yet another Native protest. The RCMP media personnel in Vancouver contacted several Vancouver media outlets to inform them of the press conference. Some of the journalists made arrangements to fly to Williams Lake on the RCMP jet. One reporter said, *'Montague did give some info* [but did not give away the full content] *on the plane – that the gist was that a local rancher and some Natives were having a disagreement over land, and that some of the people involved had criminal records.'* Not all of the Vancouver media were notified of the press conference. A few journalists learned about it from colleagues working for other outlets, but still managed to arrive at Williams Lake on time. Some reporters who could not attend made arrangements to share information with colleagues who were able to go.

According to the journalists who gathered at the RCMP detachment at Williams Lake, the mood at the press conference was sober. The RCMP officials described shooting incidents that they connected to the Sundance.[3] They laid out the weaponry that had been confiscated from two Aboriginal men who, the police said, had been at the Sundance.[4] The police played a tape of a CBC Television news story that included a clip from the videotaped program, 'Defenders of the Land.' The journalists remembered the segment of the videotape that showed Splitting the Sky (John Hill) teaching what appeared to the police to be guerrilla-warfare tactics. According to one journalist, the videotape was shown in order to give the media an idea of what the people inside the camp were like. District Superintendent Olfert made most of the comments on behalf of the RCMP. Concerns over the activities inside the camp came from several sources: the police, Bill Chelsea from Alkali Lake, and Lyle James, the rancher who had originally given permission for the Sundance.

Some media outlets did not learn of the press conference until it was too late to attend. Steven Frasher, editor of the 100 Mile House newspaper, was incensed that the Vancouver RCMP media personnel had overlooked his newspaper. Missing the press conference meant that the editor had to play catch-up to keep abreast of the latest developments. However, the newspaper's adjustment was made easier because it had covered the story longer than any other media outlet, and the staff knew of the best news sources in the area. Personnel at the *Vancouver Sun* were similarly annoyed that the RCMP media personnel did not contact their newspaper office. According to one reporter, '*We tried to figure out what happened – we phoned up Montague and basically said, "what the fuck happened?!"*' The journalists speculated that the newspaper had been overlooked because of the way its staff had written previous news stories that depicted Natives versus RCMP, where '*we didn't necessarily do what the RCMP had told us to do all the time.*' It would have been possible for the RCMP to reach someone in the news office on Saturday morning. '*But our response was – we felt left out. The other thing is, as a journalist, when the police charter a plane, fly people to a press conference at a particular place, they want this covered, so you know they have an agenda. I mean it's quite obvious*' (interview with journalist). Absence at Williams

Lake meant that the *Vancouver Sun* reporter assigned to the story also had to play catch-up and present a news story with a different angle. The journalist conducted long-distance telephone interviews with people who provided another side of the story, one that would contrast that of the police.

The reporters who did not find out about the dispute at Gustafsen Lake first hand at the Williams Lake press conference prepared for coverage in a number of ways. Some of the regional journalists had been aware of the situation from stories of complaints raised in the British Columbia legislature in Victoria that year. Others knew that a conflict was brewing because of the faxes sent by the people in the camp and the interviews that had taken place in June. Once the story broke, journalists heard about the dispute while watching television, reading newspapers, or listening to the radio while on summer holiday. The recursion of previous news accounts informing new news stories continued throughout the coverage of the standoff.

The Williams Lake press conference was instructive for the media because it provided them with a framework they could incorporate for the opening news stories. The RCMP presentation dominated the news accounts. The group of journalists recalled District Superintendent Len Olfert referring to the kind of weaponry and the shooting incidents as *'terrorist'* in nature. They said that this shaped their perception of the situation and the choice of language in their news stories. The serious manner of the police and the display of the weapons affected the mood of the press conference and left a lasting impression with the journalists. All those presenting information provided various but concurring perspectives about the situation at Gustasfen Lake. The lack of contrasting opinions of the conflict meant the journalists had to seek out the people inside the camp for the other side of the story.

Media Converge at 100 Mile House

Some reporters went directly from Williams Lake to the smaller community of 100 Mile House after the press conference. During that first week, a flood of other journalists, mostly from the Vancouver area, also arrived at 100 Mile House. Many reporters brought enough clothes for three days – and stayed almost a month. They rearranged their lives back home, discussed with editors and producers the alternatives for coverage, and tended to their immediate needs – all while covering the story and meeting deadlines for publications and broadcasts.

Journalists rented sports utility vehicles to drive on the roads that connected the town with Gustafsen Lake. They also found out how easy it was to get lost in the labyrinth of forestry roads that link 100 Mile House to Gustafsen Lake, Dog Creek, and Alkali Lake. The last several kilometres to Gustafsen Lake were so deeply rutted that flat tires and blow-outs were common for media as well as for police. This generated extra business for the local tire store.

The Red Coach Inn, the largest and best equipped of the establishments in town, had to juggle rooms between media and guests who had reserved many months in advance. The hotel also provided accommodations for RCMP, Native intermediaries,[5] and supporters of the protest.[6] For the journalists, the first priority of the daily routine was to secure a room for the night, a process that could take as long as two hours and that had to be finalized before anything else could be planned for the day. One journalist referred to it as 'the job from hell,' because hotels and motels could not accommodate the vacationers, the bus tourists, and the enormous influx of police and media. Some journalists shared, and a few had to move to other establishments until space at the Red Coach became available. Hotel rooms were at such a premium that journalists transferred them like relay batons – as one journalist prepared to return to Vancouver, the colleague coming in from Vancouver would inherit the room.

Because the RCMP called press conferences with only a few minutes' notice, journalists often took meals as they were rushing from one venue to another, if they bothered at all. According to a local source who observed the hyperactivity and the eating habits of many of the media, it seemed that they ate a full breakfast, but lived on coffee and chocolate bars for the rest of the day. The late-night press conferences and the potential for developments at any time exhausted journalists who did not have partners to share the workload. During the first ten days after the Williams Lake press conference, many of the journalists worked with very little sleep.

Journalists also had to adapt to the scarcity of communications facilities. Cellular telephones were not viable past 108 Mile Ranch, and reporters had to obtain radiotelephones. They soon realized that the radiotelephones were not secure for private conversations. They could eavesdrop on conversations occurring between competitor journalists, the police, and the conversations held at the camp. Several sources recalled, 'Everybody was always listening!' Some journalists, like the police, developed code words or spoke in very guarded terms when talking to colleagues over the radiotelephones. The loss of privacy was particularly stressful for journalists who were camped at the isolated Checkpoint 17 and for whom this device was the only link to the outside world for professional as well as personal communication. There were many rumours of RCMP wire-tapping, and several people were convinced that the RCMP had tapped every telephone and fax machine in the region. Not all the television outlets had their own satellite dishes, and some had to rent satellite-time from other outlets with satellite trucks. However, this meant that satellite-time was at a premium in terms of availability and expense.

Breaking news just before radio-broadcast or newspaper deadlines added to the chaos. Journalists had to read their stories over the telephone to Vancouver; if a hotel room was not available, telephone dispatches took place in the hotel lobby, where there was no privacy from curious hotel guests. One journalist had to run to a restaurant down the street where he could hook up his laptop computer to send news stories through electronic mail because of an incompatibility with the telephone lines in the hotel. Another journalist recalled composing stories in a moving vehicle, 'and writing our script on our knee on a bumpy road ... it was insanity. I'm actually amazed that we were able to turn out the material we did. It was very exciting, there was a lot of adrenaline, and as things settled down and got into a routine, it got less exciting' (interview with journalist).

The possibility of a violent ending was another stress factor. Some reporters described experiencing a sickening sense of foreboding about the conflict, which was not lifted until they returned to Vancouver when their shifts concluded or, for those who remained, when the standoff ended. The shooting death of a police officer during the 1990 Oka standoff and the tragic ending of the 1993 standoff at Waco, Texas, were in the thoughts of several people at the time. There were references to these events in the early news stories of the Gustafsen Lake standoff.

For the journalists who converged at 100 Mile House to cover the standoff, adapting to the conditions of reporting meant coping with the instability of the logistics, as well as the potential for catastrophic breaking news. There was no predictable timeline for the event to climax, which created what several people referred to as a 'hurry up and wait' mentality. The journalists found the exhaustion (for about the first two weeks) brutal, and most of them considered the coverage of the Gustafsen Lake standoff more hectic than any news event they had ever covered. Media deadlines were consistent, but the short notice to attend

RCMP press conferences kept the journalists alert for a news-breaking event. Once journalists had secured their personal needs and met their deadlines, they regained some aspects of control over their situations. Yet the re-establishment of routines could do little for the unpredictability of developments. The routines could not regulate the hours of work or address the sustained loss of privacy. These conditions continued to be sources of tension, particularly for those who covered the event for the longest time.

Journalists and the People at the Camp

21 August 1995

A Sun reporter who visits the camp is told by Wolverine: '(Police) and the media, you are all part of the New World Order. They'll have to take us out in body bags.' (Chronology, *Vancouver Sun*, 12 September 1995, A3)

A few of the journalists in the region had made the trek to the camp for interviews weeks before the dispute had become a breaking-news story. One reporter recalls having a conversation with Wolverine, or Jonesy Ignace as he was known. The reporter described the scene where he was at the camp, in late July, sitting around the campfire drinking coffee with six or seven people at the Gustafsen Lake camp. '*They were fairly laid-back, but very persistent in their message – that there was a new world order, and there was a conspiracy against Native people – things along those lines.*' Soon this relaxed atmosphere was broken:

Jonesy Ignace just got up in my face, he got very emotional, saying that the media was part of the problem, an institution, part of the conspiracy, things along those lines. **How did you respond to [Wolverine's] claim that the media was part of a conspiracy?** *Well, I disagreed with him and I told him we have some ethics about objectivity and how we try to get both sides of the story. He just interrupted with, you know, 'that's bullshit!' and he started screaming and raising his voice and stuff like that.*

At that point you sort of have to pretty well have to come to the conclusion that you cannot convince anybody, so you change the topic, and try to move on to something else. **Okay.** *Because you weren't going to convince him – it became quite evident when I tried to explain what my job was and the fact of what I was doing, that I wasn't on a payroll, I wasn't a spy – he called me a spy – I said I wasn't a spy – I can attest to that I told him – he cut you off – just said 'bullshit*

you're all in this together, you're here, probably taking notes and will go back
deliver it to the police' – things along those lines. So yeah, I mean he was
confrontational on that, but you have to change the subject – what are you going
to say, what would you do to convince someone so strong in their beliefs?
(Interview with journalist)

After the Williams Lake RCMP press conference, most journalists
were nervous about going inside the camp to get interviews and elected
to make contact through their cellular telephones. One reporter recalled
being so frightened the first time he went to the camp that he clutched
his gym bag in front of his chest to shield himself from gunfire during
his walk from the driveway to the cabin. The police had indicated to the
media that there were a *'fair number'* of firearms in the camp, which
played on the reporter's mind. He said that he calmed down when he
met one of the mothers of the camp members as he was walking. The
mother talked about her son and said that he was not the violent sort –
but she did not know the others in the camp.

Another journalist felt as though the people in the camp were very
nervous and watching their visitors' every move:

Drove along that road – gravel road ... then took the right off that gravel highway
– and then you drove on these massive potholes. They could see you coming from
all angles, when they watched ya. We drove up to the barbed wire fence, and you
got out of your vehicle, and you presented yourself. And Wolverine was there,
and Suniva was there, Sheila was there and Tron was there ... And then – we
spent four or five hours with them that night – trying to figure out some of the
nonsense from reality. And I'll never forget that night – we came out about ten
o'clock, it had been a 15–hour day, as we got off that road and on to the main
gravel road – our tire blew up! [laughs] *It surprised us!* [The journalist
described having to unload the gear in the vehicle to get at the spare tire
and the jack.] *And sometimes the younger Natives would say 'Okay – go – now*
go' you know like, 'we're doing visiting now.' And there was an obvious, real
tension there, pressure – and so I'd say, 'Okay, we're done, Okay we're going' and
[the young Natives would say] *'Leave! Now go!' you know like, trying to*
control the area again. So we went back to town. (Interview with journalist)

Despite the nervousness on both sides, a few journalists did get in to
talk to the people inside the camp, and they brought in gifts, such as
cigarettes and coffee. The meetings often took place while they sat around
the fire. There were minutes of silence; some Natives covered their

faces to prevent identification. A few reporters and photographers ven-
tured into the cabin, but this triggered immediate defensive responses
from some of the members of the group. According to one journalist,
some members of the media were attempting to capture pictures of
firearms. One reporter had a sense that the people were heavily armed,
but he could not tell if the lookouts behind the trees were armed. Other
journalists also observed that the young men who guarded the perimeter of the camp acted 'very, very nervous' (interviews with journalists).

During this part of the standoff, several different 'experts' provided
background information on the Sundance ceremony. In some of these
news stories the Sundance was identified as a religious practice brought
into the area from the Plains Indians' tradition, which was not part of
the traditional Shuswap culture. This information was used by newspaper columnists to challenge the camp members' justification for their
right to the land.[7]

The television and newspaper coverage distinguished two different
discourses in the camp concerning the approach taken for the protest.
One side emphasized that Percy Rosette had a vision that the Gustafsen
Lake site was sacred land, which made it appropriate for the Sundance.
This group eschewed violence as a means to acquire the property. The
other side, most often represented by Wolverine, sounded militant and
agitated. Wolverine talked of a conspiracy by a new world order that
had an agenda to decimate Native people.[8] On more than one occasion,
Wolverine referred to the fact that his group was so committed to
remaining on the land that they would only 'come out in body bags.' He
said that if events took this turn, then Canada would have to explain its
actions to the world.[9] Members of the camp refuted the RCMP allegations to the media that there had been shooting incidents and that they
had illegal weapons. They told the journalists that the RCMP 'say
anything to the press to make us look bad in the public eye.'[10] However,
a shooting incident originating from the camp on the morning of
24 August that had been announced in an RCMP press release was
confirmed on a Native website. The incident became a national
news story.[11]

Within a few days of the media's descending from Vancouver, the
BCTV crew fell out of favour with members of the camp. The television
station broadcast an impromptu interview attempt between a BCTV
journalist and a couple of people from the camp one morning outside a
restaurant at 100 Mile House. BCTV played the segment later that
evening on the news, and the next time the BCTV crew drove out to the

camp, some of the people from the camp threatened the reporter. He retreated quickly to the van. Although BCTV returned to the camp area once more, the crew did not go into the compound but stayed behind the fence. Word of the incident at the camp with the BCTV journalist quickly spread among other members of the media. However, not everyone was sympathetic: *'They made statements about the Natives, and they made inferences and stuff, in their items, that – either they are true, and they can stand by them, or – it's just satisfying part of the crowd – part of the audience that's back home saying – "there goes those damn Natives again" or whatever. So, you know, it's one of the things about being in the field – you have to look people back in the face and say, "you said it" or "you did it"'* (interview with journalist).

Only a few reporters were able to develop and maintain a positive rapport with the people at the camp, and in response to the attitudes in the camp towards the media, some redoubled their efforts to develop trust and be more considerate. Nonetheless, proof of these efforts was tested in the media publications, and many people did not appreciate the light the journalists cast on them in some of the news stories.

In order to evaluate the media's representation of them, people in the camp and their supporters monitored the news coverage from several outlets. In the 100 Mile House area, there were three newspapers available: *Vancouver Sun*, *Vancouver Province*, and *100 Mile House Free Press*. Those television viewers who did not have cable or a satellite dish watched BCTV and CFJC (a CBC affiliate). Canadian Press news stories were generally unsympathetic to the camp and frequently labelled the group as *rebels*, *renegades*, and *squatters*, but I learned that Canadian Press reporters were still welcomed into the camp. When I asked one of the journalists about this anomaly, he said that the people in the camp did not read any of the articles from Canadian Press because the newspapers that included Canadian Press articles were not sold in town.

Even at this stage of the standoff the discourse analysis of newspaper stories reveals that the greatest attention continued to be paid to the militant views held in the camp. The quotations and paraphrases from the camp leadership were most often the most volatile and extreme of pronouncements. The resultant media characterizations in the newspaper stories show that the images of the camp were co-constructed by the media, the camp sources, the police, and government officials. The news accounts emphasized the hostility of the group and characterized their demands as outlandish.

Media Coverage of Ovide Mercredi, Grand Chief of the Assembly of First Nations

24–26 August 1995

> Mercredi arrives and visits the camp – but gets a cold reception. (Chronology, *Vancouver Sun*, 12 September, A3)

The Cariboo Tribal Council invited Grand Chief Ovide Mercredi to come to Gustafsen Lake to intervene with the people at the camp.[12] For the journalists, the grand chief's arrival at the standoff seemed to define the story as a national news event, and more media congregated at 100 Mile House. The RCMP told the media that they would give Mercredi two days to negotiate a settlement, but that, in the meantime, the RCMP would continue making their own plans to remove the people at the Gustafsen Lake camp.[13] At the first meeting, the journalists arrived at the camp in advance of Grand Chief Mercredi. As they approached the camp gate, young Native men asked for their names and checked to confirm whether the camp leaders would allow specific journalists inside. This procedure created some hard feelings among several members of the media about unequal access, and the preferences of the camp shifted the competitive advantage to outlets that normally had to work harder to secure news opportunities. One journalist noticed a parallel in the camp's selection of reporters: *'See, it was almost – what Montague was doing to the media in town, the Native people were doing to the media out at the camp'* (interview with journalist). When one journalist wandered into a bushy area that shielded the cabin from the Sundance arbour, he noticed the security measures provided by the young men acting as lookouts. Their camouflage clothing allowed them to *'fade back in the bush like a hologram,'* and they were communicating with *"clickers and other things."* As soon as the journalist walked into the area, one of the lookouts emerged and advised the reporter, *'You're out-of-bounds, go back over there'* (interview with journalist).

The journalists who were left at the fence attempted to listen to the conversations between Mercredi and the camp leaders, and many of the news stories that day were based on this information. *'We were allowed to go in – not right to the meeting, but fairly close, close enough that eventually we discovered that we could hear most of it, if ... there were only a few of us* [listening near the fence], *and we shut up ... There were about eight of us at the end, perched along the fence, and we could overhear – hear every word. Umm – which was doubtless why Mercredi didn't want us back the next day'* (interview with journalist). However, one of the journalists permitted inside the camp said that the distance of the other journalists hampered their coverage of the event. He said that other journalists lacked an understanding of the style of interaction between Mercredi and the leaders of the camp. *'Now everyone else could get shots a hundred feet away, but of course you couldn't hear it, and you could only partially see it, so I could get Mercredi's face through the fire, Wolverine – everybody there ... There was no song-and-dance, there was no exchange – there was a lot of yelling and stuff – but it was yelling of emotion, not at someone, like 'Mercredi, you're an idiot' or 'Wolverine, you're stupid' or something. It was all directed at the emotion of the moment ... It was respectful ... And, of course, the other media can hear this a bit – they're holding their mikes over the fence, and ... they had their cars parked so that they could hear bits and pieces. But they were putting the mikes over the fence, and it was 50–60 feet away, and I was six inches away'* (interview with journalist).

After Grand Chief Mercredi left the camp, one reporter was lingering, talking with two RCMP officers who were parked on the road, when he heard a rifle discharge. The reporter recalls that it sounded like the shot originated from the bush: *'I mean, it was close. The one thing you knew was that this was not – I mean they were not* [firing] *up at the main camp. No way. It scared the shit outta the officers too. Naturally they said, "get outta here!" And so we departed. They departed briskly in the opposite direction –'* **Oh?** *'Oh, yeah, they were really scared too. 'Cause, I mean, they were not set up for anything, they were not ERT guys or anything ... whether they were saying, "we are bored, now go away" or – sending us a sort of farewell greeting after Mercredi'* (interview with journalist). A few of the journalists accompanied the convoy with Grand Chief Mercredi to the Dog Creek Community Hall for another meeting with local Native people, local chiefs, some RCMP officers, and Lyle James. On the way, the RCMP pulled Mercredi's car over to enquire about the reported gunshot. They surmised at the time that somebody possibly had fired a gun as a salute (negative or positive) after Grand Chief Mercredi had left.

By Grand Chief Mercredi's account, a degree of trust had been established between himself and the people at Gustafsen Lake during the first meeting.[14] However, the vast majority of newspapers did not convey this optimism. The *Vancouver Sun* refer to the negotiations with Mercredi as 'dramatic' and a 'clash over ways to seek justice.'[15] In the *Vancouver Province*, the majority of the account provided a description of the panicked response by the media and RCMP when the shot was fired near the camp and a pejorative depiction of the campsite. The meeting was briefly referred to as Mercredi's 'first unsuccessful negotiations.'[16] In the *Victoria Times Colonist*, the headline focused on Mercredi's appeal that the people risked death, and the accompanying Canadian Press news account featured a lead-in about the shot fired after the meeting.[17] The *Globe and Mail* reprinted Canadian Press news stories from several Canadian cities (all originating from 100 Mile House). The *Winnipeg Free Press* and the *Charlottetown Guardian* featured similar lead-ins that centred on the gunshot fired after Mercredi left the camp. The reprinted news story from the *St. John's Evening Telegram* focused on Mercredi's warning to the camp that they risked death if they refused to leave.[18] The accounts that provided details of the meeting schematized the negotiations in terms of appeals by Mercredi and demands and refutations by Wolverine, not alluding in any sense to the fact that they had established trust. The news narrative of Mercredi's warnings about the camp members' unyielding position put them in peril, and the gunshot that day supported the RCMP's frame of the conflict. Indeed, most of the newspaper stories emphasized the shooting incident, although the firing of the weapon took place after the meeting had concluded. The above analysis plus a check on the lexical frequencies of subsequent news stories indicate a pattern of representation that characterized Mercredi's negotiation efforts at the camp as a 'failure.'[19]

Several factors may explain the media representations of that first meeting with Grand Chief Mercredi. The news characterizations of the negotiations depicted the interactions as hostile, a more extreme but plausible interpretation after Wolverine's comments prior to the meeting.[20] Newspapers require headlines and lead-ins that summarize the central meaning of the event, both of which have a predilection to sensationalize aspects of a situation. Angry-sounding debates, dire warnings, and gunfire are dramatic, and they were the focal points in the newspaper sample. However, the context of the coverage also helps to explain the news texts. For example, it is reasonable to assume that reporters who witnessed the meeting could provide richer details than those relegated to the barbed wire fence. The data confirm that the camp leaders did not allow the majority of reporters inside the camp.

In addition, news production and editorial policies may have been at play. The only print reporter (from the large media outlets in the sample) who was allowed inside felt constrained by the editorial practices of his outlet. This journalist explained, *'You were really limited in what you could do, other than report on Ovide Mercredi's words ... And there's also a con-*

sciousness that there's a limited concentration span; if you had attempted to explain at length the context and explain Mercredi's words ... it would really be lost, it would be chopped. The editors were going for the drama, they weren't going for the philosophical ... It was a drama event' (interview with journalist). The generic, but limited, media accounts can be explained; the reporters whom the protesters allowed inside the camp shared their audiotapes of the meeting with associates at the fence. Although audiotapes provide accurate quotations, other non-verbal communicative details are missing, such as body language, gestures, facial expressions, and eye contact. Furthermore, an awareness of the positioning and impression management that underlies such negotiations, as well as a knowledge of Native communication styles, would have provided a broader interpretive base for understanding the situation. However, there was no evidence of these elements in the above-mentioned newspaper stories. Only one exclusive photograph of Grand Chief Mercredi with Percy Rosette and Wolverine, taken by a local newspaper journalist after the other media had left the camp, shows them in a lighter mood.[21]

The police and government officials, who were not present during the talks, would have obtained most of their information from the broadcasts and news stories from the larger media. They later commented on the futility of the talks and proceeded with their operation as planned. The majority of people interviewed for this study did not suspect that the media had made distortions in their reports of the meeting. The portrayals were consistent with the news stories of the coverage of the Williams Lake RCMP press conference. The group at the camp appeared to be hostile, as evidenced by someone near the camp firing a weapon.

Closing off the Camp to the Media

On the evening of Ovide Mercredi's first visit, the RCMP enacted the next stage of their operational strategy. They cut off the camp's cellular telephone; they set out a spike belt and barricades; and they prohibited unauthorized entry to, or exit from, the camp. Some of the journalists remained near the camp, but RCMP officers told them to return to the town.

The following narrative details the experience of one media crew member who attempted to contest the access boundary created by the RCMP.[22]

As soon as we came out of the gravel road ... there was an RCMP car there. And that's when I said 'Joe [not the actual name], *I don't think we should be leaving.' Joe said, 'Well, we'll go a little further and then we'll be able get to an autotel'* [where the telephone link will be possible] *... And that's when we found that log-cleared area. And pulled off there. Because the RCMP helicopters were flying – looking for people, 'wonder who's in there and not in there?' All the media had gone ... So we didn't have to go anywhere. We could stay there – and we waited. And then we got a call from our people in the east, who'd said that ... they didn't want to send us out without bullet-proof vests and gas masks. Because of the danger the RCMP had said there was to be, and there were guns and everything else.*

And as we drove a little further, the RCMP had set up checkpoint 20 – the 20-kilometre mark in the road. And I saw this, said – 'Joe look!' They had spike belts out; they had guys with night vision glasses. They had full machine guns – I'm not sure of the technical term, but machine guns. Full bullet-proof vests, and the whole works. And we drove down and I said, 'Joe, I don't like this. Something's going on here that doesn't make sense to me.' They were geared up ... And a guy [RCMP] *came over and said, 'Your driver's licence, please?' I said, 'Yeah,' and I gave it to him. He said, 'Thanks very much.' And he turned and walked away – like now we're supposed to drive out. [I] put it in four wheel drive, and booted back – and spun out and took off back towards the camp. 'Cause I just wanted to get a chance to think here a minute. I wanted to figure out, you know, Montague – RCMP Montague – promised we could come in on Saturday, for the next meeting with Mercredi – it's on tape, it's on camera ... We were given permission to come back in Saturday. And I had a good debate with Joe about this – that why don't I stay?*

But at that point, I felt I had more trust for the Natives than I did for the RCMP. Just because – sure, we'd heard 'genocide' ... we heard all that stuff over and over – but, I mean, at least they'd talk to you. And so anyways, we sat out at that dugout – we marked the truck with [a sign that read] *'news' and stuff. We got a phone call on the autotel from the 'highest as the high is high' – that we had to leave. We weren't prepared with bullet-proof vests or gas masks. There was talk about gas; gas would've been smart to calm everybody down – if it came that far. There was talk of gas – like tear-gas or something – dropped from helicopters, or whatever, and we weren't prepared. We didn't have gas masks and we didn't have bullet-proof vests.*

We respected their wishes and we left. That night, I didn't sleep a minute. Got back to the hotel ... and I said to Joe, 'We blew it.' ... And in fact, we got back into the vehicle at eleven o'clock that night and drove back, to try and get back out there, and they [RCMP] *said, 'Oh, no – you'll have to come back at first light ... I said, 'Damn, I should have just gone with my gut.' My gut was to stay.*

Because I knew – sure enough the next morning, the road's all blocked. Police escort. Checkpoint 20's as close as we could get. Twenty kilometre mark in the road. And there we sat – all our vehicles lined up. Waiting for Mercredi to come through. I said, 'Peter' [Montague]. *He showed up – I'll never forget – in these mirrored sunglasses, big round ones, the little rims, the mirror in his eyes and – the glasses, and he said, 'Mr Mercredi has asked that there be no media in there because it affected the dialogue yesterday' or whatever, whatever.* **Is this what Mercredi said?** *This is what Montague says Mercredi said. And I looked at* [my colleague] *and I said, 'I understand what's been started – and we've been fucked. We've been dicked.'* (Interview with journalist)

Another journalist stated: *'When he first came, Mercredi said several of us* [media] *could witness the negotiations. Then we left that night and saw that a spike line had been laid out. We were told Mercredi didn't want media. I'm not sure if that was ever true or not. I'm not sure whether we ever got to the bottom of this. Mercredi was surprised to learn that media were not allowed in and didn't immediately answer. There was confusion over who had asked for the media ban. We were told by officers that night that we would be allowed to go back over to the other side the next morning, but we were not'* (interview with journalist).

That morning, during the RCMP press conference at the Red Coach Inn, one journalist said that the media liaison had announced that there would be no further media access to the camp. Shortly thereafter, the journalists proceeded to the camp, behind Grand Chief Mercredi's van. They stopped at a railway crossing on Exeter Station Road, and one journalist jumped out of his vehicle to talk to Mercredi. According to this journalist, Mercredi asked, *'Are you guys going to come in today?'* Apparently, Mercredi did not know about the RCMP's closure of the camp to the media, and he told the journalist that he had not made this request. He also did not know about the cut-off of the cellular telephone at the camp, a fact that he soon learned from the people inside. Later, Mercredi told reporters that he had spent so much of the second meeting listening to the anger and frustration in the camp because of the latest RCMP initiatives, that the mediation talks showed little progress. *'A lot of faith had been put into what Mercredi could do. What really came out of ... the press conference* [later that evening] *was how Mercredi ... felt he had been sandbagged by the police ... I see that weekend as a real turning point. Mercredi got sent in without being told that they* [police] *had cut off the phone. So he went in that day and basically got nowhere in the bargaining, because the people in the camp were so angry that the phone had been cut off, and basically those were his two days, and that's really all he had a chance to do'* (interview with journalist).

Several hours later, Grand Chief Mercredi issued a scathing press release about the RCMP activities' interfering with the discussions on the second visit. His criticisms were not lost on the journalists who lingered near the camp after that first meeting. These journalists also believed that the RCMP had been duplicitous when they assured them of future admission into the area but then laid out a spike belt on the road and put up barricades. A year later, when I conducted research interviews, a few of the journalists postulated that Mercredi's media ban had originated as part of the RCMP's plan to control the perimeter and the communications at the camp.

The following afternoon, the RCMP agreed to give Mercredi another opportunity to negotiate at the camp.[23] Minutes after this plan was finalized, there was a breaking-news bulletin that two RCMP officers had been shot at several times while in their vehicle. It was reported that they were saved from being killed only because they were wearing thick, army-type flak jackets.

Interpretations of the Barricades and Closing off Camp Communications

The RCMP's strategies of barricading the primary road to the camp and cutting off the camp's ability to communicate with anyone other than law enforcement personnel probably had the strongest influences on the media characterizations. The RCMP did not likely anticipate at the time that these common law-enforcement practices would result in the escalation of stress inside the camp, the altering of news-gathering processes, and the magnification of the RCMP's power to interpret the event to the media. These outcomes increased the risk of violence as well as the potential for media distortions. This situation is best understood through the examination of how the RCMP, the people inside the camp, and the media interpreted the barricades.

The RCMP

The explanation offered by District Superintendent Olfert and Sergeant Montague for cutting off the communication link at the camp was that it was an initiative of the RCMP's operational plan instituted to resolve the conflict. The RCMP were concerned that the people inside the camp were receiving instructions over their cellular telephone from people on the outside, such as the Sundance leader, John Hill, and lawyer Bruce Clark. The RCMP believed that such outside interference would strengthen the resolve of the people inside the camp to remain. Advisers may have been encouraging them to hold out for a wider political and legal impact by pressuring for a ruling from the Supreme Court of Canada on Clark's constitutional argument.[24] This influence was seen to undermine police negotiations and to keep the issues at an ideological level. Furthermore, the RCMP were concerned that the cellular telephone had been used to draw supporters into the camp, adding to the number of people involved. The assessment of police officials was that many of these outside supporters were motivated by curiosity or by support for the larger question of Native rights regarding land claims. The supporters may have perceived the people in the camp as innocent victims. The police believed that camp leaders had not advised the supporters of the threats of violence and shooting incidents perpetrated by some of the people associated with the camp, or, if they did, that these events were portrayed as fabrications. If the supporters thought that the issue was strictly one of land claims and human rights, it was likely that many other people would become involved. The media plan was both to reinforce the idea that the people in the camp were employing illegal means to promote their cause and to dissuade people from coming to the area. The police decision to cut off telephone communication was intended to stop outsiders from interfering with the police negotiations and to prevent any more people from joining the group at Gustafsen Lake.

Similarly, the RCMP officials asserted that the establishment of the RCMP barricades was a tactical decision to minimize the potential for violence and injury. There was a concern that a groundswell of supporters might converge on the camp, making the situation more volatile and difficult to defuse. The RCMP had already established that there were several weapons in the camp, and unrestricted public access increased the possibility that more armaments would be brought in.[25] From the perspective of the police, open communication and unrestrained access to and from the camp could escalate the seriousness of the situation and increase the potential for violence and loss of life. Thus, setting up the barricades was an attempt to control the perimeter of the camp, to contain the people inside, and to ensure that supporters and armaments would be prevented from entering the camp.

The Camp

The prevalent perception inside the camp was that the barricades and the restrictions on communications was forewarning of an RCMP agenda to kill everyone in the camp. William Lightbown, a Native elder who had been inside for several days, and three others decided to leave the camp soon after the barricades were established. In an attempt to prevent loss of life, they hoped that by talking to the police and the media they could resolve the situation.

The small group was detained at the RCMP checkpoint. According to Lightbown, the RCMP officers said, '"You can't come out – you've got to go back in," and I laughed, I said, "You're kidding? You can't stop us from coming out." I said, "Who the hell do you think you are?" I said, "You can't order us around on our own land, and tell us we can't come out of that camp." I said, "You might be able to bullshit the rest of the people," I said, "but you're not bullshitting me!"' The RCMP officers at the checkpoint held the group there for two hours. 'They said that they would have to contact Ottawa, which tells me that Ottawa was informed on an ongoing basis – non-stop, through this whole process. And the word that came back – they said, "Well, Ottawa said that we have to let you through" and I said, "Well, of course you have to let us through – there are no options." So they let us through.' While detained, he had his first contact with the RCMP tactical squad (ERT): 'with masks on – hoods pulled over, and all you could see was their eyes' (interview with William Lightbown).

The RCMP and the people in the camp had contradictory interpretations of the situation, and neither side acknowledged the validity of the other's view. They seemed mutually suspicious, and it is understandable that actions taken by one side might be interpreted as a threat by the other. Because the polarized perceptions held by these two groups, the media became a site of struggle for the RCMP and the camp to define the situation to the public in order to gain widespread support.

The Media

For the journalists, the barricades signified the loss of a valued media source and of an essential competitive advantage. The barricades increased the dependence of the media on the police for information about the camp and the activities behind the barricades. This, in turn, increased the potential for abuse of police authority. One reporter stated,

'*So that really turned the whole Gustafsen Lake for me, right there ... It took away our advantage – really took away our advantage. And we're all on the same level of playing field right now. All of us. A men's playing field. Completely controlled. "Trust us, they're happy. Trust us, they're eating. Trust us this and trust us that." And from that point on, it became a real battle, because we (not only in my opinion) had to try and figure out the stories and figure out what's going on, but then we had to fight kind of a bureaucracy who knew what was going on and we just weren't being told*' (interview with journalist).

One reporter concluded that cutting off the media was a trade-off in the RCMP's tactical justification for the barricades. He recognized that there would be a cost for the control of media access: '*There is a danger in keeping them* [journalists] *in complete ignorance and dependant utterly on* [the police] *for information. Because, particularly in retrospect, on how they* [the police] *conducted themselves ... had we had a camera in there or a pool arrangement, they* [the police] *would have been able to say "hey – we can prove it." It's the same thing for the other way around too. Media exist for a reason in this country. We were, to a certain extent, prevented from doing our job, which is recording events as they happened*' (interview with journalist). A few of the journalists found that cutting off media access to the camp contributed to the pack journalism that they said characterized the coverage of the standoff. During the research interviews, several of the journalists surmised that the RCMP had invited the media to cover the event, but that the barricades helped to bring them under the control of the RCMP.

Not all the reporters, however, were concerned about the lack of access to the camp. Some of them believed that for such unstable conflicts, the media should not have access to a group that was so volatile. Few journalists said that they would have gone to the camp after the barricades were set up. Some of the most strident critics of the RCMP agreed that safety was an issue and that they were not willing to take the risk of covering the event from the camp or anywhere else inside the barricades.

The barricades severed relations between the media and their sources at the camp and altered the competitive standing between the journalists. Journalists who had gained the trust of camp members were unable to use them as a valued news resource and to competitive advantage. Conversely, the barricades did little damage to reporters whom the protesters turned away. Indeed, the barricades returned competitive potential to them. It is not clear whether the media playing field became flattened as a consequence of the barricades or by the lack of availability of alternative sources who might provide lucrative information for competing journalists. In this situation, the most valued source would be one who could provide contrasting information for the public about the camp.

The RCMP's control over camp communications and the barricades blocked the people in the camp from contesting the police to the media or their supporters. Once the RCMP had established a telephone line for discussing a settlement, the police negotiators were the only group with whom camp members could voice their concerns until Native intermediaries arrived. The RCMP did not relay these concerns to the media. In addition, the people in the camp did not have the social standing or the credibility to challenge the RCMP, especially without concrete evidence. Therefore, the barricades provided the police with the opportunity to shape the interpretation of the standoff to their best advantage.

The Barricades and the Media Characterizations

The RCMP erected the barricades on Saturday evening (26 August 1995). By the following day, some of the journalists and television camera crews had set up a makeshift camp and unloaded their equipment for filming. On Sunday afternoon, after the attack on the police, they moved the barricade three kilometres further down the road. This location became known as Checkpoint 17.

The barricades created a before-and-after time marker, with specific news contexts associated with each phase. Before the barricades were erected, the media had been able to drive to the camp and, provided they had permission from the occupants, go inside. Journalists witnessed gunfire near the RCMP helicopter and observed the tension and the security measures taken by those in the camp. After the barricades were in place, eyewitness accounts of incidents at or near the camp were impossible. Even at Checkpoint 17, the journalists were so far from the camp that it was impossible for them to hear any sounds of gunshots – despite the fact that 'thousands of rounds' (on 11 September) were exchanged between the RCMP and the protesters. There was no way to confirm whether the RCMP was giving the full story, the degree to which that story was sanitized or exaggerated, or if they were giving any part of the story at all.

The barricades confirmed two outposts for the media. The Red Coach Inn became the setting for all RCMP press conferences, and the message boards provided times of news briefings. Many informal discussions between journalists and supporters of the camp took place in the Red Coach Inn parking lot. In town, media portrayed the event from the press conferences at the Red Coach Inn or along the main thoroughfare of the town. Checkpoint 17 became the secondary news centre. That checkpoint, marking the closest allowable proximity to the camp for the media and the public, was situated on the primary road that all RCMP and ERT used to get to the RCMP field operation, Camp Zulu. Native intermediaries used this road when travelling to and from the camp at Gustafsen Lake. In spite of police warnings of the danger of the area, a local couple living adjacent to Camp Zulu travelled this road to go back and forth to town. Since waiting for anything exciting to happen on this road was boring and tedious, many journalists preferred to spend most of their time at 100 Mile House and would travel to Checkpoint 17 only occasionally. If journalists worked in teams, often one would cover the news in town, the other at Checkpoint 17. Only a few members of the media stayed at the checkpoint for extended times – usually television camera crews who commuted in shifts. An exception was one CBC cameraman, who spent 22 days at the checkpoint without returning to town. Journalists at Checkpoint 17 slept in their vehicles, and for the last few days CBC-TV brought in a motor home for its crew. While the majority of the journalists remained in town and attended press conferences for official statements, those who stayed at the checkpoint were able to get different off-the-record information from the police. Because of the length of time the journalists and police spent together at the checkpoint, they developed a better rapport than most of their counterparts at 100 Mile House.

The barricades also magnified the prominence and power of the RCMP media relations team in the characterization of the event. The media became almost fully dependent on the media liaisons for updates on the conditions and developments behind the barricades. The RCMP could give out information, or withhold it, at will, and the media became vulnerable to the police and their discretionary power to control and limit new information. In effect, the *police* defined what was news. Announcements of minor developments took on heightened importance; as one journalist quipped, 'Even a press conference that said little or nothing was still a news event.'

Some journalists, however, did not confine themselves to Sergeant Montague as the only RCMP source. They developed informal channels to get insider information. For instance, those from the Vancouver area had had previous contacts with Vancouver RCMP while covering other news stories. The journalists might strike up conversations during chance meetings in town or at Checkpoint 17, although the information did not have the legitimate authority of the formal press conference.[26] But the details did contrast with the vagueness of the RCMP press releases, a typical complaint of the journalists. As one journalist commented: *'Anyway, one of the things that was interesting to me was that the RCMP media relations was never really too keen on was the fact that I knew quite a number of the officers, from just having been around. And periodically, when I found them, they would talk to me. I mean, the theory was supposed to be that absolutely nobody talked to you unless it was Montague and Ward, and whoever they set up. And so – I'd ... find a story by running into one of them at the grocery store, you know.'* **Their guards were down when they talked to you ...** *'Cause they're all buddies! I mean, they're all buddies of mine!'* (interview with journalist). Informal sources never became major influences in the news accounts, but the details provided were helpful to the media during the question period of the press conferences.

The barricades and the ensuing restriction of information and sources for updates increased the pressure among the journalists to obtain fresh news in order to convey a sense in their stories that the event was not static. Fresh news had become scarce. Journalists could develop supplementary stories from secondary and peripheral sources, supporters of the protest or politicians in Victoria. In Vancouver, news wires and colleagues provided subsidiary stories in which the situation was analysed from the perspectives of a variety of experts and academics across the country. Sometimes such a narrative would be the most important story of the day, shifting peripheral information to the central part of the event. Competition among journalists at 100 Mile House for new angles increased, and promises of exclusive news opportunities (such as a fly-over of RCMP Camp Zulu) became hotly contested commodities. With increasing numbers of people coming into town to support various sides of the conflict, the journalists usually found someone to interview. On occasion, reporters would combine supplementary sources with an updated summary of the conflict to create *new* news. Thus, the journalists, with the assistance of news sources and news opportunities, were able to move the story and hold it in the public attention. Nonetheless, with the exception of lawyer Bruce Clark and the Native intermediaries (who, for limited timeframes, had police permission to visit the camp), the above alternative sources were unable to furnish any current information about the camp that contrasted with the RCMP perspectives.

Some of the television journalists became aware that the repeated visual backdrop of the town during news updates could lead the public to assume that the action of the event was in the town, rather than several miles away. One journalist said that in his reports he continually emphasized that the camp was actually 35 kilometres away from where he was standing and that a spike bar and a barricade on the forestry road prevented closer media access. The journalist wished that he could have announced that none of the media really knew what was going on. He said that he held back from making this disclosure while on the air because he believed that it would have been inappropriate.

The establishment of barricades also provided the impetus for journalists to listen to the police scanners and radiotelephones, which the police negotiators used for a time while talking to the people in the camp. After Grand Chief Ovide Mercredi encouraged the RCMP to open a telephone line to the camp, journalists could hear interactions between the camp and the police negotiators for approximately 10 days. Local businesses sold out of radio scanners, and almost everyone was listening – media, shopkeepers, local residents, and ranchers. The police periodically scrambled frequencies, and they used code words. Until the RCMP established a low-frequency telephone link with the camp, the possibility of listeners among media, supporters, and local people always existed. The journalists did not find these conversations particularly newsworthy, however, except when the source was the people in the camp. On such occasions, some journalists 'jumped on it.'

Journalists used the radio scanners, which picked up interactions between members of the RCMP, as a reference to probe the media liaison during press conferences. On one occasion, a journalist overheard two officers talking about a 'Native person stepping on a stun grenade' and behaving in a disoriented fashion; one laughed to the other, '"Looks like another drunken Indian on a Friday night!" Yet when you asked Montague that same day if anyone in the camp was injured or disoriented from a stun grenade, Montague said, "I can't comment on that."' Another reporter remarked: 'Quite often if you couldn't get the full picture of what was happening, you could at least sense that something was happening and sometimes get specific information that you could go to somebody and say, "What is this?"' One journalist recalled hearing requests for the media as witnesses: 'The people in the camp made frequent requests for media on the *radio. Their biggest concern was being treated fairly.'* Eavesdropping on the radiotelephone also allowed listeners to form impressions of the mood in the camp. One such instance was a poignant conversation between a parent (outside the camp) whose daughter remained inside. The parent was pleading with the daughter to come out. The journalist recalled that she said that she *'couldn't come out,'* and then the line was cut off. Listening on the police radio-telecommunications also gave the journalists an appreciation of the relations between the RCMP negotiators and people inside the camp. The journalists frequently heard agitated and hostile remarks coming from the camp side of the conversations. Several of the journalists remarked that the RCMP negotiators demonstrated *'a great deal of patience'* (interviews with journalists).

From the time of the Williams Lake press conference, the RCMP replaced the camp as the most important news source and began describing the people in the camp as dangerous. The RCMP's labelling of the illegal activities associated with the camp as acts of terrorism radicalized the group for the public record. Similarly, the Vancouver journalists attending the Williams Lake press conference took the lead away from the town newspaper in covering the conflict. In general, the Vancouver journalists had little or no background knowledge of the local community or the previous years' Sundance ceremonies. Yet, after the Williams Lake press conference, the group's news value grew in proportion to the wider media reach, but the presentations during the press conference did irreparable damage to their public face.

Camp members made efforts to contest their damaged reputation in the media, but these attempts were undone in several ways. If they intended their demands for an audience with the queen and their vows to 'come out in body bags' to gain positive media attention, it had the opposite effect. The news characterizations of the declarations accentuated the radical stance of the group. Camouflage clothing, tight security, and surveillance of media at the camp conveyed an impression to the journalists that the group was militant. Camp members asserted control over their information to the media by ousting at least one journalist from an influential news organization and by refusing entry to several of the others. These events not only influenced how some of the journalists regarded the camp, they also had a limiting effect on the witnessing and variety of the media interpretations of their negotiations with Grand Chief Mercredi. On the other hand, two shootings originating from the camp took place in the presence of media, and these incidents became important news stories. After the barricades were set up, the group at the camp could not repair or maintain relations with the journalists and present themselves in a more positive light. The strategies employed by the leaders to control the media demonstrated that the people in the camp had the willingness and some agency to manage their public image. Nevertheless, many of these initiatives appeared to sabotage their group, which may have compounded the negative impressions of the camp in mainstream media portrayals.

The barricades provided the RCMP with a near-hegemonic control over the definition of the situation at the camp given to the media and prevented the people in the camp from having a media voice or witnesses. However, the media adapted to the situation by expanding in other directions. At the checkpoint, in the town, and through telephone interviews and police radio-telecommunications, they found legitimate, and not so legitimate, ways to recover from losing the camp as a central source. Nevertheless, these alternative sources could not effectively challenge the dominant frame of the situation offered by the RCMP. The RCMP stated that their intention for putting up the barricades was to prevent the conflict from involving more people and more weapons and thus becoming more volatile. Yet the barricades contributed to conditions of news reporting that increased the potential for distorted media coverage of the event and the people involved. We will examine these occasions in the following chapters.

CHAPTER THREE

Show of Force

When Ryan asked how many people are in the camp, Ignace laughed and said, 'Why are you asking that? There's an Indian behind every tree here.' Other rebels could be heard laughing over the radio phone.[1]

Vancouver Sun, 31 August 1995

The negotiation of information and the outcomes in the news accounts is the central analytical focus of chapter 3. The news-gathering process invariably requires some form of exchange. When people provide information or a perspective about some element to the media, it gives them (aside from other rewards) an opportunity to take a more distinctive role in the construction of the news. News sources with power, status, or news appeal have a greater potential to influence the dominant frame in news stories and a chance to sway public opinion. The media, in turn, benefit by having needs such as information, authentication, and balance satisfied. However, the reciprocity between the media and their sources does not necessarily reach a balance. The media are often typecast as the exploiters in the exchange. Nonetheless, it is assumed in this case study that news sources have varying degrees of agency to control their stock of information, although it might still be in high demand by the media. News sources may also be in competition with each other to influence the dominant perspective of the news. A further complication is that the media themselves may want to portray a news story in a particular way, and will adjust the presentation of its sources and their information accordingly. These situations may lead to struggles and manoeuvring between media and their various sources.

The negotiation of information between spokespersons, the press, and the spectators was most frequently found during the press conferences at 100 Mile House. The successful disbursement of information by spokespersons and clarification of information by journalists required knowledge of the norms and routines of press conferences and an understanding of the nuances of performance for spokespersons, media, and the public audience. Yet those in attendance did not commonly understand this media convention, which led to some communication conflicts.

Some instances of information exchange connected the media coverage more directly with the RCMP operation, and these incidents are given greater analytical attention. The negotiations between media sources and the media took the forms of *barter*, *coercion*, and *appropriation*. The specific cases in this chapter include the media's use of police radio-telecommunication, the RCMP's engagement of a journalist in a police initiative, the shooting episode of 4 September; and the RCMP's confiscation of CBC videotapes of the camp. The analysis of these incidents may be compared with the negotiation strategies that the RCMP used during the standoff. Dr Mike Webster, an RCMP psychologist, gave me two articles he wrote for the *RCMP Gazette* that detailed these negotiation techniques; they involve providing cues that would likely encourage someone to be compliant without carefully considering the situation and alternatives. The articles did not describe the negotiation techniques as being limited to the people inside the camp.[2]

Shooting Episode: The Flak Jacket Incident

27 August 1995

> At 3:40 p.m., two RCMP officers are shot in the back as they and two others protect three forestry workers brought in to clear fallen trees from a road. The two officers get burns and bruises from the slugs that rip into their bullet proof vests, but otherwise are unhurt. Their truck is hit dozens of times. (Chronology, *Vancouver Sun*, 12 September 1995, A3)[3]

The following is an excerpt of Sergeant Montague's perspective of this incident, and his recollections of how he conveyed the news to the media:

The day that we got shot ... there was an awful lot of emotion. I was sitting in a restaurant, talking to some media. We're having a coffee, about 2:30 in the afternoon, if I remember correctly – and the UTV cameraman came in. He was dead white and he was sweating – and he sat down and he said, 'You don't know, do you?' And I said, 'I don't know what?' And he said, 'Your members have just been shot.' And I said, 'This is no time to be making jokes.' He said, 'No I'm not.' He said, 'Peter – they just got shot – I don't know if they've been killed, or what.' So – I went out to our command centre – the screaming and the yelling, and the stuff that was going on – oh, man.

Panic? I would say – there was some panic because we couldn't distinguish through the radio communications – they were so poor – if they were dying ... if they needed medical attention – what they were saying is 'We don't know how badly we are hurt – we know we've been shot.' Cause they could feel the burning sensation and the numbness. But never having been shot before, they didn't know if the bullets had penetrated, or if they were just going to fall over and die – like – they didn't know. So, they're yelling for all this stuff, and – you know – the other members are trying to get going the other way, and they were yelling on the radio, 'We don't know where we are going!' and 'What's going on?' And – it was pandemonium – it best describes it.

When we finally got the members to the hospital, and had to go out and deal with the media – my message was, 'Low key. Low key. No – don't raise the level – just low key. Everything's fine, we'll deal with it.' And we went out there with that message. That our members have been shot, and we're a professional police force, and we will deal with the situation in the appropriate manner. And there was no heightened level of emotion – purposely – it was subdued. And that was to keep our people confident that everything was fine here. Tell the public – no one's going to over-react. And we maintained *that message, until September the 11th, and that was the day of the gunfight.* (Interview with Sergeant Montague, 27 May 1997)

At the checkpoint, the journalists heard the crackling and disjointed police communications over the radio and the message that ambulances were on the way. The ambulances came flying past a few minutes later. All they could hear on the radio were snatches of information about shots being fired, but they were not sure what was going on. At 100 Mile House, news of the shooting brought some journalists racing up Exeter Station Road, but by the time they arrived at the checkpoint, there were no further developments: 'There would have been a photographer up there at the blockade to – you know – to take that photo – up at the actual road block kind of thing. So, our sense was that something happened.' At Williams Lake, another reporter who was preparing to interview Grand Chief Mercredi, relayed this update to him: 'His face went – "Oh my

God!" – he looked really worried.' One television crew hastily turned around while on the way to an interview with rancher Lyle James when they received a call on the radiotelephone 'that three officers were killed!' Another reporter saw the two officers walk up to the ambulance and get in and the ambulance drive away without sirens. Later, at the press conference, some of the reporters thought that Sergeant Montague looked visibly upset. They asked him if he would name the officers who had been shot, but he would not release that information.[4] Journalists considered that this shooting incident 'changed the whole situation' for the police, with the potentially fatal shooting of two of their members.[5] Another journalist recalled, after the flak-jacket ambush, 'I heard cops saying, "I'd love to plunk one of those bastards"' (interviews with journalists). Although the RCMP media liaison perceived that he was successful in subduing his internal reaction to the situation, his performance was not thoroughly convincing for his audience of journalists who prepared the news stories.

Off-the-Record Meeting

29 August 1995

Reports gained by phone anger RCMP. (Headline, Vancouver Sun, 30 August 1995, A3)

And so there was a bit of a closed-door meeting – 'All the media – into a room – let's talk.' **How did you feel about that meeting?** Actually, I was kind of excited – I knew that I hadn't done anything wrong! And I was talking – I was sitting beside [a colleague] and said, 'You didn't put anything on the air, did you?' And he goes, 'No.' And I said, 'Neither did I! So let's just sit back and watch the people squirm who buggered, eh?' (Interview with journalist)

It was tempting for the media to include information gathered from scanners and radiotelephones in the news accounts after the barricades were established. However, publishing this material without the permission of one of the parties involved in the telecommunications is illegal. Permission would not likely be forthcoming from either side. The RCMP had already indicated that they would be tightly controlling information, and there was no legitimate way of reaching people inside the camp. In this study, the media's use of radio-telecommunications is considered the appropriation of police (and, in some circumstances, camp) information without consent. Some of the media outlets published excerpts of the conversations for at least one news story. They included the *Vancouver Province*, CBC Radio, and the *Vancouver Sun*. BCTV filmed reporters listening in on radio conversations, and the radio conversations could be heard. These publications and broadcasts came immediately to the attention of the RCMP media team, which also was monitoring the news coverage.[6]

Sergeant Montague announced that he wanted to convene an off-the-record meeting with accredited journalists immediately following the press conference.[7] The following is a composite of the accounts of this meeting that RCMP media personnel held immediately after the regular late-evening news conference on Tuesday night (29 August 1995).

Two journalists took immediate exception to the fact that Sergeant Montague had arranged for the RCMP cameraman to record the off-the-record meeting as part of his RCMP training tapes: *'And in walks this cameraman, and he's recording all this. And I said, "What is he doing here?" "He's recording this." And I said, "If it's off the record, it's off the record – if he shoots, I go!" And another [journalist] gets up: "I'm goin' too!" You don't get to pick and choose what [they] get to shoot. It's all for the training video.'*

One journalist paraphrased Sergeant Montague's speech:

'You can't do this, (you know) Jesus Christ, I've been goin' to bat for you guys, you know that if it weren't for me, you would have no coverage, the checkpoint would be back at the highway on Highway 97, you wouldn't be allowed any access, there'd be no news conferences. My superiors [he said] don't want to give you guys anything, they just want to shut it all down.' That's what he said. And ... he proceeded to empower himself by using the stance that if it weren't for him, we would have no coverage – of course, forgetting that this was a democratic society – and I found it quite interesting.

A lot of the media people were upset. Personally, I found it not humiliating but insulting – we're all professionals and here we are being told that you know if you're not good little kiddies you're not going to have any cookies, basically ... I can remember him marching into the basement of that hotel and [he] said, 'If anybody uses any dialogue from there ...' And it was like he slapped us on the wrist. And I – remember turning to [a colleague] and saying, 'The only one that can slap me is my boss.'

George Garrett, [a senior radio journalist from Vancouver], the voice of reason, calmed things down, said basically that what was done was done, but that no one would do this any more ... Everybody [the media] were chastised like

*children. Montague was taking control of the situation, threatening to shut down
all of the media access. It was a show of force – a bullying tactic.*

According to my sources, Montague left the meeting and gave the
journalists the option of complying. He asked them to make a decision
and then get back to him – by coming to his hotel room and letting him
know. One journalist analysed the situation as follows: '*So the weird
thing is: (a) He's wanting everybody to make the same decision. He's wanting
the group to decide – so it creates a sort of group mentality. (b) He's asking
reporters to decide – now maybe CBC-TV reporters have more power ... but
that's not my job. I don't make decisions like that. I'm not ... It's not my role*'
(interviews with journalists).

Unwittingly, a radio journalist at Checkpoint 17 continued broadcasting live 'hits' for the 8:00 p.m. and 9:00 p.m. evening news, including
recordings from police radio-telecommunications. When the journalist
returned to the hotel, he was confronted by Sergeant Montague (para-
phrasing what Sergeant Montague said): '*"Do you have any idea what
you have done?!" He sounded morally outraged. "You risked the lives of all
the people out there!" All I remember is that it took me a long time to get over
it'* (interview with journalist).

The reporters from the *Vancouver Sun*, convinced that eating supper
was more important than waiting for a press conference, inadvertently
skipped that late-night press conference. When they returned, they
were inundated by other journalists telling them about Montague's
intimidating reprimand. The *Vancouver Sun* reporters spoke with their
editor, and the decision from the desk was that the reporters should file
their stories as usual. The editors and lawyers in Vancouver would
determine if the stories with the unauthorized source would run. They
continued to be printed, and the *Vancouver Sun* also immediately published a news story about the meeting, effectively taking it from the
realm of off the record to that of the public record.[8] All of the other
journalists who had submitted incriminating stories for print pulled
them or quickly edited out the contentious parts.

During subsequent press conferences, *Vancouver Sun* reporters said
that they felt ostracized by the RCMP media liaison because of their
publications of police radio-telecommunications and they recalled that
Sergeant Montague ignored their questions during press conferences.
The journalists brought this situation to the attention of their editor.
Frequently, journalists from other outlets reintroduced the same questions, knowing the RCMP media liaison would more likely answer

them. More than one journalist was critical of the *Vancouver Sun*, not necessarily because of the legal or ethical issues, but because of the unfair competitive advantage publishing from the unauthorized source gave them. Occasionally, journalists from competing outlets asked the RCMP media liaison during press conferences if and when the RCMP were going to press charges against the *Vancouver Sun* for publishing information obtained illegally. Although the journalists were aware of the friction between the RCMP media liaison and the *Vancouver Sun* journalists, few of them believed that Sergeant Montague's treatment was extreme.

Many of the journalists continued to use the information to pose questions during the press conferences. As they did with other unauthorized information, a few journalists subtly incorporated the material into their news stories in order to create a nuance, without actually stating that they had *heard* the information via the police radio-telecommunications.[9] The *Vancouver Sun* occasionally published information from the radiotelephones, embedding the transcripts within its news stories. Thus, the *Vancouver Sun*'s decision to continue printing unauthorized information provided the most overt case of media appropriation of information, but it was by no means the only media outlet that challenged the RCMP's control of its information.

Several members of the media believed that the reporters from the *Vancouver Sun* were breaching journalistic ethics, thus undermining the professional standards of the larger group. The resistance offered by the *Vancouver Sun* also challenged the RCMP media liaison's threat to further reduce police information, a consequence that would hurt all of them. That the *Vancouver Sun* did not seem to suffer from this act of rebellion and actually enjoyed a competitive advantage over all of the media outlets added to the resentment within the group. The journalists' condemnations of *Vancouver Sun* reporters also functioned as a form of validation of the RCMP dictates (and the law) by putting pressure on the *Sun* staff to conform. Hence, the peer pressure applied to *Vancouver Sun* reporters was motivated by professional standards, competitive factors, and, indirectly, the RCMP media liaison.[10]

This closed-door meeting between the RCMP media liaison and the media was not a chastisement of journalists who were eavesdropping on RCMP negotiations. In order for the RCMP to advise everyone to cease listening, they would have had to call a town meeting. The reprimand more likely was issued because the media were spreading negotiation information to the public outside the local area.[11]

Creation of a Media Celebrity

The lawyer Bruce Clark, who some of the people at the camp identified as their legal counsel, contributed little to the resolution of the standoff. However, he did play a major role as a frequent media source and as a topic in the media coverage of the standoff. Clark came onto the scene of the Gustafsen Lake standoff just as Ovide Mercredi was preparing to exit. It was unknown to the RCMP at the time that Clark had been in the shadows of the dispute since at least January 1995. At about that time Percy Rosette and John Stevens had asked him to represent their case for the Gustafsen Lake property. Clark was preparing a number of legal cases involving Aboriginal land disputes to be forwarded to the queen at Buckingham Palace. He had been testing his legal argument regarding Aboriginal territories for several years. All that was required was for the court to rule favourably on one of these cases to set a precedent that might alter the protocols regarding the resolution of Aboriginal land ownership. Until this point, Clark had been unsuccessful in his attempts to have his argument validated in the Supreme Court of Canada.[12]

When Clark first arrived at 100 Mile House, the media sought the opinion of the RCMP concerning his claims to represent some members of the camp. The RCMP, however, did not validate or acknowledge Clark or his role as a legal representative. After the negotiations between Mercredi and the camp were discontinued, the RCMP suddenly changed their position regarding the lawyer. They announced to the media that Clark would be working with them to resolve the situation, and they eventually allowed him into the camp. Several hours later, Clark emerged with a declaration advising that the people in the camp chose not to withdraw from the property but instead would wait for the British Columbia Court of Appeal ruling on Aboriginal claims. Clark held up a shell casing found near the camp, which he alleged had come from an RCMP weapon. He defended the camp for shooting at RCMP officers, stating that they were acting in self-defence. On the next day, the RCMP advised the media that Clark was no longer part of the police negotiation team. In the meantime, Clark travelled to England in an attempt to have his petition heard by the queen and then returned to 100 Mile House to appear in court for some of his clients. During the court session the judge held him in contempt, and he was put in jail. After another court appearance, he was sent for a 30-day psychiatric examination, which extended past the resolution of the standoff.

Why did Bruce Clark become such a media celebrity at Gustafsen Lake? The answer is provided in a montage of responses from the journalists.

He was a colourful character, and you're not going to avoid colourful characters in a story like that. It's a bonus when he's a bit like that. Because – it makes for great TV – and he can't come across so much in print, but on TV, people could see this guy, plus he's flamboyant – Montague is pretty much as dull as dishwater ... Clark was flamboyant – and he dressed ... and he's yelling and he's swearing ... And most of the other people up there – the Natives, the non-Natives, the townspeople are either not very articulate or they're just not great interviews. And then somebody like Clark comes along – the flashy lawyer from Ottawa, with these weird glasses that cost a fortune – he's an obvious for the media because he's different, plus he also claimed to represent the people in the camp, which was a big part of it. I mean, if he just blew into town and said that he wanted to represent the Indians, then he wouldn't have got ... he would have got a bit of coverage ... He went into the camp, he knew Wolverine; Wolverine and these other guys said he was the greatest lawyer and they respected him ... The fact that he was colourful was a bonus for the media. (Composite of remarks taken from interviews with journalists)

Journalists also saw him as volatile, and they suspected that he exaggerated the accusations of harm being inflicted on the people in the camp. They described him as a consummate actor. He appeared calm, but as soon as he entered the courtroom, *'he'd turn on like a light switch.'* At the same time, a few journalists considered that Clark's distress about the denial of public access to the court on the day he was charged with contempt might have been legitimate. According to a journalist who was present, Clark objected so violently, it aggravated the antagonism of the police and the judge: *'He should have known that they were after him ... He could have diffused it, or he could have not fallen into the trap, but he decided to push the envelope'* (interview with journalist). The timing of Clark's arrival was also a factor in his celebrity status at Gustafsen Lake. There were no developments in the standoff. The barricades were up, and the number of stories that contrasted with police accounts were at a premium. According to Gary Mason, editor of the *Vancouver Sun*, news of the standoff was beginning to drag, and Clark injected fresh interest into the story. Clark's media visibility continued throughout the standoff but peaked during his two stays in the 100 Mile House vicinity.

Clark's period of positive media coverage coincides with his brief stint with the RCMP negotiation team.[13] Once the RCMP had disassociated from Clark, he was maligned by the police, the attorney general, and the media. Clark's claims of solidarity with the camp, combined with the loss of the camp as a media source due to the barricades, positioned him as the superimposed face of the people at Gustafsen Lake. The newspaper stories accentuated his appearance and his behaviours with unflattering photographs and descriptions in the news text.[14] Labels such as *rebel* and *renegade*, which news stories used to describe the people in the camp, were gradually incorporated into the description of Clark.[15] Journalists and others closely involved with the resolution of the protest concurred that Clark's own behaviour may have done more to damage, rather than to help, the credibility of the people inside the camp. This analysis confirms that the media accentuated this outcome.

Why did the RCMP reverse their public assessment of Clark and include him in their operational plan? The Gustafsen Lake trial revealed evidence that implicated a member of the media. Very few of the media realized at the time of the standoff that the RCMP had engaged George Garrett, a CKNW Radio journalist from Vancouver, to act as a messenger between them and Bruce Clark just before the police publicly announced their support of Clark's involvement. The following is an excerpt of George Garrett's interview for this study.

Peter Montague, the media liaison for the RCMP, came to me and he said, 'Can you find Bruce Clark?' And I said, 'Sure.' **Why do you suppose he came to you?** *I was a conduit ... I found out later why ... But first of all, 'Can you find Bruce Clark?' And I said, 'Sure.' 'Would you give him a message for us? I said, 'Yes.' – 'Tell him that we'd like to talk to him.' I said 'Sure.' I knew he was staying at 108 Mile Ranch ... so I drove up there and interviewed him, told him I was relaying a message from the RCMP that they wanted to speak to him. He said, 'That's fine.' And I said, 'Would you mind going on tape, and you can just tell me on tape what you want to tell them, and I'll play the tape for them.' 'Yes, I'd be glad to.' And he directed it specifically to Sgt Montague, and it was to the effect that, 'Yes, he'd be glad to cooperate, please feel free to come and see him, whatever.'*

So, I acted as a messenger between the RCMP and Clark and made no bones about it. I put it on the air – it was sort of embarrassing – trying to inject myself into the story, which is not a good thing to do. **Why do you suppose that they didn't just ask an officer to go up to where he was staying?** *I don't know.*

That would've been the simplest thing. I would've told them where he was. I just said, 'Yes I knew where he was,' and that was that.

So, I took the message to the RCMP, and the cameraman for the RCMP (with my knowledge) was videotaping as I played the tape for Montague and others in the RCMP, in the detachment at 100MH. And I don't remember what I said, or what jokes were said, or whatever, but I played the tape for them in any event, and got their response and did a story on it ... I didn't have any idea I'd done anything wrong.

It came out at the trial – George Wool, one of the lawyers, made an issue out of the fact that I was helping the RCMP. And there's a touch of irony here in that George Wool is a former RCMP staff sergeant, who knows full well how people interact, whether they're media, police, or whatever, and there's a pretty good trust relationship that's built up. And if I say one thing, I think I have the trust of police generally, and the RCMP included, in this province, because I've been around for 40 years, and I have been known for not betraying a trust. So, I thought I was doing nothing more than trying to expedite a situation, and help bring a resolution to it.

I later found out ... that it was Mike's [Dr Webster's] psychology to involve Clark – to have him go in – and they anticipated that he would come out with guns blazing, so to speak – that he would be an antagonist. What they wanted to do was let Clark self-destruct. Which he did. 'Cause he went into the camp – after all this – let's get Mr. Clark involved etc., etc., then he comes out and accuses the RCMP of doing ... whatever he said ... and the thing went downhill from there. And apparently Mike Webster had anticipated that's exactly what Clark would do. And – you know, he'd been held up as the guy representing the Natives, and knew all about going to the queen, and so on – it was bloody ridiculous. But – they wanted to let him show the public what an idiot he is. And sure enough, he came out with that kind of an attitude, he was featured at interviews [promoting] this idea that this was a Native land claims case that should go to the queen, it should go to the Privy Council, and on and on it went. He was involved in a court hearing for one or two of the people who had come out of the camp. And he went berserk in court ...

So, the RCMP strategy was to make him self-destruct on his own volition, which he did, added, I think, to the image to the public that these people were kooks or criminals – or whatever. **So, knowing that, how do you feel about your participation in that whole scene?** Well, I did it in good faith. And I thought it was properly motivated. **On your part.** It was on my part, and I thought it was on their part too. I thought that they were genuinely desirous of getting him involved, hoping he would resolve it.

Had you known at the time that there was a psychological ploy, would you have willingly participated? *I don't think so. I guess hindsight is 20-20, but if you know you're being used in an improper way, then I think you draw the line and say 'Wait a minute.'* (Interview with George Garrett, 29 May 1997)

During the trial, the senior defence lawyer argued that Garrett's participation in the RCMP strategy crossed professional boundaries. He had inserted himself into a news story, and he had lost his journalistic objectivity by collaborating with one of his news sources. In the defence counsel's estimation, the RCMP ploy was to assist in the negative characterization of Clark and, in the process, the people inside the camp. Garrett's participation was likely more damaging to his professional reputation than that of Clark or the camp members. A few journalists who know George Garrett considered that his involvement in the RCMP plan was *'worse than what CBC did'* (a topic that will be covered later). The journalists whom I interviewed after George Garrett's trial appearance said that the fact that Garrett is so well respected in the media community and that he is considered their *elder*, saved him from peer censure. One journalist commented, *'Put anyone else into that equation – you'd get a different outcome.'*

The RCMP's request to Garrett was coercive because they did not provide him with the details of the extent to which his cooperation would involve him or their actual motivation for this request. The police did not give Garrett sufficient time to evaluate his professional involvement in the request or to speak to his employer or other colleagues, who may have been better able to critically evaluate the situation. The original RCMP request for Garrett to find Bruce Clark expanded into his agreeing to tape the interview, which situated the request as a reciprocal arrangement. The favour netted Garrett a news story, and it provided the RCMP with material documentation of Garrett's interaction with Clark. The RCMP request was enlarged again, and he agreed to present the tape at an RCMP strategy meeting. Although Garrett was aware of the videotaping during the meeting, he had not been advised at the time of the original request (to find Clark) that this meeting would be video recorded. This progression of favours and commitments exacted a higher cost from Garrett than that to which he initially agreed, resulting in his being drawn deeper into the police initiative, and as a result, he was accused of being an RCMP collaborator. Garrett's involvement in this police strategy was not mentioned as causing any strain in the police/media relations at the time of the standoff. At least as a partial consequence of Garrett's role, however, Bruce Clark did not leave 100 Mile House as he had originally planned, and he went on to draw primarily negative media attention, which discredited the people in the camp.[16]

Coverage of the Attack on the RCMP Suburban

4 September 1995

'The militants, who set up camp in June, fired on an RCMP emergency response team a few kilometres from the camp late Monday and then stalked them during the night,' Ward said. The armored vehicles helped extricate some team members Tuesday, although others were still in the bush surrounding the camp. 'This is the fifth incident where members of the RCMP have been shot at,' Ward said Tuesday. 'It's become clear that we must deploy armed personnel carriers to provide protection to our members.' Ward initially said police officers returned fire Monday night, but he later said that had not been confirmed. ('Army called in after Mounties shot at again,' *St. John's Evening Telegram*; reprinted in the *Globe and Mail*, 6 September 1995, 8 (CP))

5 September 1995

Shooting prompts police to bring in four armored personnel carriers. Four RCMP officers who came under fire from armed native Indians later ignored opportunities to shoot their attackers, an RCMP official said Tuesday. 'They showed great restraint,' Cpl. John Ward said of the decision by the four officers, members of the emergency response team, not to fire on armed natives who followed police when they retreated from the camp. ('RCMP Exhibited "Great Restraint," *Calgary Herald*, from the *Vancouver Sun*, 6 September 1995, A3)

The details provided by the RCMP to the press at the time conflicted with the episode that actually took place. None of the journalists in the early part of the fieldwork mentioned this shooting incident as being significant in terms of the media coverage. There was no sense of anything being untoward until the topic was discussed at the trial, almost a year later. The *RCMP Report to Crown Counsel* is used here to summarize the shooting episode as it occurred, as opposed to how it was reported by the media. Three RCMP vehicles carrying constables were driving down 1100 Forestry Road, and gradually the second and third vehicles lost sight of the lead vehicle. The second vehicle, carrying four constables, encountered a muddy section, which is referred to in the report as a 'mud bog.' It was at this time that some of the occupants 'heard a popping sound.' They noticed that the right side mirror collapsed towards the truck. In the *RCMP Report to Crown Counsel* it is stated that the officers in the second vehicle assumed that they were being fired upon, hence they returned random fire. During the investigative interviews by the RCMP shortly after the episode, only one of the occupants of the last vehicle attested to hearing gunshots originating from the side of the road. The other three passengers could not see anyone from the roadside firing at the vehicle ahead, although they witnessed shots being fired by the officers in the vehicle ahead of them. The day after the alleged shooting, a police and service-dog search of the area found 'one old shotgun shell casing.'

Although the RCMP investigating team realized, within 24 hours, that there was little evidence to support the original account of the shooting incident, there was only one minor correction given to the media: the earlier statement that the police officers had returned fire was retracted. There was no correction to the assertion that the officers had been stalked by people from the camp. The only evidence contained in the *RCMP Report to Crown Counsel* that might support that claim was trampled grass around a nearby tree and identifiable footprints in the mud. Other than the old shotgun casing found on the ground, the only other shell casings were found inside the police vehicle that was allegedly under attack. These casings would have come from shots fired by constables inside the vehicle, who had indeed returned gunfire. There was no indication to the journalists at the time that the incident may have been a case of frayed nerves on the part of RCMP officers on patrol. One journalist described the press release of the incident and the depiction of the officers being stalked as '*very convincing.*' According to one journalist, '*The truck episode with the mirrors – was never corrected. Initially this was an innocent mistake. But failing to correct this as fast as they could exaggerated the seriousness of the incident*' (interview with journalist).[17]

According to defence lawyer George Wool, taped conversations between the people in the camp and the RCMP negotiators confirmed that Wolverine had advised the negotiators that the reported shooting incident (heard over CBC Radio) was not true. Wolverine accused the

RCMP of 'bullshitting.' Wool asserted that 'The police knew right then that they had a timely denial of that media event' (interview with George Wool, 29 May 1997). The police vehicle was taken away for forensic examination, and on 16 September it was stated in the released forensic report that the mirror could have been hit by a foreign object, such as a tree branch. This conclusion was also included in the RCMP Report to Crown Counsel. None of the findings of the police interviews or the results from the search for evidence, nor the results of the forensic report were provided to the media during the time of the standoff, when it was a national media event. Yet at about the same time as the news coverage of this shooting incident, B.C. Premier Harcourt confirmed, in the Victoria Times Colonist, that the armoured personnel carriers (APCs) had been ordered two weeks earlier.[18]

The information released about this incident breached the protocols of the RCMP Operational Manual, which was in effect at the time of the standoff. (See appendix 4 for excerpts from the RCMP Operational Manual II.16 Media/RCMP Relations protocols.) The manual represents the codified norms of communications between the RCMP and the media during police investigations; provisions are outlined that call for information that is released to the media to be 'relevant, timely and reliable,' and to 'keep a record of information given to the media to protect against misquotation, exaggeration or sensationalism' (Section C.3:1872/93-04-23 and Section F.1c:2114/94-11-17). Any information released to the media should not 'result in injury, injustice, or embarrassment to anyone' (Section F.1d:2114/94-11-17). When I asked Sergeant Montague, the senior media liaison, about the press releases of this shooting episode, he stated, 'I can't deal with that, because I wasn't there.'[19] Other RCMP officials interviewed in this study acknowledged that 'mistakes were made,' and that the mistakes with the media were largely due to the hectic pace and sustained stress during the standoff. This was not the last time during the standoff that the media relations personnel contravened their own protocols.

Media Witnessing the Arrival of Armoured Personnel Carriers

5 September 1995

Four military armored personnel carriers roar past the outer perimeter, headed for the camp area. Police say the National Defence APCs will be used to transport RCMP patrols. (Chronology, *Vancouver Sun*, 12 September 1995, A3)

Checkpoint 17 was the name assigned to the location of the barricades on the main forestry road leading to the camp. It marked the entry point to a different reality, one that the police controlled. Journalists could not pursue their curiosity, they could only imagine what was beyond the barricades and around that curve in the road. Over time, the police and media who regularly stayed at the checkpoint developed a camaraderie. There was none of the aloofness between most of the journalists and the police that was evident in town. Police officers shared rations (which one journalist said were much better than his canned food), and they would throw a football or sit around on lawn chairs when nothing was happening. On warm sunny days, the media would drop the back doors of their 4 × 4s, take off their shirts, lie back, and sunbathe: '*It was a bit like sitting at the beach, waiting for something to happen.*' One afternoon, a colleague on the telephone from Vancouver said that there had been a news-flash on the Internet that a policeman had been shot at Gustafsen Lake – the comment inadvertently came over the journalist's speaker – and everyone heard it. '*Everybody just jumped – especially the policemen! But it turned out to be nothing. It was some hoax. But it showed that everybody was tense all the time, waiting for something to happen*' (interview with journalist).

The level of stress during the conflict was not particularly noticeable in town, except during some press conferences when the RCMP announced serious shooting incidents. The tension was more palpable for journalists and police working closer to the camp. At Checkpoint 17, one journalist recalled, one of the police officers wore two flak jackets instead of one, "*in that heat!*" On one occasion, two RCMP officers sitting around a campfire with journalists late at night were spooked by sounds coming from the bush, which they thought might be a sneak attack by the protesters. One of the officers who went into the bush to investigate inadvertently fired his gun. The journalists ran for cover, and a group of ERT personnel converged on the area. Although the noise turned out to be a grazing cow, the officers were relieved of their duties that evening. The following day, Sergeant Montague announced during a press conference that it had been a '*quiet night*,' and he refused official comment on the shooting episode.[20]

When the APCs, also known as Bisons, filed passed Checkpoint 17 on 5 September, it was one of the biggest news stories of the standoff witnessed by the media. The arrival of the APCs was all the more shocking to the journalists because the police had been denying various media queries about whether the military (or military equipment) was going to be called in. One of the television camera crews at Checkpoint 17 had received a vague tip from police officers a few hours earlier: *'I had my tripod set up, longshot – ARRRRR – and they came flying by, all four of them, with the guys standing proud as daylight up there. They shot through ... And then I phoned back to 100 Mile House – and it was like – Highway 1 to Nowhere – coming up ... So that was a big turning point, that – a really big turning point – because that was a real show of force'* (interview with journalist). Journalists at Checkpoint 17 made hasty telephone calls to colleagues, who were sound asleep at 100 Mile House, and then to the main desks at Vancouver.

At 100 Mile House, reporters were waiting to hear the official word about the APCs. *'And the police aren't – they aren't commenting, so everybody's tense again – wondering "What's going on? What's going on?" And the cops aren't there to say anything. So you're scrambling to find Montague – you don't know where he is – he might be in his room, or maybe in the detachment – trying to get him to tell us what is going on, 'cause he's the only cop there who would ever tell us what was going on ... The next news conference, whenever that would be – maybe in an hour after something happened – might be two hours. He would – he would tell you what was going on – as much as he wanted to tell you'* (interview with journalist). Within minutes of the telephone calls from Checkpoint 17, a brigade of journalists jumped into their vehicles and barrelled down the forestry road (as quickly as they could) to see the video footage. By the time the media arrived, the APCs were past Checkpoint 17 and parked three kilometres ahead at what would later be revealed by the RCMP to be Camp Zulu. The RCMP did not inform the media until the end of the standoff that the police had brought in four additional armoured personnel carriers, on large trucks, from alternative forestry roads in order to avoid detection. Later in the conflict, when the RCMP allowed a media pool into Camp Zulu, four of the APCs were neatly lined up in full view. Unknown to the media (at the time) was the fact that the RCMP had strategically positioned other APCs closer to the camp.

The coverage of the APCs satisfied media needs with a critical development they could report, with the bonus of validating their media efficacy: *'We were there!'* The video footage was seen across the country on television, and photographs were shown in most newspapers across Canada the next day. They were shown again in subsequent news stories chronicling the event, as a reminder of the RCMP's show of force. Even so, the journalists whom I interviewed did not consider the impact on the audience and did not critically assess how the media may have been serving the police. Nor did they ask themselves who had the most to gain from this coverage. The significance of that media coverage (besides gaining a top story) was that it uncritically transmitted the RCMP's message of their prowess to the public. The visual image of the armoured personnel carriers evoked a war rhetoric that had the potential of inflaming audiences supporting any side of the conflict.[21]

Press Conferences at 100 Mile House

The press conferences at 100 Mile House were the central mechanism for authoritative information dissemination during the standoff, and they played an integral part in the media characterizations. Many reporters considered the Red Coach Inn, the venue for most of the press conferences, to be the information hub during the standoff. Originally, the RCMP media relations team held press conferences at the local RCMP detachment, but this location soon became infeasible because of increasing numbers of media and additional equipment. The management of the Red Coach Inn offered to accommodate press conferences in its main meeting room in the basement.[22] When the supporters of the Gustafsen Lake camp requested their own place to talk to the media, the management allowed them to use the vacant service station next door.[23] Most of the television newscasts of the standoff included video recordings of the press conferences, and all depended on the RCMP press releases for quotations and summaries of developments. In addition, provincial Attorney General Dosanjh arranged teleconferences at the hotel with journalists through his adjunct communications officer.[24]

The RCMP controlled the timing of the press conferences, and aside from breaking-news announcements that could be made at any time, these conferences were regulated to coincide with television news broadcasts. As soon as the police had posted a notice of a press conference in the lobby, journalists would scramble to find their colleagues. The scene was chaotic: reporters were running around, banging on doors, and calling out that the press conference would take place in an hour – or less. It was even more disorganized because, owing to the frequent room changes, it was difficult for them to remember where their colleagues were staying. '*It was messy ... and it was messy, and everyone was exhausted. But no, I've never seen anything like it. We'd have news confer-*

ences at seven in the morning and one at night ... we were all really ragged' (interview with journalist). Despite their competitive relationship, the journalists felt a responsibility to look out for each other, to make sure that nobody was left out. During the entire time of the standoff, the RCMP media team did not contact Steven Frasher, the editor of the *100 Mile House Free Press*, about pending press conferences. Occasionally journalists whom he had befriended thought to contact him. He felt as if he was *'excluded from* [his] *own backyard.'*

Press conferences provided the platform from which the RCMP could advise the media of new developments, for the record. In accordance with RCMP regulations, the RCMP provided press releases in English as well as in French, which usually necessitated the participation of two RCMP spokespersons. Although as a rule the RCMP took centre stage, other spokespersons participated, such as Ovide Mercredi (while he was in town) and a few of the Native supporters (until other arrangements could be made). For about the last ten days of the standoff, Native intermediaries provided the media with updates about the camp.

Press conferences also were the site of negotiations and struggles for media sources and the places where the media constructed news stories. The media had brought with them their aggressive press conference style from Vancouver and recreated it at the 100 Mile House Red Coach Inn meeting room. One journalist described the press conferences as *'a clash between people who needed information for the sake of filling in 30 minutes, and knowing that some of the police were getting adept at serving it up in the most dramatic fashion'* (interview with journalist). Press conferences also were open to the public, and supporters of the camp were usually in attendance. Along with various members of the media, a few of the spectators attending the press conference would ask questions, and sometimes those questions would be rather pointed; in response, Sergeant Montague appeared to get upset and *'stomp away, and the rest of us media would have nothing.'* According to the journalists' recollections, some of the spectators seemed not to understand that a press conference is for the benefit of the media, not the public. Once the RCMP media liaison established the rule that he would answer questions only from the media, the press conferences returned to the usual format.

A convention of the press conference is the strict identification of the participants and the appropriate communicative roles that they play. Typical press conferences allow spokespersons and media personnel as the two groups of participants who engage each other in providing and clarifying information that is to be incorporated into news stories. Media and media spokespersons consider spectators passive guests. If spectators initiate enquiries during the media question period, official interlocutors interpret this as an interference that threatens a breakdown in the speech event. The complication here was that, for much of the standoff, the RCMP media personnel were the only official source of information about the camp and the police operation. The press conference was the only possible venue for interaction between the audience and the police media liaison.[25] When the conventions of press conferences excluded the public audience as active participants, the lines of enquiry were restricted to aspects of the event that enhanced news stories. In the case of the press conferences during the Gustafsen Lake standoff, members of the media may not have been asking the same questions as would concerned citizens and relatives of the people inside the camp. Although order was restored once the RCMP media liaison began answering only those questions initiated by the media, many months afterward I met Aboriginal people who believed that the RCMP media personnel had silenced them.

RCMP media team members were conscious of their performance during presentations. Either they attempted to convey emotional detachment from the content of the press release, or they presented an emotional response to create a particular impression for the media.[26] Journalists are keen observers of people's reactions, however, and they were watching the RCMP media liaison for coherence between the content of what was said and the emotional tone used when the press release was conveyed. One journalist noted, '*It was quite clear that some of what the police were reflecting to us and what sounded like angry statements – were really reflections of fairly frightened, alarmed, and confused cops. Montague probably reflected that fear more than once when he came out to give his statements*' (interview with journalist).

A phrase that Sergeant Montague repeatedly used at the press conferences with the media was '*the multifaceted operational plan*' that the RCMP were carrying out. A few journalists thought the phrase was an obfuscation that sounded impressive but held little meaning. The media liaison also advised the media, on more than one occasion, that they were part of this plan. He also told them that they were working together with the police to carry out this plan. The phrase became a standing joke in some of the newsrooms in Vancouver and back at 100 Mile House: '*And in the Red Coach, somebody would say, "Oh, what are you having for breakfast?" and I'd say, "I can't tell you that. It's part of my multifaceted operational plan for the day!" sort of thing ... You realize the stupidity of it. Like, you're joking about it – because that's sort of the best way to be critical about it.'* Another journalist grumbled, *'To this day, that phrase makes me want to get a beer!'* (interviews with journalists).

At first the journalists also found it awkward to adjust to the press releases given by some of the Native spokespersons, who, in their view, seemed to have difficulty communicating information that the media could render quotable, partly, perhaps, because their media liaisons were not trained to deal with a large group of journalists, as was the RCMP media team. One journalist considered that the problems in communications may have stemmed from a fear of being misquoted, perhaps a carryover of the stereotype of mainstream media held by Native people. Another observation was that the spokesperson would leave the podium immediately after giving a prepared statement without asking the media if there were any questions, which was a crucial component of the press conference. The journalists found that these spokespersons seemed to become more at ease at the podium over time, and the pattern of communication for press conferences came more in line with the expectations of the journalists. Later in this chapter, we will explore other reasons why communications with the intermediaries were more problematic than the media realized.

As the only legitimate venue for RCMP information dissemination, press conferences guaranteed a large media presence. Some journalists complained that attending the press conferences was hardly worth the effort when there was no breaking development. The scarce supply of information resulted in the journalists' starvation for news, which characterized much of the Gustafsen Lake standoff media coverage. This chronic situation would also have an effect on the reporting of information presented by the RCMP at the press conference that advised them of the most violent shooting episode (discussed more fully in chapter 4). Because the media needed to preserve credibility with their audiences, they had to continue the illusion of presenting authentic accounts, although few of these could be independently verified. To raise the issue of not being able to confirm much of what the RCMP were advising would directly call into question the credibility of the police source, and that might jeopardize media credibility as well. Of those working for newspaper outlets in this research that covered the Gustafsen Lake standoff, only the *Vancouver Sun* reporters discussed how the lack of media witnessing had influenced the news coverage of the standoff. These accounts were printed at the conclusion of the standoff.[27]

The creation of a second press conference site for supporters of the protest allowed supporters to speak on topics that they believed were not forthcoming from the RCMP-dominated press conferences next door. The people who spoke there did not have to adhere to the norms of press conferences. The second venue provided a platform for those who did not agree with the RCMP definition that the conflict was a law enforcement issue. Instead, the supporters asserted that the dispute at Gustafsen Lake was connected to the history of colonialism and the lack of resolution of Aboriginal land issues in British Columbia.

Nonetheless, this content had only limited appeal for the mainstream media personnel gathering news. The primary reason offered by the journalists was that much of the information was repetitious and was limited in its newsworthiness, at least for the conventions of large media outlets. Historical information does not evolve; news does. The journalists were interested in fresh news about the camp. When the supporters made reference to what was going on in the camp, *'We would say, but how do you know? – You weren't there!'*

In addition, the vacant service station (although providing a space at a time when space was in short supply) was less likely to convey the officialdom, authority, and credibility associated with the Red Coach Inn. The physical appearance of the service station and the lack of amenities combined with the lower social status of the camp supporters who spoke here made this media centre an impoverished alternative. Although it was close enough to the hotel to allow easy access for the journalists, it was far enough away that some journalists would not feel obliged to walk next door, especially if the information was not re- garded as newsworthy. A test of this argument (although a supposition) would be to imagine a reversal of players and locations. I speculate that, if the camp supporters had held press conferences in the hotel conference room, and the RCMP had held press conferences at the vacant service station, the status hierarchy most likely would have been reversed – or, at least, have created a sense of discontinuity.

RCMP Confiscation of CBC Television Videotapes

6 September 1995

Meanwhile, the RCMP arrived at the Vancouver newsroom of CBC-TV Wednesday with a search warrant and demanded video cassettes contain- ing coverage of the Gustafsen Lake standoff. The television station turned over the tapes after receiving word from a lawyer that the RCMP's warrant was legal, said CBC senior producer Connie Monk. 'As a general rule we don't like handing over tapes and we don't hand them over,' said Monk. 'But we also comply with the law.' The RCMP did not go to other Lower Mainland television stations. ('Police seek assistance to end stand-off,' *Vancouver Sun*, 7 September 1995, B1)

There were two instances when the RCMP demanded CBC-TV videotapes with legal search warrants. On 23 August 1995, a few days following the airing of a segment from the videotaped program, 'Defenders of the Land,' provided by Gustafsen Lake supporters, the RCMP presented a warrant to the CBC Vancouver headquarters for this video recording. On 6 September 1995 the RCMP demanded all of the videotapes that had been taken inside the camp by the CBC camera crew. According to police sources, the police confiscated the material because they lacked physical evidence for a criminal investigation. They wanted confirmation of the identities of the people in the camp, the number and types of weapons, and scenes that showed the terrain and the defensive positions that those inside might take against officers. The videotapes provided scenes that had useful evidence for laying criminal charges. One clip showed two people in the camp shooting at an RCMP helicopter, and another captured some camp members unselfconsciously walking around with weapons; a few of these weapons appeared to be AK–47s.

The journalists felt that handing over the material would breach a trust with their sources. The representatives from the camp had voluntarily turned over 'Defenders of the Land,' to the CBC Television outlet, perhaps naively unaware that the videotape contained incriminating evidence against their group. At the time, the camp representatives did not sign a waiver to acknowledge the risks for broadcasting this videotape. This is not a standard procedure for the CBC, nor is it for most media. Later, when they allowed a CBC Television crew to film inside, people in the camp also may have trusted that the broadcaster would not allow any harm to come to the camp as a result of the filming. Nonetheless, according to media convention, subjects are solely responsible for their behaviour while on camera.[28] A journalist commented that the RCMP had exploited a trust between the CBC crew and the people in the camp who had allowed them access: '*They showed more – damning stuff of the Natives, but they still had the respect of the Natives. The CBC had the tape of them shooting at the helicopter ...*'[29] They [the RCMP] *go*

through every shot on the tape that was there – that the CBC *cameraman took –*
'cause it's used as evidence – and that's a whole different story, whether that's
right or wrong, or whether they used the crew's access to get in there – I have a
real hard time with that. But they were in no position to argue – 'cause the
cameraman could've been taken from the line, arrested' (interview with
journalist). Ironically, the confiscation of media products lent credibility
to Wolverine's earlier accusation to a journalist that the media were
'spies working with the police and that they would take notes and deliver them
to the police.'

The media's objectives to gather and present news and the RCMP's
objective to conduct a criminal investigation overlapped in the case of
the Gustafsen Lake standoff. Although the media outlet may not have
deliberately compromised the camp, its inability to protect the tapes
did jeopardize their media sources. In both of these situations, once the
television outlet had possession of the video property, the people in the
camp relinquished control of it. At the same time, it appears that the
television outlet had little control of the video recording.[30] The above
analysis is not an attempt to minimize the known facts that the people
in the camp were in possession of illegal weapons, that they shot at
police helicopters, or that they shot at police officers. It is not to suggest
that the police, as law enforcers, should not benefit from the assistance
of citizens in conducting investigations, especially when evidence is at
a premium. The difficulty is that the media, particularly the CBC as a
public broadcaster, is supposed to be independent of political or legal
authorities. The RCMP's confiscation of the video materials created a
relationship wherein the outlet became an extension of the law enforcement agency. The structural features between the police and the
media during the Gustafsen Lake standoff will be discussed further in
chapter 7.

Media and the Meeting at Alkali Lake

A meeting was called for the 17 bands of the Shuswap Nation on
Thursday, 7 September at Alkali Lake. This gathering was partly in
response to an invitation from the RCMP for assistance from Native
chiefs and elders to facilitate the resolution of the conflict. The purpose
of the meeting was to plan for and organize a team of Aboriginal
intermediaries that would speak with the people in the camp, a strategy that might promote a peaceful settlement.[31] The gathering at Alkali
Lake gave some members of the media opportunities to meet local

Native people and participate in some of the spiritual ceremonies. Alkali Lake has the distinction in the area of becoming a dry reserve. The Natives there have taken a proactive stance on the alcohol addiction that had plagued their people for many years.

At Alkali Lake, the Native community set the agenda and conventions of the event, which obliged the police and media to comply. Journalists were not allowed in during the meetings, which at one point included elders and the police and then only Native people. The local Native interpretation was that the conflict was *'a Native problem for which a Native solution'* would be found. Three of the journalists were invited by the Shuswap community to witness and participate in the pipe ceremony preceding the talks. The meeting at Alkali Lake provided opportunities for journalists to speak with Native people on a less formal basis.

> *So those of us who were at Alkali, who were fortunate enough to get stuck out in the sun and have to stand around and – eventually, the Indians started to take pity on us, and they would chat with us ... This is how it transpired. I asked them, 'Look, I don't understand what you are doing here. I want to report on it accurately, I want to be able to explain to my readers what it means that you are doing. Can you explain to me the conditions and the roles that you are going through here?' And as soon as they could see that I was interested in what they were doing, they were willing to tell me. And eventually they – a group of them came out and said, 'Well, if you want to come in and watch the ceremony, then you can watch the ceremony. No taperecorders, no notes, no nothing. They came and they set us in a certain place and we ended up – I think eventually – ended up participating ... Even the RCMP officers there ... also ended up participating in the ceremony. After that we were excused, and it continued on ... They were nice people. Sweet, really gentle people. And you have to respect that. Later on they insisted we go on a sweatlodge [ceremony], so we did a couple of 'sweats' ... You could understand the pressures that were being exerted on the community, and the way for them to resolve their problems was not going to come through a conflict with the RCMP. It had to come through a different resolution through their own community. And that's I think what eventually did settle the dispute.* (Interview with journalist)

The meeting at Alkali Lake between Native leaders, elders, and RCMP officials was a strategic situation that shifted the news event to a peaceful, Native community setting. It was not structured and predictable according to media conventions, RCMP timelines, or the interpretive frames heard so far. Journalists had to be more conscious of cultural and community sensitivities in their interactions with Native people. Such interactions may have challenged mutual stereotypes, and it helped the journalists to appreciate the difficult position of local Native communities in this conflict. Although the dominant frame of the media coverage continued to come from the RCMP characterization of the standoff, the rapport between Native people and the media on that day did have a positive effect. The journalists' narratives of their interactions at Alkali Lake were not the product of a schedule of interview questions. The journalists initiated the discussion more than a year after the standoff.

Inclusion of Native Intermediaries

Matthew, president of the Shuswap Nation tribal council,[32] said earlier Sunday that significant progress had been made in talks between the elders and rebels. He said the site of the stand-off has evolved from 'a defence-oriented camp to a peace camp.' ('Hopes falter for deal with rebels' *Vancouver Sun*, 11 September 1995, B1)

B.C. Attorney General Ujjal Dosanjh was unimpressed. 'A peace camp does not have AK–47s; peace campers don't shoot at the backs of police officers,' he said. He said he welcomes the elders' involvement 'if they are attempting to defuse the situation, disarm these individuals, turn them over to the police, let the law take its course.' ('Native leaders tightlipped after meeting,' *Victoria Times Colonist*, 11 September 1995, a1; reprinted in the *Globe and Mail*)

Matthew also tried to clarify his weekend comments referring to the occupation as a 'peace camp,' despite the shooting incidents. He said the term was meant to hark back to the site's previous use as a venue for sacred sundance ceremonies. ('Three natives shot in firefight,' *Victoria Times Colonist* 12 September 1995, a1; reprinted in the Globe and Mail)

Native elders, on the invitation of the RCMP, initiated talks inside the camp in an attempt to settle the dispute peacefully.[33] The intermediaries were respected elders and chiefs from a variety of Native communities. Nathan Matthew, chief of the North Thompson Band and chairperson of the Shuswap Nation, was one of the Aboriginal chiefs who had attended the meeting at Alkali Lake. He described his involvement during the standoff and also relations with the RCMP and the media: *'things at GL* [Gustafsen Lake] *had escalated. We wanted a non-violent resolution.'* The Aboriginal leaders established several teams made up of the people who had attended the meeting at Alkali Lake, and Chief Matthew was to be one of the media liaisons at the press conferences. The discussions ended between 2:00 a.m. and 4:00 a.m., and then another ceremonial sweat was held.

According to Chief Matthew, once the Native mediation teams had been established, they set up at 100 Mile House. The police briefed them daily. The main goal of the intermediaries was not to deal with the media, but to establish contact with the people in the camp. However, the committee of chiefs and elders decided that they needed to have contact with the media because of the way that the RCMP was characterizing the situation. Consequently, there was considerable time spent *'strategizing how we could cool the situation down and support a peaceful resolution.'* Chief Matthew considered the relationship between the intermediaries and the other First Nations supporters to be *'good.'* *'We had our own briefing session with them in the space we had across the lane from the hotel.'* Chief Matthew said that the tasks of arranging for delegations into the camp, communicating with First Nations individuals and organizations, reviewing legal options, and maintaining an organized intervention were *'hectic and exhausting.'* He himself did not go into the camp but performed other tasks, including providing many of the press releases at the Red Coach Inn news conferences. He described the mood of the camp as *'very defiant, growing tension. We thought we had discussed with the RCMP that their goal was to contain the area – but the RCMP was increasingly moving in – tightening the perimeter ... We had a concern that the RCMP were doing more than containing the area – we knew that this could lead to violence with the increasing tension.'*

The day before the firefight, Chief Matthew stated during a press conference that the intermediaries were in the process of turning the camp into a *'peace camp.'* *'This was to counter the actively aggressive nature of the RCMP* [referring to the tightening of the perimeter around the camp]. *The media portrayal of Gustafsen Lake was that it was a war zone – they* [the media] *lapped it up – the blood and guts. We thought that we could* [turn this negative image around] *if we referred to the camp as a "peace camp."'*

Chief Matthew described the press conferences and the self-monitoring done by the intermediaries while providing information to the media:

A lot of attention was paid to the television cameras. We would give our media releases after the RCMP gave theirs. There were never any questions after, so we left. Our version was not the same as the RCMP. We became even more cautious when we felt the RCMP were putting on even more pressure on the people inside. **Did you think the Native negotiating team was given fair access to the media?** *We didn't engage in protracting a dialogue with the media. We didn't initiate any comment. We became very aware that the RCMP was orchestrating the event to the media. They said one thing – then did another. They weren't supposed to put any more pressure on the people in the camp, but they did. We wanted a buffer zone, but this was continuously being diminished. Both sides were armed to the teeth – well, the army was anyway.*

Chief Matthew was unable to monitor the news during the time he was directly involved, and he was concerned about how the event and the people inside the camp were being depicted by the RCMP and the media (interview with Chief Matthew, 17 February 1998).

Although they remained in this secondary media role, the Native spokespersons were able to provide a different view of the camp than that offered by the RCMP. They gave information that the people inside might not have shared with the RCMP negotiators or that the RCMP negotiators would not want the media to learn: fears of a police assault, food and drinking water shortages, and the mood inside the camp. This was the kind of information that might generate public sympathy. The input to the media from the Native intermediaries became an avenue for contesting the RCMP characterization of the 11 September firefight. However, the Native intermediaries were operating on the assumption that certain disclosures to the media might jeopardize their access to the camp.

Relations of Power in the Exchange of Information

The unifying theme in this chapter has been the analysis of the complexities of the negotiations between media and sources in the struggle to contribute to the framing of the news stories. Sources do not have equal abilities or status to influence news stories. In the case of the Gustafsen Lake news coverage, the RCMP had the greatest status by being the law enforcement agency called in to investigate various weapons and shooting offences. They were also the only group with specially trained staff and a set of codified protocols to deal with the media. Another advantage of the RCMP was that they had a media plan from an early point in the dispute, and, more than any of the other stakeholders, they were systematically monitoring the media coverage as well as public opinion. All of these factors provided the RCMP with superior resources to deal with the media. Compared with the other groups (the camp, the supporters, and the intermediaries), who seemed to be operating on a more ad hoc basis, the RCMP were by far more sophisticated.[34]

A central consideration for media sources was impression management, both for themselves individually and for the group or ideology being represented. I consider in this study that all sources (save, at this point, the people inside the camp) had a degree of control over their impression management. However, not all sources used this to their advantage. During the Gustafsen Lake standoff, impression management also hinged on its being validated by authority figures, such as the RCMP or community leaders. Akin to proximity to the RCMP was the importance of sharing the same venue to provide news information. Thus, the supporters' request for their own venue for press conferences may have contributed to decreased attention from the media.

An aspect of impression management was the ability of groups to control their stock of information going to the media. For Sergeant Montague, the goals for his media plan included maintaining police security, supporting RCMP morale, and ensuring favourable public opinion. Nonetheless, the RCMP were unable to fully control police information, whether over radio-telecommunications or through its members' speaking informally with the media. Until the RCMP established secure radio-telecommunications with the camp, there was potential for a breach in their security. The closed-door meeting provided the media liaison with an opportunity to use the RCMP's power and influence to dissuade the media from publishing from this source. The RCMP's reminder that the procurement of this source was illegal practically assured media compliance. For Chief Matthew, the goals for the press releases from the Native intermediaries included providing a more humane perspective of the camp and maintaining support from the RCMP as intermediaries. This meant that the Native spokespersons had to be selective in what they told the media in order to portray a contrasting image of the camp that did not interfere with the peaceful resolution of the conflict. The Native spokespersons did not depend on radios for their interactions with the camp, and therefore they were in a better position than the RCMP to control the information going out to the media. In contrast to the other media sources, with the advent of the barricades and loss of its cellular telephone connection, the camp lost control over their stock of information to the police. This shift increased the likelihood of unfavourable media characterizations of the people at the camp, because details about the camp and the activities behind the barricades came from a law enforcement perspective. Another development that signified the camp's loss of control of their information was the confiscation from CBC-TV of the videotaped recordings taken of the camp. The video materials offered the RCMP incriminating evidence of illegal activities and identified individuals in the camp.

On the other side of the exchange were the media. Media appreciate material from their sources that make gathering news easier. Conversely, they are critical of information that is irrelevant, unreliable, vague, and difficult to quote. Ironically, the journalists found that controversial and mercurial lawyer Bruce Clark furnished some of the most satisfying media copy during the standoff, although the media (in general) did not present him in a positive light. At the same time, many of the difficulties for the media during the Gustafsen Lake standoff were caused by insufficient information provided during the RCMP press conferences. Journalists sought out a variety of supplementary sources to provide background information or to assist them in questioning RCMP spokespersons, but these sources did not provide the depth of information required for such a serious conflict. A reverse situation occurred during the media coverage of the 4 September 1995 shooting incident: RCMP press releases offered information and full explanations before they were verified, resulting in media misrepresentations of the episode and the camp. From these examples, one could assume that, ideally, media should witness the events they report. The news coverage of the arrival of the APCs, however, exposes the weaknesses in the media in their simply witnessing without a critical evaluation to address the underlying agendas of the players orchestrating the event.

In this chapter, occasions when the negotiation of information between the media, the media sources, and the RCMP was connected to the RCMP operation also have been identified. The *Vancouver Sun*'s decision to continue publishing unauthorized police information was the most obvious case of the media's appropriation of police property, although other outlets also used various unofficial sources to supplement their news coverage. The RCMP's request of the radio journalist to act as a messenger appears to have been part of a successful ploy to neutralize the lawyer Bruce Clark, to prevent him from interfering with a police-negotiated settlement with the camp. Another instance was the

RCMP's confiscation of video materials of the camp from CBC-TV, which compromised the CBC's detachment from the RCMP operation. The above cases show that the lines between the media and the police were not definitive, a structural characteristic that will be discussed further.

The outcomes of the methods used by the RCMP and the media in negotiating information include the coverage of various shooting incidents on 27 August, 4 September, and at Checkpoint 17. The RCMP media team attempted to convey information that maintained favourable impressions of the police and to convince the public that they were in control of the situation. Despite their efforts, all the narratives and facts surrounding the shooting episodes underscore the extent of the stress within the RCMP. The impression management strategies, implicit or acknowledged in these incidents, reveal patterns in the media portrayals that are confirmed by the newspaper coverage. Events most likely covered in the news include shooting incidents that were characterized as being initiated from the camp (as opposed to the friendly fire at Checkpoint 17). Another pattern is that these news stories presented the RCMP as in control and showing restraint and, conversely, the people in the camp as dangerous and criminal.

On the afternoon of Monday, 11 September, 75 Natives representing 25 bands, including a delegation from the Native intermediaries attended a meeting of British Columbia Native chiefs at Merritt. After the meeting, those in attendance issued a press release stating 'the people at Gustafsen do have our support.' Some of the delegates expressed their anger about the RCMP operation. They recognized that there might be repercussions if the standoff ended in bloodshed.[35] While this meeting was taking place at Merritt, the most violent episode of the standoff was unfolding at Gustafsen Lake.

CHAPTER FOUR

Out of Control

I saw the tape of the blast and it looks pretty scary, because the smoke was incredible. *That's not smoke – it's dust.* It was dust? *It was dust on the dusty road, yeah. Yeah.* Not smoke? *No. No. A little bit of it would be smoke, but that was all dust ...* It didn't look like dust to me, Peter [I laughed]. *Oh, yeah. Well, some of it was going to be smoke, but most of that was dust – we know that because we tested it out there. We – we – but we didn't expect that much dust.*

Sergeant Peter Montague, interview, 27 May 1997[1]

The firefight of 11 September 1995 and the shooting episode of 12 September 1995 offered the greatest contrasts of media coverage during the standoff: saturation – and silence. The firefight was the most violent episode of the standoff. It was also the occasion for the most damaging media portrayals of the people in the camp. In contrast, the RCMP never reported the shooting episode of 12 September 1995 to the media. The two incidents illustrate how the RCMP operational plan and their internal network of communication had a direct impact on the media coverage of the standoff.

Information control takes on a heightened importance for players who have invested heavily in representing themselves in the media as being exemplary in conduct during situations that might damage their reputations. The RCMP media strategy in response to the 11 September firefight demonstrates this point: it was to counter potential negative public backlash on any offensive measures enacted by the police against the people in the camp. Yet the Native intermediaries, who at this point were dealing directly with the people at the camp, could have derailed this initiative. Not only did they have the only legitimate means of obtaining an alternative interpretation of what had happened, but they had their own media strategy to counter the RCMP's damaging portrayals of the protesters. The timing of the implementation of the media strategy also figured into the success of the RCMP media plan, because, at this point in the standoff, the media were primed for a major break in the story. With their starvation for fresh news, constant deadlines, competition with other media outlets, and restricted legitimate sources of information, most journalists were not in a position to evaluate critically the RCMP firefight press release.

These two episodes also reveal how media stereotypes were constructed from the point of origin in the RCMP operational plan and disseminated to a national multimedia audience.

Preamble to the Firefight

According to Sergeant Peter Montague and RCMP psychologist Dr Mike Webster, the RCMP's conflict management strategy to end the standoff was twofold: the ERT would apply consistent pressure to gradually tighten the perimeter around the camp in conjunction with the negotiation efforts. They wanted to make it easier for the people in the camp to leave and difficult for them to remain inside. The day before the firefight, the RCMP negotiators allegedly had notified the camp that the perimeter that separated the camp's safe zone from the no-go zone would be tightened. This would render the well and the firewood out of bounds. This initiative is consistent with the RCMP's response to barricaded situations in urban settings. Cutting off access to heat and electrical power creates pressure for the barricaded party to surrender. The RCMP argued after the firefight incident that the water in the lake was safe to drink, and in their interpretation, the camp was not being deprived of a fresh water supply. There is no information available as to who in the camp received the message about the new perimeter or whether everyone in the camp knew about this change. However, the *RCMP Report to Crown Counsel* indicates that one of the individuals (shortly after the final arrests) advised police that Wolverine (the leader at the camp who usually spoke to RCMP negotiators over the radio) did not tell the others about the restricted perimeter.

Firefight

11 September 1995

The day starts quietly, with another delegation going into the camp. But shortly after the native Indian negotiators emerge, gunfire erupts. (Chronology, *Vancouver Sun*, 12 September 1995, A3)

11 September 1995

Police and rebels in shootout after explosive device damages a camp truck. Police say rebels claim a woman in camp was injured, a man missing. ('Anatomy of the B.C. standoff,' *Toronto Star*, 18 September 1995, A4)

The primary controversy during the trial testimony regarding the 11 September firefight and the shooting incident on the following day was that the ERT was given orders to shoot to kill.[2] According to District Superintendent Len Olfert, the commanding RCMP officer of the Gustafsen Lake operation, the ERT command may have altered the terms of engagement at about this time, but he flatly denied that there was a general 'kill order,' as such.[3] Interviews with District Superintendent Olfert and Sergeant Montague, suggest that the ERT initiatives were not made known to the two senior officers at the time of the standoff. Olfert and Montague recall that the basic plan was that, given the opportunity, the truck used by the people in the camp would be disabled and its occupants arrested, and they would not be allowed to return to camp.

Interpretation of the RCMP Wescam Recording

The firefight had a witness with a visual record: the RCMP wescam[4] aerial video-recording that was shown as evidence at the Gustafsen Lake standoff trial.[5] The episode began at about 2:00 p.m. on a Monday afternoon (11 September 1995) as the Aboriginal intermediaries were preparing to drive to the camp for talks. Before the RCMP could clear them to enter the perimeter, gunfire erupted in the direction of the camp. The entourage was kept back and one of the elders had a heart attack.[6] It was confirmed during the trial that three people with a dog had taken the truck to bring back some water, in anticipation of the arrival of the intermediaries.

A few of the camp leaders before the standoff

People in the camp examining the news coverage early in the standoff

The first meeting between Grand Chief Ovide Mercredi and members of the camp

Exclusive photograph taken after the first meeting between Grand Chief Ovide Mercredi and members of the camp

Gunshot damage to the RCMP Chevy Suburban from the shooting episode on 27 August 1995

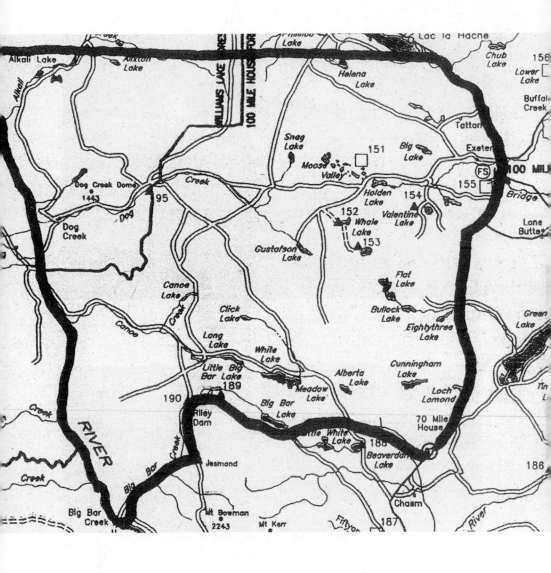

Map of the RCMP 'No-Go Zone' public notification

Aerial photograph of RCMP Camp Zulu

Armoured personnel carriers during the media tour of RCMP Camp Zulu, 15 September 1995

Non-Native street demonstration at 100 Mile House protesting the standoff

Live audience during the 11 September 1995 firefight press conference

Damaged red truck from the 11 September 1995 firefight

Media tour of the Gustafsen Lake camp, 24 September 1995

The RCMP wescam aerial video recording provides an eye-witness account of the truck explosion and activities that took place immediately afterward: *The truck from the camp can be seen driven along a dirt road, and at some point, an explosion occurs. A large, dark plume of oily smoke billows up approximately 30 metres.*[7] *The video shows that the smoke is very dense, blocking the view of the truck for several seconds. A light-coloured dog can be seen immediately emerging from the back of the truck. The dog runs away from the truck. An APC is seen ramming the front of the truck, pushing the front of the truck into the cab section. The dog is shot several times and is last seen lying on the ground* (interpretation of the RCMP wescam video-recording, S. Lambertus). According to George Wool, senior defence counsel, the explosion propelled the truck's battery several metres down the road, and it blew out the oil pan – *'that's a substantial force'* (interview with George Wool, 29 May 1997).

The remaining part of the account is a synthesis of the *RCMP Report to Crown Counsel* and trial testimony. One of the male occupants and a female occupant ran into the forest towards the lake. They began swimming in the direction of the camp, and an APC moved into position to attempt to arrest them. Warning shots were fired at the couple, and they were ordered to surrender with their hands above their heads. At some point, the woman was shot in the arm while she was in the water. Gunfire from the treed area was directed at the ERT members standing in the APC, and they ducked inside for safety.[8] The APC moved into the vicinity of the shots being fired and began chasing an armed male, who was on foot. This man was later identified as Wolverine, one of the camp leaders. The APC became disabled, and it was one week before the cause was determined. The armed man (Wolverine) allegedly fired at the APC, then made his way back to camp; the subsequent shift of attention from the APC towards the armed man provided the male and female the opportunity to swim across the lake and return to the camp. Many shots were heard, and eventually the disabled APC was hitched to another APC and towed to safety. It was established in court that much of the gunfire during the episode might have been crossfire between two APCs.[9] The fracas lasted about 45 minutes.[10] At the end of the firefight, the RCMP retrieved a loaded AK–47 rifle and a hunting rifle from the truck, and they found an ammunition clip on the ground nearby. Neither the RCMP nor those in the camp knew the whereabouts of one of the male occupants of the truck. One of the passengers from the truck was wounded. The dog was killed. The truck from the camp was destroyed, and an APC was disabled.

The Press Conference

Many of the journalists, as well as supporters, heard fragments of information over the scanners and radiotelephones during that afternoon, and they knew that something serious had taken place. One journalist recalled, 'What I could tell from the radio transmissions – there was a helluva lot of somethin' flyin' out there, because both sides were breathless, and goin' nuts – like Stop! Stop! Stop already!! It was quite something to hear first hand' (interview with journalist). The journalists had to wait several hours for the press conference to confirm any information. The press conference, held in the early evening following the firefight, was fraught with electric tension. The room was packed with journalists, as well as supporters and various Native people concerned about the situation. A few journalists recalled that it appeared to them that RCMP media relations officer Sergeant Montague came into the room with a police escort. 'After the so-called firefight, he was very serious. My impression was they had been caught off guard – he was very serious.' One journalist remembered,

> The press conference took place late in the day – the cell phones 'went for a dive,' with all of the media trying to access their desks at the same time. He came across like they'd screwed up – it's like when someone knows they have done something wrong, and they're trying to put their best face on – that's how it came across. They tried to show they had been on a defensive course, that they had come under a hail of bullets after the truck had blown up. We never heard about the dog [being shot], it was probably not significant at the time. We were told that thousands of rounds were fired, and that the officers barely came out alive, and that the shots were coming from all sides, and there had possibly been one injured, and that possibly one person might leave [the camp]. I had a sense that Montague was covering up, we always know they wouldn't tell the good stuff, [but on this occasion] we had the sense that things got out of control – that's what scared us ... We had no sense that the RCMP had everything under control. I don't think they were equipped for the situation.' (Interviews with journalists)

Hotel staff said that the RCMP had about ten fully armed RCMP personnel waiting behind the meeting room and in other rooms in the hotel, in case the press conference got out of hand. However, I could not confirm this information with the RCMP.

Comparative Analysis of Newspaper Coverage of the Firefight

As evidence of the crisis of the firefight situation, the RCMP reversed its usual tactic of dispersing sparse information to the media and, on this occasion, released extensive details of the action behind the barricades. The media coverage of the firefight is significant for several reasons. First, the RCMP did not verify important details of the confrontation before holding the press conference. Second, the RCMP used this occasion to enact a media strategy to identify names and criminal records of suspects. To some extent, this information appeared in all of the newspapers in the cross-Canada sample. Third, the *Vancouver Sun's* version of the episode included unauthorized information about the firefight, which, while providing an alternative perspective to the RCMP press release, nevertheless broke the law. Last, the media coverage of the firefight transmitted the most vilifying characterizations of the people in the camp during the standoff.

The following is an excerpt from the Canadian Press story that appeared, the *Globe and Mail* on 12 September 1995.[11] The unverified information is identified with an asterisk (*). The punctuation and spelling from the published account have been retained. (See appendix 5 for the full *Globe and Mail* account.)

1. *Three natives were shot during a firefight Monday with RCMP using armored personnel carriers outside an armed camp in the B.C. Interior. It was not known how serious their injuries were.

2. Rebel leader William Ignace, known as Wolverine, 'advised our negotiators that three people were injured as a result of the gun battle,' RCMP Sgt. Peter Montague told a news conference.

3. When RCMP suggested helping the wounded leave the camp, 'his response was that nobody was leaving the camp and the conversation ended.'

4. Monty Sam, a Shuswap native, went into the camp after the gun battle, said Sam's wife Jeannette Armstrong.

5. Montague identified some of the camp's leaders, saying that 'for reasons of public interest, the RCMP is now compelled to inform the public as to whom we are dealing with at the camp. [close quote missing]

6. *'There's a criminal agenda which is continually being advanced by the criminal element in that community,' he said. 'They have usurped

any legitimate goal and objectives of the local people with their own self-serving criminal agenda.'

7. The gun battle began when a pickup truck tried to go outside a 'no-go zone' around the camp, he said.

8. But an aboriginal negotiator said police knew the pickup truck was coming out of the camp to meet native elders. 'The RCMP were well aware that these people come out of the camp, come up to the road and sit awaiting the arrival of the delegation,' said Gordon Sebastian.

9. The truck was disabled when it drove over an 'early warning device' police had put in a logging road in the zone, Montague said.

10. *The two or three people in the truck then grabbed weapons and ran into the bush, he said.

11. *A Bison armored personnel carrier on loan from the Canadian Forces then joined the fray but experienced mechanical difficulties when it was hit by fire from an AK–47 assault rifle, Montague said.

12. *A second Bison was called in but both vehicles 'came under heavy fire' so police started shooting back, he said.

13. He said police recovered an AK–47 and a hunting rifle from the truck.

14. *It was the seventh time police have been fired on.

The above excerpt demonstrates how the RCMP interpretation of the firefight episode dominates the news narrative. Responsibility for the alleged shooting of three Native people is subsumed in the passive construction of the news lead. The news story reveals a hierarchy of sources, privileging the RCMP spokesman who is quoted first and most frequently. The RCMP spokesperson relays police communications with the Aboriginal protest leader in the camp, but the reported transaction implies that the protest leader has little regard for those injured. The RCMP media officer employs the sanitized descriptor *early warning device*, to describe the RCMP weaponry that caused the explosion.[12] This usage contrasts with the numerous references to the protesters' aggressive use of AK–47s. Although there is some attempt to include challenges offered by Aboriginal spokespersons to the RCMP's interpretation of the incident, the police information is more believable. Their proximity to the actual situation and their status as law enforcers put the RCMP in a position to offer details of the incident that no other sources could provide. The quotations from Native sources are situated later in the story; the diminished effect of the placement of this information is in keeping with the ranking order of news sources. Because they appear mid-point in the story, these details will not likely be remembered by the reader, and they are more susceptible to being edited or cropped by a client newspaper.

The asterisks in the above excerpt indicate the extent of the inaccurate information released to the media. Contrary to the *Globe and Mail* news account, only one of the truck occupants was injured. The people exiting the truck were unarmed. The APC was not disabled because of the protesters' gunfire, and the source of the 'heavy fire' on the second APC had not yet been determined. One of the shooting incidents included in the tally did not occur at all. This unverified information is most damaging to the characters of the people in the camp, but is consistent with the repeated allegation of a 'criminal agenda,' which is an interpretation, rather than a statement of fact. The dominant frame of the story follows the version offered by the RCMP – that the protesters were the aggressors – forcing the police to defend themselves.

One can appreciate the power of this typical account to influence mainstream audiences by considering the potential audience reach and the solid reputation of Canadian Press within the news industry. As a cooperative news service, Canadian Press provides news stories to up to 90 newspapers across Canada.[13] Its journalists intend their stories to resonate with the news values of client newspapers. As a conservative news supplier, Canadian Press has a mandate to supply reliable news, gathered responsibly. This necessarily implies that the news cooperative gives a high priority to law enforcement authorities.

The following is an excerpt from the *Vancouver Sun* account of the firefight, which contains transcripts of the RCMP radio-telecommunications. The punctuation and spelling from the published account have been retained (see appendix 6 for the full *Vancouver Sun* account).

1. After the gunfight, Montague said, RCMP contacted the camp and spoke to Jonesy Ignace, who goes by the name of Wolverine. Ignace told the RCMP that three people were injured, including an unarmed woman.
2. When RCMP asked Ignace to return everyone to the camp so the injured could be removed, Montague said Ignace told them 'nobody was going to leave the camp.'
3. Wolverine let fly a string of expletives and accused police of betraying their promise not to hurt the campers. 'You murdered one of our women, you bastards,' he screamed over the phone. 'It's payback time, you motherf—ers.' (Ignace later referred to three people being injured – not killed – in the firefight.)

4. Police asked if anyone in the camp wanted to come out, but Wolverine said no one would leave.
5. Later, Percy Rosette, one of the spiritual leaders in the camp, accused police of double-crossing the campers. 'Everything went wrong with your people. It was a bomb,' he said. 'You people started firing first again. Your people sent bombs.' He said no one would come out now because they believed the police would kill them.
6. Still later, another person in the camp, who refused to identify himself, picked up the phone and told police to back off or they would be killed. 'I'll tell you something before you tell us. You are going to listen. That wasn't very nice what you done, and you better expect we are going to engage you. We are not going to back down. All you f—ing people get out of here now or we're going out now and you'll be answering for a lot of shit, and this will spark the fire worldwide.' (*Vancouver Sun*, 12 September 1995, A1[14])

This news excerpt draws the reader into the post-firefight scene and refutes the RCMP's contention that the people at the camp were the aggressors during the firefight. It also provides a speech event that otherwise would have remained private between the RCMP negotiators and the camp (except for several individuals in the local vicinity who were eavesdropping with radiotelephones). The passage with the protesters recreates a drama that the police did not mention at the press conference. Social actors not previously heard, make allegations against the police in the heat of the moment, using discourse not staged for the public. The account provides a believable alternative framework for understanding the firefight.

The *Vancouver Sun's* news story directly challenged the RCMP's press release, but it is not surprising that the newspaper offered the greatest resistance to the RCMP's attempts to monopolize news information behind the barricades. In contrast to the conservative ideology of the Canadian Press, the *Vancouver Sun* has a reputation for challenging government and police authorities.[15] Its news values encourage investigative and critical reporting, more so than for journalists working for news services. According to Gary Mason, the *Vancouver Sun* news editor who orchestrated the Gustafsen Lake coverage, the *Vancouver Sun* advised journalists at 100 Mile House to continue incorporating unauthorized radio transcripts, although editors in Vancouver made final decisions for publication. The inclusion of this illegal source provided the newspaper with a competitive edge over the other media outlets, which infuriated several journalists (as discussed in chapter 3). Although the RCMP media liaison previously had threatened legal action against media outlets who published accounts derived from RCMP communications channels, the *Vancouver Sun* was the only media outlet to defy this edict. The police addressed this issue several months after the standoff, when they issued a written warning to the newspaper (see chap. 3, n.11). The *Sun*'s standing as a successful newspaper in the province and the financial resources available to defend their actions in court strengthened the editors' resolve in breaking away from pack journalism. However, the potential audience impact of the *Vancouver Sun* news story was limited, because it was restricted to print media and to audiences residing in British Columbia.[16]

Issue of Corrections

The release of unverified information led to significant contradictions between the media coverage and the actual incident. The *RCMP Report to Crown Counsel* confirms that the people were unarmed when they left the truck and that the APC became inoperable after driving over a tree, which damaged the steering mechanism. Descriptions of the firefight published in the Canada-wide newspaper sample are presented in table 4.1.

In the 18 newspapers across Canada consulted for this study, there were 14 stories detailing the firefight, all of which advised that the occupants left the truck with weapons. The *Calgary Herald*, *Regina Leader Post*, *London Free Press*, *Vancouver Sun*, and *Vancouver Province* mentioned that the occupants fired at the RCMP when they emerged from the vehicle. Thirteen newspapers reported that the APC was disabled because of gunfire either from the occupants in the truck or from the camp. The *London Free Press* did not refer to the armoured personnel carrier. The *Victoria Times Colonist*, *Vancouver Sun*, *Edmonton Journal*, *Saskatoon Star Phoenix*, *Winnipeg Free Press*, *Toronto Star*, *Globe and Mail*, *Montreal Gazette*, and *St. John's Evening Telegram* quoted Sergeant Montague as saying that the gunfire was specifically from an AK–47 assault weapon. None of the 18 newspapers (during the period of the standoff) corrected the misinformation about the occupants. Nor was there a correction to explain the reason for the APC's being disabled during the period of the standoff.[17]

The journalists in this research confirmed that the RCMP did not advise them of corrections during the televised press conferences. Ser-

TABLE 4.1
Details of the 11 September 1995 Firefight Published in Canadian Newspapers
(The table reproduces representative published details of the firefight. These details were also found in the Canadian Press news stories appearing in the *Edmonton Journal*,[a] *Saskatoon Star Phoenix*,[b] *Winnipeg Free Press*,[c] *Toronto Star*,[d] and *Montreal Gazette*.[e] The punctuation and spelling from the published accounts have been retained.)

Description of the truck occupants	Reasons given for the Bison/APC's being 'disabled'
Victoria Times Colonist[f] 'The two or three people in the truck then grabbed weapons and ran into the bush, he said.'	'A Bison ... joined the fray but experienced mechanical difficulties when it was hit by fire from an AK–47 assault rifle, Montague said.'
Vancouver Sun[g] 'He said the two occupants, or possibly three, jumped out of the truck and ran into the woods with their weapons. The RCMP pursued the individuals but discontinued the pursuit when the two individuals commenced firing upon our members.'	'Montague said AK–47 fire from native Indians disabled a Bison manned by RCMP emergency response team members.'
Vancouver Province[h] 'Montague said two natives ran into the trees carrying weapons with them, and began firing at officers.'	'He said RCMP officers came under such heavy fire that one of the APCs was disabled.'
Calgary Herald[i] 'Montague said two natives ran into the trees and fired at officers.'	'Montague said "thousands of rounds" were exchanged and one APC was disabled.'
Regina Leader Post[j] 'The truck's occupants bailed out and opened fire on Mounties in a Canadian Armed Forces Bison armored personnel carrier.'	'The shooting was so heavy the military vehicle was disabled and another Bison had to come to the rescue, Montague said.'
London Free Press[k] 'Montague said police pursued the two or three people but stopped when they were fired upon.'	No mention of Bison
Globe and Mail Published *St. John's Evening Telegram* (CP) version 'The two or three people in the truck then grabbed weapons and ran into the bush, he said.'	'A Bison ... joined the fray but experienced mechanical difficulties when it was hit by fire from an AK–47 assault rifle, Montague said.'
Published *Victoria Times Colonist* (CP) version	

TABLE 4.1 (concluded)

Description of the truck occupants	Reasons given for the Bison/APC's being 'disabled'
'The two or three people in the truck then grabbed weapons and ran into the bush, he said.'	'A Bison ... joined the fray but experienced mechanical difficulties when it was hit by fire from an AK–47 assault rifle, Montague said.'
St. John's Evening Telegram[l] 'The two or three people in the truck then grabbed weapons and ran into the bush, he said.'	'A Bison ... joined the fray but experienced mechanical difficulties when it was hit by fire from an AK–47 assault rifle, Montague said.'
100 Mile House Free Press[m] 'Two or three people in the truck grabbed weapons and fled the vehicle, Montague said.'	'When one of the Bison armored personnel carriers (APC) came on the scene it "came under fire initiated by the camp occupants," and was itself disabled.'

[a]'Natives wounded in firefight,' *Edmonton Journal*, 12 September 1995, A1 (CP).
[b]'Natives wounded in firefight,' *Saskatoon Star Phoenix*, 12 September 1995, A1 (CP).
[c]'Natives hit in shootout,' *Winnipeg Free Press*, 12 September 1995, A1 (CP).
[d]'B.C. Indians, RCMP trade fire at camp,' *Toronto Star*, Tuesday 12 September 1995, A10 (CP).
[e]'Three Indians injured in shootout with Mounties outside B.C. camp,' *Montreal Gazette*, 12 September 1995, A6 (CP).
[f]'Three natives shot in firefight,' *Victoria Times Colonist*, Tuesday, 12 September 1995, A1 (CP).
[g]'Three rebels feared hurt in wild shootout,' *Vancouver Sun*, 12 September 1995, A1. The *Vancouver Sun* also named and identified seven individuals and their previous criminal records in 'Criminal records detailed,' 12 September 1995, A2.
[h]'Criminal agenda has shoved aside legitimate goals, cops say,' *Vancouver Province*, 12 September 1995, A5. The *Vancouver Province* also named and identified seven individuals and their previous criminal records in 'It's a rogues gallery, cops say,' 12 September 1995, A5.
[i]'Three natives shot rebels say,' *Calgary Herald*, 12 September 1995 (VP,VS and CP). In the same story the *Calgary Herald* also published the names (but not the criminal records) of William Ignace, Joseph Ignace, and John Hill.
[j]'Gunfire at B.C. native protest,' *Regina Leader Post*, 12 September 1995, A1 (CP). This story resulted from a press conference later in the day, which clarified information; the previous assertion in other CP accounts, that 'thousands of rounds of ammunition' had been exchanged, was corrected.
[k]'Three natives shot in B.C., rebel leader tells police,' *London Free Press*, 12 September 1995, A9 (CP).
[l]'Natives shot in gunfight,' *St. John's Evening Telegram*, 12 September 1995, 1 (CP).
[m]'Bullets shatter peace prospects,' *100 Mile House Free Press*, 13 September 1995, 1. Because the *100 Mile House Free Press* is a weekly newspaper, it printed the firefight story on 13 September 1995; all of the other news stories were published 12 September 1995.

geant Montague asserted that he corrected the information regarding the 'armed and shooting' description of the truck occupants, citing as evidence the fact that the media did not report this detail in subsequent accounts. He claimed that he corrected the information in an informal manner:[18] *'Every day, the media were all staying at the same hotel, and I was having breakfast, lunch and dinner with them – I mean – well, I couldn't get rid of them, I couldn't shake them, I wasn't trying to. My job was to be there and be available to them.'* According to Sergeant Montague, he had been originally advised of the erroneous information about the truck occupants, but that the next morning, the RCMP dog-master informed him that the report gave a different story, and that *'they weren't armed.'* Sergeant Montague explained that he corrected this in the morning, but he did not repeat the announcement during the following press conference. This was because *'there was no reason to, because we had already advised everybody.'* Of the 18 newspapers sampled in this research, only in the *Regina Leader Post* story (from Canadian Press) was it specifically mentioned that Sergeant Montague had corrected his previous announcement of 'thousands of rounds of ammunition' to 'several hundred rounds' being exchanged.[19] This confirms that the Canadian Press journalist at the news site had included the update, but that client newspapers in the sample may have deleted it. According to the media liaison, a week after the firefight he learned that the mechanic repairing the APC found that the mechanical failure was due not to gunfire, but to the APC mowing down a tree (interview with Sergeant Montague, 27 May 1997). By the time this fact was known, the RCMP's attention was focused on the resolution of the standoff and the arrangements for people to exit the camp.

Yet the manner in which the RCMP corrected information to the media reveals a contradiction in the RCMP's justification for providing detailed information about the firefight 'for reasons of public interest.' Informal requests made to journalists by the RCMP to correct or to omit certain details in future news stories are not equivalent to a formal public notification of a correction through the media. If corrections are not conveyed at the podium where the original press release took place, the errors are not publicly acknowledged with the same vigour and legitimacy as the original mandate of releasing information 'for reasons of public interest.' Informal notifications reduce the significance of the errors, and members of the media are less likely to report them because they were not provided within the context of quotable, official information. In addition, it cannot be assumed that the public would take note of subsequent omissions of erroneous details. Future news stories would more likely offer summaries, not such details, so the news practices in themselves might have suppressed erroneous details. If corrections were provided to the media outside a press release situation (such as that described by Sergeant Montague), these occasions likely excluded spectators as witnesses. This live audience would have included family and friends of those inside the camp, people who would have been keenly interested and affected by the corrections. That the changes were seldom acknowledged in the media materials implies that the media and police were possibly in collusion to withhold information that might be important to the public. Casual corrections do not provide the record for police accountability to the public that a television broadcast would have allowed. My assessment of the motivation, 'for reasons of public interest,' which was used for the announcement of the criminal agenda and criminal records finds the application of this motive to be inconsistent, because the RCMP disregarded a parallel obligation to correct misinformation previously announced.

Release of Criminal Records

The RCMP's release of the names and criminal records was another aspect of information control that contributed to the media's characterizations of the firefight episode. The media outlets that published or broadcast the names and criminal records include the *Vancouver Sun*, the *Vancouver Province*, BCTV, *Newsworld*, and CKNW Radio.[20] Along with print and electronic media audiences, those in the camp were listening to CBC Radio. Yet the RCMP intimated the criminality of the protesters to the media before the firefight. According to one reporter, Sergeant Montague made a passing reference to criminal backgrounds during the flight to the Williams Lake press conference. During the trial, a training video was shown in which Sergeant Montague told two radio reporters that most of the people in the camp 'had been convicted of murder.' Sergeant Montague testified that the statement was 'obviously a mistake on my part – I shouldn't have said convicted of – capable of, but not convicted of.'[21]

Central to understanding the RCMP's press release outlining the criminal records to the media is that the RCMP had anticipated this strategy in the media plan. According to Sergeant Montague, in a memo dated 1 September 1995, he had advised that a public announcement of criminal records should be made, and that the RCMP should profile the criminal elements in the camp during a press conference. *'Now we did that on September 11. This was written on the first of September; on the 11ᵗʰ of September we did implement that particular action.'* Sergeant Montague asserted that the announcement of the information was justifiable because of the seriousness of the situation. It was imperative that the public be made aware of the lack of legitimacy of the group. *'We had to bring the focus out in the event that the RCMP had to make a physical move, and go in there and with fire power, so that people wouldn't think that we're going in there to deal in a violent nature with innocent people, unarmed people, and people who were really trying to advance an agenda regarding a Sundance or a spiritual situation.'* According to Sergeant Montague, it is stated in the Federal Privacy Act *'that – a person's right to privacy is basically excluded when interests of the public overrides it ... And in our opinion, the public interest overrode the right of privacy here.'*[22] Sergeant Montague denied that the release of the juvenile record was inappropriate, because it was used to *'advance a criminal investigation.'*[23] He went on to explain, *'Of course it's in our policy manuals that we will respect the privacy of all individuals, and you cannot release the record of an individual unless there's a specific purpose to do it. It's the same thing with dangerous sexual offender alerts or pedophile alerts that – when the interests of the public is paramount, and it overrides the person's right to privacy – the section in the* Federal Privacy Act *applies to that in Section 8 subsection 2m. And that's what we relied on, and that's why we did it'* (interview with Sergeant Montague, 27 May 1997).

Journalists discussed the releasing of names and criminal offences: *'It was information – we took it at face-value – didn't question it – it was a clear motive –* [the police] *wanted to show people in a negative light – nobody was puzzled.'* One of the names and records released pertained to a juvenile crime, and the journalist noted that he *'didn't notice at the time – to my shame, didn't know until just recently ... I don't think anyone noticed ... That's what happens when you get a bunch of overstimulated reporters in a room and throw a lot of information at them. There is a compulsion to publish information – no question about not using it – it wouldn't have occurred to us not to use it.'* A frequently cited reason for the publishing of the names and criminal records was the scarcity of information (after the barricades went up): *'We were so starved for information, we were so happy to get something* [relating to the press conference where the names and criminal records were released] *... We didn't even question the ethics – we were just starved for information. Even the editors, they said it was okay to print this, they said the* [people in the camp] *were thugs and the public has a right* *to know.'* One journalist admitted that normally his outlet refrains from publishing such information: *'Under normal circumstances, we don't – especially if a person is charged with a criminal offence, or about to be charged, we refrain from mentioning their criminal record, because – it's prejudicial. And it could cause a mistrial.'* Another journalist found that the RCMP release of criminal records was typical for organizations that are sophisticated about public relations and have professional spokespersons: *'They tend to put a spin on things that might not be there. So while – personally, I think – I definitely – I guess it seemed that they were trying to struggle to gain control over the situation which they didn't have. But within the context of the way people work with the media – it's kind of not – not the most amazing things. Its just one of those things that happens ... But to rattle off the names – the way he did – did take us by surprise ... But certainly some of the charges that were read off had nothing to do with the standoff and were meant to severely inflame public opinions about some of the individuals in the camp. Some of the charges got to be quite the jokes around town'* (interviews with journalists).

The announcement of the names and criminal records included people not in the camp at the time and one individual who claimed to have never been in the camp.[24] A few of the journalists remembered that Johnny Guitar, named as one of the criminal elements in the camp, was a spectator during the press conference. *'I recalled that so-called Johnny Guitar was actually standing there in the news conference when his name was read out.'* **So, what did you think?** *'It was a mistake by the police. I don't think that they were trying to manipulate when they did that. I can accept that – knowing them, knowing who they are and knowing how they operate that they – I can accept their explanation'* (interview with journalist). John Hill, who had been mentioned in the list, also was not in the camp at the time. During a telephone interview with a journalist, he denied the relevance of his former prison record and accused the police of a 'smear campaign' by releasing the criminal profiles of people involved in the dispute.[25]

The RCMP media liaison stated that the seriousness and violence associated with Hill's and Guitar's criminal records were indicative of the potential for violence from the camp. Although Hill was not in the camp at the time of the firefight, the RCMP were aware that he was leading the camp during the early stage of the conflict. Sergeant Montague stated that Guitar was at the Adams Lake and Douglas Lake protests, and that RCMP intelligence associated Guitar with the dispute at Gustafsen Lake, even though he was not physically at the camp:[26]

'So, no – we didn't inadvertently say anything about somebody being in the camp when they weren't. We knew who was in the camp.' He stated that at the press conference he had made the distinction that *'these people are not in the camp. That Hill was in the camp, and a person like Guitar is not in the camp – he's here ...*[27] *So no, we didn't – put out any sort of information which wasn't accurate with respect to those criminal records'* (interview with Sergeant Montague, 27 May 1997).

Of the nine individuals identified in the newspapers as having criminal records,[28] four were never arrested or charged in conjunction with the Gustafsen Lake standoff. One of these four was never proved to be in the camp. Two people who were not arrested were associated with the most serious crimes, and their names and charges were announced first. Thus, of the 18 people charged at the conclusion of the Gustafsen Lake standoff, five were identified as having previous criminal records, although one of those named, in fact, had none.[29] The *Reasons for Judgment* did note that four others had prior records: two were considered minor, one involved mischief and theft, and the last had two convictions for robbery. The nine remaining adults included wives who were with their husbands, Native and non-Native supporters, environmentalists, and human rights activists. One was an occupant in the truck at the time of the firefight. After the conclusion of the standoff, Attorney General Dosanjh of British Columbia and Sergeant Montague defended the release of the criminal information.[30]

A few news stories during the standoff included comments from Native people about the way in which the media and the RCMP were portraying them. In particular, they found offensive and misrepresentative the description of the camp as being composed of terrorists, extremists and squatters: 'I do not think we are really squatters or trespassers on our own land' (Union of B.C. Indian Chiefs President Saul Terry, quoted in the *Vancouver Sun*, 29 August 1995, A3[31]). Some comments concerned the release of criminal records and their connection with Native people who have prior records but who were not involved in the standoff: 'Bill Lewis, a Metis who supports the rebels at Gustafsen Lake, said he was particularly incensed when the RCMP released old criminal records of native Indians there. "I have a criminal record, but I am an ex-criminal," said Lewis. "They always forget the 'ex' part. I guess it's my ex-file." He cited the devastating situation on reserves, which, he said, leads to social problems like alcohol and drug abuse as the reason many more native Indians have criminal convictions than the broader community' (*Vancouver Sun*, 13 September 1995, B4[32]).

Smear Campaign

In a broader sense, the RCMP press conference after the firefight was the enactment of a strategy to ruin the credibility of the protest, and the people involved. The suggestion to do so originated from District Superintendent Len Olfert and was discussed at a strategy meeting on 1 September.[33] It was during this video-recorded meeting (which became trial evidence), that Sergeant Montague stated, 'smear campaigns are our specialty.'[34] Although he insisted that he intended this comment to be facetious, Sergeant Montague did not deny that there was a 'smear campaign' during our interview. 'But I don't mention "smear campaign" in my media plan – but you can interpret it – by putting out criminal records we were smearing these people's reputations – you can say that, and you'd be justified in saying it. But – we're not running a smear campaign, we're running a truth campaign – the brutal truth – it's never been done before – and we know that people are going to be some ticked off, but – there's gonna be – there will be repercussions – but we're going to do this so that the public know what we're dealing with.' Sergeant Montague explained that the strategy was about 'reducing their credibility.' He described it as 'all part of a psychological warfare – you bet it was.' It was not an initiative that was a response to a crisis; rather, 'It was well thought out, not done in a haphazard manner – we carefully talked this out.' The media plan was presented to District Superintendent Olfert on 1 September 1995, but 'we didn't use it until the 11th of September – because we didn't want to use it? The only time we used it was because of the gunfight.' **It was because of the gunfight?** 'Oh, absolutely – the September the 11th gunfight?' **Yes.** 'Absolutely.' **Okay.** 'Now we realized that, you know – if this thing gets out of control – the public have to know what we're dealing with here. We're not dealing with a bunch of innocent people in there, and this is no Sunday-school picnic.' Sergeant Montague's admission that the situation had gotten out of control is an indication that the intention behind the release of the criminal records was to get the situation back under control.

Sergeant Montague read from the memo that he had prepared as a media plan, in which he explained that the RCMP had interpreted the agenda being promoted from the camp as 'one of violence being promoted by Wolverine and his thugs' (see 'Issue Two' of the unclassified memo, found in appendix 7). It was important for the RCMP to make the public aware that 'our actions are being precipitated by the criminal actions by proven criminals, before the force makes any physical move.' Sergeant Montague said that the impetus to utilize the strategy presented itself *'when that gunfight happened.'* He also said that the public advisement of the criminal elements in the camp was important for the morale of the ERT, who were aware of this information. *'They all watch the news – and they say, "thanks a lot – finally – someone is telling it like it has to be told."'* Sergeant Montague believed that the announcement would reduce any public criticism of the RCMP operation. He said that if the people in the camp did not have criminal pasts, the RCMP would have conceptualized the dispute much differently. Sergeant Montague explained that having a criminal record and continuing to resort to violence – *'It's an indication that the person has an attitude and is an indication that the person is still defiant of the law and will go to any measures that he wants to or she wants to go to – by taking the law into their own hands.'* Another little-known fact at the time was that the RCMP were receiving faxes and telephone calls from various groups and organizations supporting the camp, warning the RCMP of dire repercussions *'if anybody lost their lives.'*[35] The RCMP were worried about an influx of supporters who would *'make the situation worse again. And we didn't want that. All we wanted to do was – resolve it in a peaceful manner ... And then start dealing with the issues – because we knew that there would be a lot of issues to deal with'* (interview with Sergeant Montague, 27 May, 1997).

The success of the 'smear campaign' rested on the RCMP's knowledge of the kind of news that would have the greatest appeal, their knowledge of news production practices, and their authority as the most important media source. At the press conference the RCMP's provision of vilifying details of the firefight contributed to sensationalized media coverage. This press conference was a dramatic event, and the RCMP tailored their press release to command the dominant frame of the news stories. The extraneous details served a rhetorical function in the RCMP interpretation of the situation, because they accentuated the drama of the news narrative, and they added to the impression of reliability of the RCMP account. The errors in the information likely were believable to an uncritical audience because the descriptions were consistent with previous RCMP portrayals of activities associated with people at the camp. The press release announcing the firefight was loaded with negative character judgments of those in the camp, and it subtly contrasted these judgments with the positive character of the RCMP. By the same token, the press release avoided references that would have drawn any public sympathy towards the people in the camp. The sequenced appearances of spokespersons during televised broadcasts of the press conference affirmed the importance of the

RCMP over all other sources. This ordering presumed a hierarchical structure of news, paralleling the hierarchical social status of the media sources.

For the media, the situation at the firefight press conference was the most important happening since the standoff began, requiring speed and focus to get the stories ready in time for the deadlines. Compared with other press releases, there was more information given out, and there was little time for the journalists to consider the appropriateness of the information. They were 'starving for information,' and the RCMP news conference offered the promise of a 'feast.' Most of the journalists assumed that the facts provided were accurate, although several recalled sensing that the RCMP media liaison was covering up some elements. Aside from the unauthorized radiotelephone communications, the reporters could not confirm the basic facts of the situation because the RCMP did not allow them beyond the barricades.

Walker Incident

12 September 1995

> A member of the encampment walking to the dock to wash in a 'no shoot' zone is fired upon by two RCMP members, who testify they were shooting to kill. (Chronology, *Vancouver Sun*, 21 May 1997)

None of the people who knew of this incident reported it to the media during the standoff. It was brought to public attention by the media during the trial, when the RCMP wescam video was shown in court. In its chronology the *RCMP Report to Crown Counsel* does not refer to the incident, but does refer to Wolverine's comments after his arrest, 'someone had got shot when he was down by the lake, trying to get some water.' This incident contradicted the assurances of safety that people inside the camp had received after the trauma of the firefight.[36]

In the RCMP wescam video of this incident the following action takes place. *It is a sunny morning, and a male individual is seen walking along a dirt road surrounded by open field, towards the lake. He is attired in a jacket and casual slacks. The walker casts a long shadow as he saunters down the road, with his hands clearly at his side. The individual is seen removing his jacket, and he throws it over his left shoulder. He steps off the road, and begins walking across an open field. After several steps, a gunshot blast lands between his feet spraying up dust. He runs back towards the road, dropping his jacket.*

Two more gunshot blasts hit the dust near him. He lies down on the ground without moving (interpretation of the RCMP wescam video, S. Lambertus). Although three shots were fired from high-powered weaponry about 1,000 metres away (just over one-half mile), the individual was not harmed.[37] He lay on the ground for several minutes, then he returned to camp, presumably without further incident.

According to the evidence presented in the trial, the individual was described on the ERT radio communications that morning as wearing camouflage clothing and face paint and holding a rifle at port-at-arms position and stalking the RCMP. The ERT radio transcript, which was presented in court and printed in newspapers, relates how officers across the lake decided to deal with this individual. In the radio transcript presented in court, one officer asks another, 'Can we get authority from Zulu to make his day unpleasant?' An authorization is given over the radio to shoot at the person. The ERT member testified in court that his orders were to shoot to kill. It was conceded during the trial that (although this fact was not immediately visible in the wescam video) the man did have a rifle slung over his shoulder, but he was casually walking and not stalking. It was also determined in court that the individual was walking within the agreed-upon safe zone, but this was not communicated to the officers who fired the shots. The senior RCMP officer who gave the authorization to shoot told the court that he based his decision on events from the previous day (the firefight) and the previous shooting incidents with RCMP members.[38]

During the Gustafsen Lake standoff, the shooting incident with the walker was a non-event. When the episode was made public several months later, it raised questions as to whether the episode was deliberately withheld from the media liaison to keep it from the public for as long as possible. During the interviews for this research, both Sergeant Montague and District Superintendent Olfert denied any deliberate plan to withhold information about this incident from the media. Sergeant Montague explained: *'I had found out about that particular event about mid-October. I was never told about it. I was never told to deal with it. I don't think a lot of people even knew. I didn't until – I mean, the RCMP were forthright about it at trial, and they stood up there and said why they did it – and – but it was nothing that I ever had to deal with. I – matter of fact, when I heard about it in October, I said, "Are we talking about the same event here? Why wasn't I told? Like, what happened here?"'* (interview with Sergeant Montague, 27 May 1997).

Similarly, fellow officers did not advise District Superintendent Olfert of the incident until several weeks after it occurred. He stated that the orders to shoot came from the ERT command that was operating from Camp Zulu: '*I wasn't a part of that decision.*' He said that the decision would have been made by the senior officer at the site: '*I'm not going to second-guess him.*' District Superintendent Olfert explained that ERT senior officers traditionally use their own judgment on how to deal with specific situations. Ideally, the efforts of the negotiators and the ERT were being balanced to contrast the '*velvet glove*' with the '*iron fist.*' District Superintendent Olfert advised me that the ERT had their own assignment, one that was separate from that of the RCMP negotiators. This fact was confirmed during the trial. He stated that because of the way in which the communications worked between the various components of the operation, the ERT did not report their activities until well after the standoff (interview with District Superintendent Olfert, 17 February 1998).

Chief Nathan Matthew and the other Native intermediaries learned about the walker incident that same evening from the people in the camp, but they noted, '*the RCMP didn't confide in us.*' Yet contrary to their previous objective to offer the media alternative perspectives of the people involved in the conflict, none of the Native intermediaries informed the media of this shooting incident. According to Chief Matthew, making the media aware of this shooting incident would have antagonized the RCMP, and in response the RCMP might have denied the intermediaries future access to the camp. This would have put the lives of the protesters and the RCMP at greater risk. The intermediaries believed that the best chance for a peaceful resolution was through their direct talks at the camp and through their roles as brokers between the camp and the police. Consequently, the power of the RCMP to control and select information to apprise the media suppressed the only other legitimate media source.

Consequences of the internal communications of the RCMP regarding this incident extended beyond the RCMP. According to the trial testimony, the incident contributed to dissention among the ERT members.[39] In the RCMP media plan, the non-event meant that the casting of the people inside the camp as criminals supported the depictions of the previous day. The police still defined the situation – silence in itself is a message. The police responses to both situations were consistent. The response (or lack of one) to the media maintained the positive public image of the police and the criminal characterization of the people inside the camp. The media did not have to repair inconsistencies in their portrayals of the protesters as the aggressors, which the incident with the walker would have required. By the time that this second violent episode in as many days was made public, the standoff was over, and concerns for a mass convergence of Native people in support of the camp had long since dissolved. The lack of media coverage of the walker episode during the standoff underscores the distinction between the realities that existed on either side of the barricades. It also points to the institutional mechanisms within the RCMP that determined how much of the reality behind the barricades they would share with the public. One can appreciate this void in the news coverage as an outcome of a lack of media witness, the intermediaries' limiting information to the press, and the RCMP's control of their information to the press through their internal chain of command.

Information Control and Media Stereotyping

The RCMP's use of information control helped them to regain their composure, to maintain the dominant perspective in the news narrative, and to ensure positive public support after two crises. They used impression management gambits that elevated the stature of the RCMP and denigrated the camp to the public. The RCMP presented the protesters as unworthy of public sympathy and themselves as showing restraint and acting in a justifiable manner. Their barricades and their declaration that unauthorized police communications were off-limits to the press further supported the RCMP's control over information. Police power to limit access to the camp prevented the Native intermediaries from mentioning the walker incident to the media.

On the other hand, the enactment of the RCMP media strategy points towards the transfer of a stereotyped construct of the camp from the RCMP to the public through the media. The RCMP correspondence, legal documents, and interviews with senior police officials confirm that the RCMP operation relied for planning purposes on a negative typology that generalized all of the people at Gustafsen Lake. The RCMP's depiction of the camp's activities as *terrorist* since the time of the Williams Lake press conference provided a schema that could anticipate adequate provision for the safety and security needs of the RCMP and the public. Less obvious at the time was that the police had also made a connection between previous criminal offences (but not necessarily convictions) associated with certain members of the camp. According to the police, the previous criminal involvement influenced their interpretations of the shooting episodes. The shooting at the ERT reconnaissance member, at RCMP helicopters, at the RCMP officers wearing flak jackets, and (assumed) at an RCMP patrol vehicle likely validated this criminal categorization. From a law enforcement perspective, *terrorist* and *criminal* reflected the instability of the situation, the lawlessness of the people, and the potential for injury and loss of life in the event of a confrontation with police. The operation required that the RCMP reduce the characterization of the people in the camp to the lowest (and worst) common denominator of behaviour in order to make them conceptually manageable for planning and strategizing.

The RCMP strategy memo of 1 September 1995 recommends advising the public of the law enforcers' generalized assessment of the group. But the memo also reveals the extent to which the RCMP professional distancing had been transformed into personal invective against the people in the camp. 'Issue Two' in the memo is identified as 'Wolverine and His Band of Thugs;' the protesters are referred to as 'proven criminals;' and the importance of creating public awareness of 'criminal actions of proven criminals' is stressed. The memo conveys a presumption that the people have already been convicted. There is no provision for defining or explaining that the majority of the people in the camp did not fall within the proven criminal category. In effect, the RCMP labelling renders these people invisible. The RCMP extended this reduction to the firefight press release.

The RCMP strategy to criminalize the protesters in the public's perception required the cooperation of the media. With their expertise in sensationalizing breaking news and their wide audience reach, the media could magnify the stereotyped characterizations well beyond the RCMP's capabilities. The timing of the release of the criminal records with an important breaking-news event also contributed to the tenor of the news characterizations. It is my assessment that the firefight would likely have been a front-page news story (or a top story for radio and television) even without the advisement of the criminal agenda and criminal records. Press announcements of previous shooting incidents paled in comparison with a gun battle that involved 'thousands of rounds.' Competition between media's outlets also increased the likelihood of the media representing the incident as fully and as dramatically as the RCMP presented it in the press conference. The inclusion of the criminal theme and criminal records elevated news that already had tremendous appeal. This point is illustrated by the fact that the *Vancouver Province* and *Vancouver Sun* made the criminal records news stories in themselves, and a few outlets included this information in their news accounts when their conventions normally would prohibit doing so. What neither the RCMP nor the media took into consideration at the time was their complicity in reinforcing a pre-existing stereotype schema of *criminal Indians* at the level of national media saturation.[40] Thus, the strategy the RCMP used to regain control over these crises influenced public attitudes and behaviours over which they had no control.

Despite the quantity of information that the RCMP provided to the media about the firefight, many suppositions and theories continued to circulate for years after the standoff. A few days after the incident, one of the ERT officers who was inside the disabled APC gave his story to the media, comparing the assault to being in the Vietnam War.[41] Some of the people that I interviewed also volunteered various interpretations of what had happened, although I did not talk with anyone who actually had been there. These alternative interpretations are indicators of a general dissatisfaction with the explanations the RCMP offered to the media at the time and, in some cases, 'spins' that served various stakeholders. There were claims by some RCMP officers that Wolverine had attempted to fire a gun directly into openings in the APC in order to kill RCMP occupants. There were allegations that the RCMP had violated international human rights by using land mines, which caused the explosion with the truck. To account for the RCMP finding only one AK–47 in the campfire, one journalist volunteered that before they surrendered, the protesters had melted down other AK–47s into an unrecognizable mass.[42] Some Native people speculated that the dog, which had been a companion of the group and was not threatening ERT officers, was killed in order to demoralize the people inside the camp. Some interviewees suggested that, considering the mood at the time, there would have been a greater public outcry if the police announced that they had killed a dog than if they had killed an 'Indian.' To explain the surprisingly little evidence of gunfire originating from the camp, one RCMP officer advised me that the people in the camp had metal detectors that they used to find and conceal their bullets and casings after shooting incidents. There were no explanations as to why there were no metal detectors found on the scene.[43] The strength of the convictions behind several of these assertions would make it difficult to successfully challenge what has become, for some, the *truth*. The RCMP's lack of full disclosure provided openings for a number of inflammatory suppositions and face-saving spins concerning the Gustafsen Lake standoff that continue to this day.

CHAPTER FIVE

Surrender

Everybody had expected it, everybody was hoping for it – and when I say
everybody, I mean the families. Media, it didn't matter to us, we had a story.

Interview with journalist

In the final phase of the standoff, the media and their sources adapted to a reduction in the stress of the situation as well as a reduction in the action. The media's dependence on the RCMP for news was easing, with more of a shift in focus to a 'Native solution' to end the standoff. For the journalists, the range of news stories about the camp expanded with the availability of Native spokespersons, who provided information about the camp, and of press conferences with Native spiritual leaders, who arrived to assist in the resolution.

Except for the occasional person voluntarily leaving the camp, there were few interactions reported between the camp and the RCMP. Still, the police media personnel used this time to reassert their presence in the news narrative by implementing the final strategies from the RCMP media plan of 1 September, which would provide full media coverage of police resources. In addition, the RCMP media personnel offered other news-gathering opportunities related to the investigation of the camp, signifying a reduced level of tension and a more relaxed hold on police and camp information. Thus, during this slow period of the standoff, the RCMP media personnel admitted select openings in their previously withheld information, allowing their interpretation of the situation to remain in the forefront.

CBC Radio Announcement of the Surrender Message

13 September 1995

> Indians agree to surrender after radio broadcasts of message from Chief
> Antoine Archie of nearby Canim Lake band assures they will not be harmed
> if they put down their guns. But only Indian negotiators leave the camp.
> ('Anatomy of the B.C. Standoff,' *Toronto Star*, 18 September 1995, A4)

The tension of the firefight abated with the help of Marlowe Sam, a
spiritual leader from the Penticton Band and a member of the Native
negotiation team, who began bringing people out of the camp. The
intermediaries and the RCMP negotiating team arranged for visits by
Native spiritual leaders. Arvol Looking Horse, a Dakota Sioux and
Keeper of the Sacred Pipe, arrived with an entourage. He held a press
conference at the Red Coach Inn and then spent an afternoon at the
camp.[1] A few hours before Arvol Looking Horse's visit, Marlowe Sam
brought someone out of the camp, who reportedly relayed a message
from the camp to the RCMP.[2]

In response, Sergeant Peter Montague asked one of the CBC Radio
reporters, Conway Fraser, and Chief Antoine Archie to comply with a
proposition from the camp.[3] The request was to broadcast a message
from a respected chief to the camp that assured them of safety and
respect if they came out voluntarily. Montague explained that the chief
did not necessarily have to be someone who was an advocate of the
camp. Sergeant Montague told Fraser that he could play an integral
part in ending the standoff, but he would not provide the details until
they arrived at the (Gustafsen Lake) RCMP Operations Command Centre, located behind the RCMP detachment. Once there, Sergeant
Montague explained the circumstances to Fraser and Chief Antoine
Archie and advised that the message had to air at 3:00 p.m., less than 30
minutes away. The proposition was that, if Fraser agreed to broadcast
the message, he would have a news scoop, and he could be the radio
representative in the media pool later that evening to witness the surrender. When Fraser asked Sergeant Montague why they did not put
the message over the radiotelephone, he was told, '*We want to do it on
CBC Radio, because CBC Radio is the only reception that they have in at the
camp.*' In addition, the camp wanted to hear the assurances on the
public record. Fraser advised Sergeant Montague that he could not
make the decision to cut into regular broadcasting and insisted on

calling his superiors in Vancouver. While speaking with Jeffrey Dvorkin from the CBC Radio office in Vancouver, Sergeant Montague also revealed that Wolverine had been monopolizing the radiotelephone. Broadcasting the surrender message over CBC Radio would ensure that everyone in the camp could hear it. Sergeant Montague gave Dvorkin about ten minutes to make a decision. In the end, the CBC reluctantly approved. Chief Antoine Archie composed a surrender message and asked Sergeant Montague to check the message over to make sure that it was worded to the satisfaction of the RCMP. The message was recorded and was broadcast at 3:00 p.m. Sergeant Montague received word that the people in the camp had not heard the message, however, so the CBC was asked to play it twice more during the next hour.

The following is the CBC Radio announcement, beginning with the introduction by the news announcer:

ANNOUNCER: There could be a major breakthrough at the armed standoff at Gustafsen Lake. Police say the Native people in the camp are ready to lay down their arms and surrender. Conway Fraser is at the RCMP headquarters and joins us on the line. Conway, what are police saying?

FRASER: Well, Bob, police are saying that a demand has come out of the armed camp that if the Native people hear a certain message from a respected chief from the Shuswap Nation, they will lay down their arms and come out. Now CBC plays a role in this, in that the occupants out at the camp can only pick up CBC Radio. So this is basically their only link to the outside world. So here now with that message, and with me is Chief Antoine Archie of the Canim Lake Band, who will speak first in Shuswap, then in English, to the people in at the camp.

Here's Chief Archie [Chief Archie speaks, beginning in the Shuswap language, conveying greetings, then switching to English]: 'People who have come out of the camp have been treated – have never been mistreated, and have been treated with respect. If the rest of the camp come out, they will be treated with dignity and respect. The RCMP have lent their support for this. I will personally be at the RCMP station, or wherever – to greet you on your arrival.' [Chief Archie closes with another assurance in the Shuswap language.]

FRASER: Now that was Chief Antoine Archie of the Canim Lake Band, and just to reiterate, that message was going out to the Native people at the Gustafsen Lake camp and – what we are getting now is that they are almost prepared to lay down their arms and surrender, based on what they heard from Chief Archie. And that's it from here – from RCMP headquarters, in 100 Mile House, Bob. (Announcement replayed on the CBC Radio program, *Now the Details*, broadcast 17 September 1995)

After the broadcast of the message, the RCMP media liaison called a meeting with the mainstream media. During this meeting, a media pool was selected – one television, one radio (Fraser), and one newspaper representative – to act as observers for the surrender. In answer to journalists' questions about how this radio message fit in with the camp visit by Arvol Looking Horse, Sergeant Montague told them that it was a 'coordinated effort.'[4] The RCMP took the media pool past Checkpoint 17 and held them there until the RCMP at the line received further instructions. However, the RCMP received word that no one from the camp was coming out that evening: **What was the response from the RCMP at the time?** *'Frustrated, I think. Because there had been a lot of work gone into trying get this particular deal arranged – and it didn't take place ... He* [Sergeant Montague] *seemed angry – I can't remember exactly what he said, but he was angry'* (interview with journalist).

The anticipated surrender failed to materialize. Among the 18 newspapers incorporated into the study, the CBC's broadcast and the subsequent aborted surrender provided front-page news stories in the *Victoria Times Colonist, Vancouver Sun, Calgary Herald,* and *London Free Press*.[5] One journalist recalls, *'At one point it became clear that we nearly had a break. It all fell apart on that one day ... and we ended up sitting outside the RCMP station listening to the radio – actually, I think the Indian families by that time were – a lot of them were gathering on the lawn, and were listening to our radios, listening to the transmission; it was a really bizarre circumstance. There was a call that went into the camp ... we ended up hearing part of what was going on. The families were sitting on the lawn. It became – it was a crestfallen circumstance, in which everybody sort of – when it became evident that today was not going to be the day. Everybody had expected it, everybody was hoping for it – and when I say everybody, I mean the families. Media, it didn't matter to us, we had a story'* (interview with journalist). At the checkpoint, one of the RCMP officers said to a journalist, as the media pool briefly stopped in on the way to the surrender point, *'"This is not going to end tonight. This is nowhere near ending tonight. This is not going to happen"* ... And, of course, the media got all turned around and went back. And one of the RCMP guys said, "Phhh – told you, didn't I? This was just a show, this was just a big show"'* (interview with journalist). One of the intermediaries, Gordon Sebastian, noted that the people would not come out because it was growing dark.[6]

Several journalists at the time questioned the ethics of the CBC broadcast, how the CBC was coerced into submission, and the implied collaboration between the CBC and the RCMP in the airing of the surrender message. Some journalists commiserated with the difficult choice that the CBC was forced to make under extreme time constraints. They considered the broadcast *'absolutely overt manipulation of the media.'* Reporters were *'sitting around scratching our heads over this one.'* One journalist said that he was immediately suspicious when the RCMP approached the CBC journalist: *'I knew Montague but* [nobody wanted] *to hear me ... Everyone felt uncomfortable about this.'* Some journalists observed the reactions of the supporters, who were upset over the choice of Chief Antoine Archie to provide the surrender message: *'He got ripped* [Chief Antoine Archie] *because he went on the air. They thought he was a patsy for the cops ... And it sort of didn't work. It got everybody riled up. Got the other side just saying he wasn't the spokesman for the – for that side. He was basically a – sort of a – sort of like a – status quo kind of Native – status quo with the treaty process ... The talk after – at the gas station – they were upset and that this move can totally backfire and make the dispute getting worse ... "This is not the guy"'* (interviews with journalists).

From the perspective of CBC Radio journalists, the request to broadcast the surrender message was highly contentious, and was the topic of *Now the Details*, a CBC radio program on which media issues are discussed. The narrator began the program by asking the question, 'Did the people's broadcasting corporation become the "RCMP Broadcasting Corporation" last week in British Columbia? Well, what would you do if the police said, "We need your cooperation. You could help end the standoff at Gustafsen Lake."'[7]

The program included interviews with CBC Radio journalist Conway Fraser, CBC executives Jeffrey Dvorkin and Robert Sunter, as well as Sergeant Peter Montague. Dvorkin stated that he felt quite uncomfortable with the request and the pressure from the RCMP to cooperate. He pointed out that the CBC was ready to help out, but he felt that the integrity of the CBC, as a public broadcaster, was compromised by complying. In his interpretation, CBC Radio personnel had become 'agents of the RCMP.' There was no time to preview the message, he had no idea what was being said in Shuswap, and he had to trust the reputation of Chief Antoine Archie that the Shuswap content was appropriate. Dvorkin said he felt that the proposition from the RCMP media personnel was manipulative and coercive. He was told by Sergeant Montague: 'lives [are] at stake,' and 'we didn't have any choice in the matter.' He described the lack of free will at Gustafsen Lake and that, at the CBC, they were accustomed to making 'informed choices'; this was not the situation in the broadcasting of the surrender message. CBC Radio staff were not given adequate details to make an informed decision. Dvorkin nevertheless appreciated that the public broadcaster would be 'held accountable for what we were putting on the radio – that was wrong – I hope there will be strong protests made ... toward the RCMP.' Dvorkin related how Conway Fraser was temporarily pulled off the story because 'we should not be reporting on ourselves.'[8] For Robert Sunter, the executive who made the final decision, and Conway Fraser, the journalist who was originally approached, the pressure of having to make a decision within a short period of time was the toughest part of the negotiation. Sergeant Montague was also interviewed during the program to explain his perspective on the situation. He stated that the surrender message was a suggestion initiated by someone from the camp and brought out by Marlowe Sam.

The following is the transcript of the radio interview between Mary Lou Finlay, host of the program, *Now the Details*, and Sergeant Montague:

> FINLAY: Did you tell them it was urgent? – It couldn't have gone out at 4:00?
>
> MONTAGUE: Yes, we told them it was urgent.
>
> FINLAY: And did you give them a sense that it was life and death?
>
> MONTAGUE: We – well – life and death – no, we didn't do that. We told them that it was a real possibility that this would end the armed standoff. And, I suppose when you – if you talk about it like that, if we could end it in a peaceful manner, as a result of a short conversation on CBC Radio, rather than the alternative – which may have to be at some point in time – I mean, there wasn't any down side to doing this.
>
> FINLAY: Who asked that it be repeated three – twice?
>
> MONTAGUE: I did.
>
> FINLAY: Not the Natives?
>
> MONTAGUE: No, we wanted to make sure they heard it – and it's a good thing we did, because they didn't get it on the first broadcast [cleared his throat] their batteries were low, or – something like that – but they caught it on the second broadcast.
>
> FINLAY: Now, did you think the CBC would comply with your request?
>
> MONTAGUE: Yes.
>
> FINLAY: Why?

MONTAGUE: We didn't even give it a second thought.

FINLAY: Because it didn't strike you as an extraordinary request – that they would turn over their airways, in effect to you, at the behest of people, that – what you describe as criminals.

MONTAGUE: MMmm. Oh, no – not – at all. I mean, we firmly believed that this was going to work. There were three or four communications with the camp after that message – and everything was extremely positive. That it was going to happen. And then, all of a sudden, the last communication we had with them – there was a change of mind, or they decided that they weren't coming out. And going to CBC with that request – we would have been, I think – well, I think that the Canadian society would have been aghast, had CBC rejected the thought of doing that – in light of everything else that has gone on in the last two months. (Transcript of CBC Radio program, *Now the Details*, broadcast 17 September 1995)

Sergeant Montague said that under similar circumstances in the future he would make a similar appeal. He reiterated that the choice was made because CBC was the only station heard at the camp – that it was not about the RCMP's taking over the airwaves, or favouritism, or taking advantage of a particular airwave. 'That had nothing to do with it' (Sergeant Montague, on CBC Radio program, *Now the Details*, broadcast 17 September 1995).

There were many inconsistencies found by the journalists and the camp supporters regarding the surrender message over CBC Radio. Several supporters and some members of the media questioned the choice of Chief Antoine Archie as the *respected chief*. It was common knowledge that the people inside the camp were antagonistic towards him.[9] Some of the supporters of the protest were suspicious that the broadcast was another RCMP initiative that would allow the police to appear proactive in the resolution of the dispute. They thought that this was a facade, adopted to characterize the people at the camp as unreasonable and belligerent when no surrender was forthcoming, in contrast to the pains taken by the RCMP to make the arrangements in good faith. Many found it inconsistent that, if the camp members had initiated the request, they would not have made the effort to listen to the radio at that time. Other journalists covering the standoff questioned the CBC's ethics in cooperating with the RCMP, but once the circumstances were made known to them, nothing more was said. Still, the CBC broadcast was soon forgotten. Neither the Native intermediary, who allegedly brought someone out from the camp with the request, nor any of the people arrested discussed the CBC Radio announcement with the media during or after the standoff.

Chief Archie, during his interview for this research, indicated that he did not question whether the RCMP or the camp had initiated the request for the radio broadcast from a respected chief. He took the RCMP at their word. He recalled some of the repercussions: *'I read a lot of people were cheesed-off because I made those comments in Shuswap. And they were saying, "Who the hell knows what the hell he said? Nobody knows what he said!"'* Chief Archie translated what he had said in Shuswap: *'[I] told them, "I am talking to you positively and not negatively." And I said "They're not going to ill treat you – they're going to treat you with respect. They will not hurt you, or do you any harm – if you come out"'* (interview with Chief Archie, 25 July 1997).

If the original request for a radio message assuring safety and respect was initiated by the camp, it was never confirmed by any of the journalists with whom I spoke. Neither did I find any record to confirm the origin of the request in the media products during or after the standoff. Although the RCMP media liaison claimed that CBC Radio was the only radio station transmission that the camp could hear, Steven Frasher (of *100 Mile House Free Press*) and I tested a radio at the site. We found that it would have been possible for the camp to hear the message over CKBX Cariboo Radio, another AM station. Since Cariboo Radio is a privately owned outlet, however, any negotiations with the RCMP for broadcasting a surrender message might not have entailed the same ethical principles that would be necessary with the public broadcaster.[10] A *Vancouver Sun* news story published shortly after the conclusion of the standoff included statements from Native spiritual leader Arvol Looking Horse, who was inside the camp when the surrender messages were broadcast. He stated that the RCMP had not told him about the radio broadcast before he went into the camp. At 3:00 p.m., when the first message was broadcast, he and the other people in the camp were in the middle of a religious ceremony. During this visit, the people decided that they would leave the camp after three days. Arvol Looking Horse is quoted (referring to the RCMP): 'They never gave me enough time ... I was shocked when I heard (the broadcast). They did not tell me what they were going to do.'[11]

The case of the CBC Radio broadcast was another situation of blurred boundaries between the police and the media. In this situation, the negotiations involved the cooperation of a radio journalist, a local Native chief, and media executives. Thus, contrary to Sergeant

Montague's assessment, the announcement did have negative repercussions. Some of the media called into question the trustworthiness of
the chief to provide an appropriate message in Shuswap over the airwaves. The involvement of the local chief also rattled the sensitivities of
the local Native communities and the camp's supporters.

By involving CBC Radio, the RCMP presented two occasions when
their negotiations with a media outlet were put on the public record.
The initial product of the negotiations was the broadcast of the surrender message. Later, the host of a radio program assessed the context of
the surrender message broadcast through interviews with some of the
key players. This second account revealed many of the negotiation
strategies used by the RCMP media personnel. The police made promises of rewards to the radio journalist for his cooperation in broadcasting a message, allegedly requested by people in the camp. Time
constraints impeded thoughtful consideration and extensive consulta-
tion at the Vancouver office. Last, the RCMP's appeals to the moral
obligations of the outlet made it difficult for the CBC executives not to
comply; they considered the request coercive, but they felt trapped,
with no alternative but to broadcast the message. The ingenuity of
presenting the contextual account of the news story was that it gave the
media personnel an opportunity to express their concerns to the public,
and the RCMP media liaison was allowed to respond. In this way, the
hidden aspects of issues of power, domination, and ethical conflicts
between the media outlet and the RCMP became another dimension of
the story. This aspect will be discussed further in chapter 7.

Media Tours of Camp Zulu

15 September 1995

RCMP takes selected media on a tour, but swear the reporters to secrecy,
holding tape and film for later release. The Vancouver Sun does not take
part in the tour. (Chronology, *Vancouver Sun*, 21 May 1997, A6)

I just got a call on my cell. He [Montague] *said, 'Be at the airport at two o'clock
with a cameraman.' That's all, and, 'Don't talk to anybody.'* (Interview with
journalist)

The RCMP media liaison arranged for television crews to fly into Camp
Zulu on Thursday, 15 September. He told the television crews to meet at

the police headquarters and to tell nobody. One journalist remembered the excitement of getting a scoop: *'I mean, seriously, if it's your competition that's going to find out, and you've got the jump on your competition because of – whatever reason you don't know why – believe me, you're not going to tell anyone ... I don't know what's going to happen, but I'm being let in on something and we got to go and find out what it is! I mean, you're not going to say to all the competition, "This terrible thing has happened. I've been given this secret something or other but, of course, I won't go because you weren't invited." Of course you go'* (interview with journalist). At the same time, journalists were becoming critically aware of the evolving dynamics: *'And that whole aspect of deals made secretly points to a control-oriented operation.'* Several of the print journalists became incensed over being left out. In response, Sergeant Montague arranged for a media pool for the following day. The *Vancouver Sun* declined and made other arrangements. The journalists allowed into Camp Zulu were told that they could not publish or broadcast stories about the camp until the standoff had concluded. The RCMP collected the videotapes and the rolls of film before the journalists left Camp Zulu, stating that they would temporarily embargo materials for security reasons. Some of the RCMP officers at Camp Zulu were unhappy that the media were allowed inside to ask questions and take pictures. One journalist who went into the camp recalled, *'Suddenly, Montague says, "We have to get out of here." Because a lot of the cops that were up there were very displeased with this media circus that was suddenly happening in their camp'* (interviews with journalists).

While the RCMP media liaison may have assumed that he was providing the journalists with a story opportunity, the fact that they could not use the photographs, films, and interview tape right away devalued them. By the time that the RCMP released the materials, the story was stale: *'One thing the RCMP never understood through the whole thing was the competition in the media. They didn't understand the fact that doing the interview then, then sharing the information after the whole thing was over, was useless, the tape was useless ... It was old news – nobody cared about it anymore. To address this point, we did feature stuff – like the ERT interview'* (interviews with journalists). The interview with the ERT member, who had been inside one of the APCs at the time of the firefight, provided an emotionally powerful war image of the conflict.[12]

The *Vancouver Sun* hired a helicopter to fly a photographer and a journalist over Camp Zulu as soon as the journalists found out that television crews were being flown in. Once in the air, the chartered helicopter pilot received a message that the RCMP had doubled the

perimeter of its secured airspace, forcing them to turn back. Nevertheless, the journalist was able to see Camp Zulu and the Gustafsen Lake
camp; the aerial view was characterized as follows: 'Over-all, the
Gustafsen Lake site looked more like a pleasant camping ground than a
heavily fortified complex. Well out of sight from the sundance grounds
the police staged their latest round of patrols at base Zulu. And beyond
a road blockaded by police cars and concrete barriers, the media waited
for the latest news release.'[13] According to a *Vancouver Sun* journalist,
who was irate over the exclusive television coverage,

We felt that we were being frozen. And that they knew that if a print reporter
went in – a reporter could talk about it differently, and would have a different
level of information. Just as the photographs that our photographer did over Zulu
showed, that there were a number of – there was a different number of Bison
actually in the camp than we had been told had been brought in. And so there was
a view that you couldn't necessarily trust anything they said. And I think
eventually that's the way we felt about it – was that we'd been lied to, and that we
had not been kept informed – we had been kept informed to their point ... The
argument that I use is that I understand that the RCMP have a reason to do what
they do. When they do their hostage negotiations, or when they're in a situation
like this, you expect them to not tell them everything. But you don't expect them
to lie to you and to manipulate the situation. And I think that's eventually what I
think we concluded was happening.' (Interview with journalist)

The *Vancouver Sun* maintained its professional distance from the
RCMP by hiring its own helicopter. It also published the only news
story about the media tour to Camp Zulu that was critical of the
RCMP's providing such a media opportunity. The *Vancouver Sun* journalists felt that the RCMP had contrived the media tour of Camp Zulu
and that this was another example of how they were attempting to
control the news narrative.

The feature interviews with the ERT member who was part of the
firefight added to the war drama – and may have contributed to the
skewing of the representation of the standoff. After the standoff, more
of the journalists began questioning how the RCMP had led them to
news stories as a way to control the characterization of the event.
Several months later, one reporter compared perspectives with another
ERT member who was also involved in the firefight. The journalist
paraphrased the officer's response: '"Well, I guess people just react differently to different things" ... He said that before they ordered the army vehicles,*

they'd done intelligence – they knew exactly what sort of fire power that they were looking at. And they ordered vehicles [APCs] *– that wasn't going to be – you know, those bullets were not going to pierce.'* The journalist's impression was that *'They* found *the most over-reacting guy to do the interview – 'cause my guy said "Huh?" You know, he said, "We knew what they had for weapons, we knew that in that APC we were perfectly safe. I mean, the only way you were going to get hurt was if you were stupid enough to stick your head out! There was no problem – I don't know why those guys were so excited!"'* The journalist cynically stated that the sanctioned interview was a case of *'we found the guy who was going to go hysterical for you, to make it sound as bad as possible.'* The journalist said that the interviewed ERT member seemed quite sincere, but that his response may not have been representative of how other ERT members recalled the situation. Another journalist came to a similar conclusion: *'The cops got what they wanted ... but so did media. The very fact that we used it* [the APC interview] *made it gospel – the RCMP knew that'* (interviews with journalists).

The RCMP's rationale for the visit, as explained to the journalists, was that the establishment of the camp was unique in RCMP history. It would be good to have it on the public record. Yet full media coverage of RCMP resources had been suggested in the 1 September RCMP media strategy memo (see 'Issue Three' in appendix 7). In the memo it is stated that the 'public must see that the RCMP is capable of flexing its muscle but will only do so if necessary.' It is implied that media coverage of RCMP equipment and facilities would be efficacious for public relations because it might instil public confidence in the RCMP's handling of the situation. With hindsight appreciation that the tour of Camp Zulu was a public relations initiative, was the tour a news event? And was it appropriate for such a highly charged, conflict situation?

Media Coverage of the End of the Standoff

17 September 1995

A dozen people leave the camp after the month-long standoff. They are all arrested. In total, 18 people face charges ranging from mischief to attempted murder. (Chronology, *Vancouver Sun*, 21 May 1997, A6)

After a few false alarms of surrender and a trickle of people leaving the camp since the firefight, the day that the remaining people left the camp was anticlimactic. John Stevens, the Gustafsen Lake Sundance spiritual leader, visited the camp for a few hours, and then the remaining people agreed to come out. The police were careful to explain to the media that this would not be called a *surrender*, because the negotiators were trying to preserve as much face as possible for the people in the camp and show them respect. Some journalists were hesitant to become too excited about the rumours that had been circulating about a resolution, in case it did not work out as planned. The RCMP told them that the occupants of the camp would be taken to the airport at 100 Mile House. A few journalists said that Sergeant Montague assured them that there would be a media witness to the arrests, but according to one journalist, on the day the arrests were made, Montague told reporters, '*"That was never in the plan – and you know it." He denied he ever said it. There were no media present* – [for the arrests] – [I] *don't how people were treated.'* Several journalists gathered in the Red Coach Inn parking lot, waiting to hear the final word. They had been told at around 2:00 p.m. that the release would take place in two or three hours.

The public and the media gathered at the 100 Mile House airport, where they watched the helicopters land with the people from the camp. The RCMP positioned the journalists closer to the heliopad so that they had a slightly better view. '*We were sort of cordoned off in a little area that we weren't allowed to leave ... It was a section where we could stand and watch the helicopters arrive*' (interview with journalist). The public, consisting mostly of Native people, had begun to line up along the fence next to the airport well before the estimated time. There were few non-Natives and few townspeople in the crowd. One journalist recalled meeting a reporter and a photographer from a Native newspaper, who had just arrived from Milwaukee. People were happy that the standoff had ended without loss of life or serious injury, and it was an emotional time for the supporters, families, and Native intermediaries. Some of the reporters attempted to interview the Native people as they were waiting. One of the journalists observed that he was being trailed by a Native male who seemed to intimidate people into not speaking: '*As soon as they saw him, they shook their heads and said they didn't want to talk to me ... I did meet two Native people who were kind of appalled by the Gustafsen standoff, and didn't think that – didn't support it at all what was happening there. And I think it was people like that they didn't want me to talk to.'*

The scene at the airport marked the transition from the end of the standoff to the beginning of the long judicial process that lay ahead. The largest helicopter of the fleet, called the '*big red tomato,*' was the first of the shuttles to land, and supporters began waving eagle feathers and beating drums. Some stood on top of vehicles to get a better view. One journalist, who admitted to being sceptical of the people involved in the protest, recalls: *'They were cheering. They were cheering the people in hand-cuffs. They were cheering the prisoners ... It was a mixture – it was like, "right on! – up the pigs" kind of thing. Which was – I thought it was unfortunate.'* The final helicopter, which held Wolverine and Percy Rosette, made a more theatric approach to the airport. Instead of flying in directly, like the others, it flew over the adjacent marsh area, allowing better visibility for the crowd and waiting photographers. According to the journalists, when Percy Rosette and Wolverine got off the helicopter, the emotion peaked, accompanied by loud cheering and waving of eagle feathers.

For many of the reporters who gathered at the airport, this was their first chance to see the people from the camp in person. One reporter commented on the appearance of some of the younger people: *'They looked like kids, a lot of them,'* while another described them as a *'sad, rag-tag group that were brought out.'* **Did they seem violent to you?** *'Well, they weren't in a position to seem violent, they were under arrest, they were surrounded by police, they were handcuffed. They were – they seemed – pretty beaten when they were brought out.'* The news accounts provided an array of perspectives from Native and non-Native leaders, RCMP officials, and private citizens. There was a consensus of relief that the standoff had ended peacefully. Nevertheless, there were mixed reactions concerning the conduct of the camp, the RCMP, and the politicians (interviews with journalists).

Once in police custody, the camp members were about as inaccessible to the media as they were when they were behind the barricades. However, the media coverage of the landing of the helicopters with the people from the camp did offer an opportunity for the journalists to interview people with a variety of perspectives. The visual effect of seeing the people who had occupied Gustafsen Lake for a month (and for some, longer), handcuffed and brought to waiting police cruisers, fit the script for a criminal versus law-and-order theme. Still, the presence of cheering supporters and comments from several Native leaders, who voiced criticisms of the RCMP and the politicians in their handling of the situation, provided contrasting frames. The RCMP's comments at the subsequent press conference shifted away from interpretations of the camp to advising the media of the arrest protocols and trial appearances. At the press conference, the RCMP officials acknowledged the assistance of various Native leaders and groups in reaching the resolu-

tion, and they commended the efforts of their officers and the restrained approach that they had taken to the conflict.

Under *normal* circumstances, the scene at the airport and the press
conference would have been the culminating news story for the journalists, after which they could return to Vancouver. Although most did
leave 100 Mile House, several returned six days later, when the RCMP
media personnel invited them on a police flight that would take them
for a tour of the Gustafsen Lake camp. This was a news opportunity
that did not require any time-limited embargoes and that promised
ample photographic and filming potential. The tour would also quench
the journalists' curiosity and fantasies about the camp, which had been
off limits for three weeks. According to my sources, when Sergeant
Montague contacted one outlet, he requested that a particular journalist
not be included in the tour. The journalist attended regardless, arriving
early enough to get an unofficial tour of the camp (courtesy of his
RCMP friends) as well as to obtain exclusive interviews from people
who would otherwise not talk to the media.

Media Tour of the Camp

24 September 1995

'I'll let the people of British Columbia be the judge of whether those who
occupy – illegally – private land and then shoot at police officers at sight
and hunt them and actually aggressively pursue them to kill – whether
they're heroes or zeroes,' Dosanjh said.[14] ('Gustafsen Lake Aftermath,'
Vancouver Sun, 25 September 1995, B1)

In the interim between the surrender and the media tour of the Gustafsen
Lake camp, the RCMP forensic team combed the area, searching for
weapons, bullet shells, and casings. The news coverage detailed the
weapons found in the camp: 'In the foxhole at the foot of a tree they
found 10 guns, a bow and three arrows, and a powerful pipe bomb. In a
firepit, they found the remains of an AK–47 assault rifle, a Lee Enfield
and an FN assault rifle' ('Gustafsen Lake Aftermath: Standoff site has
foxhole, bunker,' *Vancouver Sun*, 25 September 1995, B1). Shortly before
the arranged tour of the camp, some of the media flew to the airport in
the RCMP jet, along with Attorney General Dosanjh, while a few other
journalists made their own way from Vancouver. Some outlets did not
send journalists to the tour of the camp because of the expense already

incurred in covering the Gustafsen Lake standoff. Details of the costs are discussed below.

More than one journalist described the media visit to the camp as a fully controlled situation. *'When we were with the police, it was like a grade five field trip, where everyone was holding onto a rope – "stand here," "don't stand here."'* The police led the walking tour, pointing out various defensive constructions and sites of media-documented confrontations. The process of seeing these features and listening to the explanations offered appealed to the imaginations of many people making the tour. While reflecting afterward, one journalist discussed how the tour affected his news account: *'I think [I] described it as looking like some kind of – like a guerilla camp or something – you know, which – in retrospect, I kind of I shudder at – because that's a really loaded term.'* **But why wouldn't you use the term 'guerilla camp'?** *'Well, because I've never seen a guerilla camp. I mean, [how] do I know [what] a guerilla camp looks like? It was sort of my image of what – so – that's a term that I thought maybe I shouldn't have used.'* **Did it look like a frightening camp?** *'Yeah, there is no question. It was crude, but I think it had the potential for being quite deadly.'*

Some journalists openly joked about how the RCMP restricted their movements during the tour. *'All the media had to drive in together, and they were all going – "BAAAA! BAAAA!" Making these sounds of cattle, "MMOOO!" because they all got to stay together. We were making sounds like cows – moving around – "this is a hole," "this was the tree" "this was the ..." – ugh – this is nothing new! And so, Peter would get into these holes – "This was a foxhole." In fact, I found out later [from] some of the Natives that some of them were, you know, protective foxholes. But some of them were also built for winter. The logs – you cover them and you climb inside them.'* A participant in this study, who had been in the camp before the 1995 Sundance, advised me that a few of the structures were built before 1995. These were traditional dugout shelters, called kee-kwu-lee,[15] although the RCMP identified them during the media tour as 'foxholes' and 'bunkers.' This sceptical journalist argued, *'Sure, the inside of a car looks like it could be for shooting out of too, but it could also be for staying warm and dry. I mean ... there's a couple of things that – I knew were misleading. Now, there was a cache of guns under a tree – covered with a board. There's no argument there'* (interviews with journalists).

Several of the reporters questioned whether the attorney general's presence was required during the tour, and a few interpreted it as a way to reinforce in the public's perception the necessity of such a large police presence. *'But, I mean, when you looked around the camp, it was pretty piddly ... again, and this is the thing, it goes back to what I was saying before – with the – it's not a black and white story, right? And it never was.'* Some of the journalists felt that Dosanjh was making a pitch about how the public should interpret the actions of the people in the camp: *'"Were these people heroes or zeros – you be the judge," kind of thing – which kind of strikes me as the kind of thing that's not real; people don't speak like that – you know, I guess he's the attorney general. But he's kind of known as a guy who is ready with a quote on anything, you know.'* Another journalist stated, *'We didn't need him on the tour ... What the hell? He'd never been in there before. Montague'd never been in there. Dosanjh had never been in there.'* Some of the journalists considered his presence to be politically motivated, timed for the upcoming provincial election. *'Well, they certainly don't want to have it clouding election time. They didn't want to have this goin' on, or too fresh.'* Another journalist referred to the attorney general's appearance at the camp tour as *'running in to shoot the wounded at the end'* (interviews with journalists).

Defence lawyer George Wool was also critical of the role of the attorney general in the media coverage and his appearance at the camp: *'Well, he made the very fatal error of actually involving himself. He involved himself in the process, which he ought not to have done. He should never have been flown around in an RCMP plane and making comments about evidence or comments about what did or did not happen. That's inappropriate for an attorney general. Because his role in our society is to protect the rights of all people – at all times. Not to be selectively seen as supporting one side or the other, or making comments to the effect that "there is no other side to the story." It's inappropriate. It's not an appropriate position for an attorney general'* (interview with George Wool, defence counsel, 26 May 1997).

The tour of the camp was the finale of the media coverage of the Gustafsen Lake standoff, with the RCMP providing the journalists with an opportunity to see the camp. This was the first time most journalists had seen the camp, and they had no other frame with which to interpret what they saw. However, the police-guided tour offered a view through the eyes of criminal investigators. Although the people from the camp had been arrested and most were released on bail, the RCMP provided the media with information that would later be presented during the trial as prosecuting evidence. This included a walking tour of the sites of shooting incidents, strategic pits that offered tactical advantages, and a hideaway for a cache of weapons. Sergeant Montague read off a list of weapons found on the premises to the group of journalists who were gathered near the place where they had been stored. For many, it was easy to accept at face value the RCMP's portrayal of the camp.

Still, even for those journalists who were sceptical of the tour, the task at hand was to report what they saw and what the police and the government official told them. The RCMP and the attorney general were offering information and quotations that could produce important news accounts. There were no alternative sources available on the tour to challenge the RCMP's characterization of the camp, and the journalists had no time to return to town and seek out anybody who could offer another perspective. Only a few of them commented that the camp tour predisposed the media to promote a guilty verdict on the people in the camp. Consequently, the media coverage of the camp tour offered no critical assessment of how the media event was constructed, nor was there an evaluation of the players who were being served or abused by this news opportunity. Thus, in spite of the joking resistance offered by the journalists, they were still being *led* by the RCMP media personnel during this tour.

The final week of the standoff provided several opportunities for the RCMP to maintain the ruling definition of the situation, offering news-gathering opportunities to the media. During this period the RCMP relaxed control over information and details about their operation and the investigation. Their enthusiasm for conducting media tours of the RCMP Camp Zulu, the shot-up RCMP vehicle, the camp truck, and the Gustafsen Lake camp were more typical of the victor of a war than of police engaged in the process of an investigation.

In the analysis of the situations of the CBC Radio message, and the tours of Camp Zulu and the Gustafsen Lake camp, it appears that the role of the RCMP expanded to include the creation of news events for the media. In effect, the police were telling the media what the news was going to be. The RCMP's authoritative news appeal, their wealth of information, and the journalists' ever-present hunger for news ensured that these events would be given media attention. Exciting images of RCMP resources, battle stories with heroes, and glimpses of defensive structures at the camp were media spectacles that in themselves became news events. The interview data with the journalists suggest that the media could not ignore the availability of these news-gathering opportunities. The RCMP were the most powerful media source, and competition between outlets ensured that police information retained a high value. The investment of the various outlets in labour and coverage hooked the media into covering the story until its natural conclusion. They could not easily afford breaks in the flow of the story, and any developments, even those that may have been artificially constructed, became viable news that might satisfy their audiences. Indeed, several journalists found that the RCMP *tours* had more news appeal than the staid police briefings, far removed from the actual scenes of the standoff.

However, these constructed news opportunities were not covered (with the exception of the *Vancouver Sun*'s coverage of the fly-over of RCMP Camp Zulu) with a critical view. There were few, if any, struggles or manoeuvres between sources and the media, because the RCMP were the only source of information and the RCMP arranged for the media opportunity. The media's passivity and willingness to follow along made them ideal conduits for the RCMP perspective. Earlier in the standoff, the RCMP were displaying weaponry that had been confiscated from people connected with the camp. This was followed by periodic viewing of material evidence associated with the violent incidents and culminating with the camp. Because journalists had these eye-witness opportunities, the media provided the public with information about the police investigation in advance of a trial. Yet, other than providing graphic displays, the tours and media access to evidence offered no advancement of the news event.

Despite the diminished tension between the camp and the police, the RCMP provided news-gathering opportunities that maintained a focus on the criminality of the camp and the war conditions endured by the police. Several journalists felt that in their accounts during this time they toned down the negative characterizations of the camp. Nonetheless, the RCMP continued to dominate the news narrative with powerful images and language depicting the camp as volatile and dangerous.

Denouement

On the day after the tour, two of the journalists drove back up to the camp. *'There wasn't a single policeman* [around] *And we drove back in – just to – I wanted to spend a little time of my own in there, lookin' around.'* **How did you feel about that?** *'Oh, I felt like I was trespassing. I felt like I was – we never did go over to the sacred circle. Just – you know, we sat on the logs a bit. And we were surrounded in cattle! A day later – not 12 hours later – after the media tour. Five hundred head of cattle'* (interview with journalist).

Of the 18 people arrested, two were charged with attempted murder. The remaining 16 individuals were charged with mischief and trespassing. After the arraignment, most of the defendants were immediately released on bail. The criminal trial, including the pre-trial phase, lasted about 10 months, and the ensuing convictions and sentences were as follows. All attempted murder charges were dropped. Wolverine received the longest sentence, with four and one-half years for mischief endangering life and other offences. The remainder received sentences ranging from 6 months to 3 years for convictions of mischief endangering life, possession of weapons, mischief, and trespass. Wolverine was released on parole on 28 January 1999.

CHAPTER SIX

Terms of Engagement

... if under these circumstances, this is where you are at, this is what the terms of engagement would be.

District Superintendent Len Olfert, interview, 17 July 1998

In this chapter different aspects of stereotyping in the news coverage of the Gustafsen Lake standoff are analysed. First is a discussion of the media's construction and dissemination of stereotyped characterizations. Next is an examination of select audience responses to the media coverage. This is followed by a look at how the local Native and non-Native communities responded to the media stereotypes of their communities. The chapter concludes with an assessment of the social repercussions of the media stereotypes.

Several factors contributed to the construction and dissemination of media stereotypes of the people in the camp. During the standoff, visual, verbal, and written communications lacked variability in expression, owing to the context of the coverage, news production practices and conventions, and external influences. For long-term news events like this standoff, these and other limitations posed serious obstacles, which led to repeated patterns of representation that were transformed into stereotypes. At the time, language was one of the aspects of the coverage over which the journalists had control. Yet, as will be demonstrated, there were still some limitations inherent in language itself as well as in news production practices. The journalists' accounts contextualize the quantitative analysis of stereotype labelling, the predominant linguistic feature in the newspaper stories in the Canada-wide sample.

Stereotyping in Media Products

Photographic and film representations of the standoff consisted of those taken before the barricades were erected (which were retained for later use when access was impossible) and those taken afterwards (which were limited to specific sites). The latter group included Red Coach Inn press conferences, the street in front of the hotel, the view of the town from the golf course, the airport, and Checkpoint 17. According to one television journalist, once the barricades were established, providing accompanying film footage for television coverage was difficult: *'In television, with no pictures you're in tough – only have Montague's face, file pictures, spectacular shot of APC rumbling down the dusty road in the early morning.'* In order to refresh the audience's memory of what the camp was like, television outlets *'used the same pictures we took of the camp over and over again.'* Similarly, newspapers also showed pictures of the camp, long after access had been cut off. Other visual representations included shots of armed ERT members in town, RCMP officers at Checkpoint 17, helicopters flying overhead, and convoys of police vehicles and unmarked supply trucks as they headed past Checkpoint 17. The police also invited media photograph and film opportunities. These included the shot-up flak jackets and the RCMP Suburban; an exclusive tour of Camp Zulu (originally for the television crews, then extended); a media pool for a surrender (which was aborted); and, after the conclusion of the standoff, a post-investigation police-guided tour of the Gustafsen Lake camp.

The visual component of the media coverage promoted a wartime theme, emphasizing the power and pride of the RCMP and the danger of the situation and the people in the camp. The lack of alternative media opportunities, however, also created a poverty of visual representations of the news event: *'It was a hurting story for pictures – bad for TV – because, like it or not, TV reaches more people than anybody. And we were probably in the worst position to do those stories – because we had no information, no pictures – we couldn't even bullshit our way around our lack of information because we had no pictures'* (interview with journalist). One of the remedies was to use video footage and photographs on file. I propose that these contributed to the development of patterned representations of the conflict and the people involved. Sensational scenes are most likely those that audiences remember; repetition, for want of any other visual characterization, reinforces the extreme images. Corroborative verbal and written media communications that accompany such images support thematic patterns of stereotypes. When television media consistently reproduce these coherent presentations for their audiences over an extended timeframe – stereotypes are more likely subsumed by audiences as *common sense*.

Newspaper stories are most amenable to reinforcing stereotype themes through repetitive language use, including stock expressions and narrative themes and labels. The repetition of certain news elements, which link stories from one episode of a news event to preceding ones, contributes to the formation of a coherent news narrative of a developing event.

Stock phrases included tallies of shooting incidents from the camp to the RCMP, time markers, and summary explanations of the situation, most often found at the end of the stories. The following stock expressions are taken from the firefight news story, 'Three natives shot in firefight' from the *Globe and Mail*, 12 September 1995. They were circulated (with periodic adjustments) within Canadian Press accounts across Canada for most of the standoff. 'It was the seventh time police have been fired on.' This sentence constitutes a form of score keeping, although it is one-sided. In this case, it includes a shooting incident that did not happen. Other incidents had yet to be proved in court. During the course of the standoff, no tallies were ever published for the RCMP. 'The standoff entered its fourth week Monday in the confrontation between the armed aboriginals and police surrounding the remote piece of ranchland the natives claim as sacred aboriginal territory.' This stock explanation opens with a time marker that reinforces the length of time the dispute has lasted. The explanation oversimplifies the dispute. Not all the people in the camp were Native people. The police by far outnumbered the camp members and were better armed. The emphasis on the *sacred territory* was the rationale for land ownership, but the explanation does not allude to the camp's challenge to the provincial treaty process. The repetition of such a phrase would reinforce the narrow definition of the situation, which pitted Native and non-Native interests against each other. Tallies and time markers were techniques of extending the news narrative from a previous account to the current one, and they explained the conflict consisely while enhancing the audience's understanding. However, clarity was achieved at the cost of misrepresenting the complexity of the situation and the people involved.

The use of pejorative labels provided consistent thematic repetition in the news stories. The news excerpts, both those previously presented and those in the endnotes, show that the terms *rebels*, *renegades*, and *squatters* were inserted in headlines, lead-ins, and news narratives. The labels provided thumbnail sketches of the people at the camp and circumvented long explanations of their identities, when time and space in media products were at a premium. Nevertheless, these words were not neutral, and at the time of the standoff they cast a prejudgment of lawlessness that was consistent with the RCMP definition of the situation.

Some of the outlets had a policy (or routine practice) concerning the appropriate use of language to characterize Native people even before the Gustafsen Lake standoff. Journalists working for these outlets found that editors quickly changed any deviations from what was expected. Some outlets debated the language used to identify the people in the camp, so that it would be consistent throughout the coverage: '*You know, this whole debate was one we all had. At some point in time, somebody was favouring calling them "campers" and everyone sort of, like, laughed at that one – like no, they're not campers*' (interview with journalist).

All of the journalists recalled that the RCMP introduced the label *terrorist*, the strongest language to describe the activities of the people in the camp, during the Williams Lake press conference: '*They had created an impression that ... these were people who were volatile and violent ... as a matter of fact, that's what marked the beginning of the full coverage of the event, was when police held this news conference.*' The journalists commented on the influence of that press conference on the media coverage: '*The RCMP started calling* [the people in the camp] *"terrorists" – it jumped right out at me. From the beginning this set the tone. It biased the tone against the people in the camp. I never once used the word "terrorist." It is inflammatory and didn't help understanding the issue*' (interviews with journalists).

Several journalists considered that the intensity of the language employed by the RCMP media sources gave tacit permission to use whatever language they wanted: '*You're getting your information from police, or politicians, getting your descriptions of the people and what's happening, and you tend to pick up their descriptions.*' Another journalist stated, '*But certainly, once the words "terrorist" and "bestiality" start getting thrown around, you have to decide whether you're going to let that influence you or not.*' Some (from print and electronic media) admitted using *terrorists* in their news accounts of the early part of the standoff. One journalist said that it was easy to justify this characterization because of the shooting incidents early in the conflict and the guerilla-warfare attire worn by several of the young men at the camp. Wolverine's manner towards the media and his language were other influences: '*Wolverine was very belligerent.*' Wolverine's use of *body bag*, '*is the kind of phrase the media would repeat in reports – it showed where Wolverine was coming from.*' One journalist said that CBC Radio ended up deciding on 'Natives in the camp and non-Native sympathizers' and similar phrases. Canadian Press journalists said that they selected *rebels* because it was not as extreme as *terrorists*. A few journalists commented that it was difficult to find neutral descriptors that would allow the audience to make up their own minds.

Journalists covering the standoff from 100 Mile House recalled that the people at the camp and their supporters became upset with the media's use of *rebels*. '*They didn't like us calling them "rebels."*' **Why?** '*They felt they weren't "rebels" – they were defending their own land.*' Some of the journalists acknowledged that the use of inflammatory language was excessive. '*I felt we (the media in general) overused "rebels" – I avoided it as much as possible. I didn't use "armed" at first, until it was obvious the people in the camp were using them.*' Several of the journalists used the term *squatter*, although they knew that some people disagreed with its appropriateness in the situation. Some journalists considered the people at the camp to be squatting on the rancher's property, but they also knew that the camp (and many other Native groups) believed that all unceded land in the province belonged to Native people.

Language was most noticeable to journalists who returned to Vancouver and saw subsequent news stories filed by their colleagues back at 100 Mile House: '*I would hear editors talking about getting some of that language out and replacing it – or, more often the case, you'd hear the next day in the post-mortem of the newspaper editors saying, you know, "Why are we doing that? What are we calling them that for?"*' **What would you suggest would have been more of a neutral way?** '*I called them "protest-ers." I think I tried to stick to that word – "the protesters."*' However, at times even this word did not seem to provide a good fit: '*accepting the police word that two of their members have just been shot in the back, while they tried to protect two unarmed forestry workers – protesters doesn't seem an adequate word to describe those guys who would shoot like that, if in fact that happened.*' Occasionally, conversations overheard on the police radio-telecommunications might generate sympathy, but at other times, '*you'd hear stuff that would make your blood run cold because it seemed to be so violent in their nature, sometimes. So, it was a real emotional mix for anybody covering that, I think, at least for me, anyway.*' Of the journalists inter-viewed, only one of them held the belief that the politicians and the media neutrally represented the people in the camp.

Several journalists appreciated that choice of language is a central aspect in objective journalism. One reporter remembered, '*Every once in a while, we were told* [by the editors] *to tone down the language.*' Some journalists noted that the RCMP also tempered their language and tried to play down references to people in the camp, probably to the other extreme. At the mid-point of the standoff, the *Vancouver Sun* dropped its use of *sundancers*. According to one of the *Sun* journalists, this was because it was no longer certain that the conflict was about a Sundance. Another reporter felt that the insistence of his editor on using *rebels* and *renegades* was '*wrong, wrong, wrong ... I don't refer to people as rebels. That's a loaded term ... I think I eventually gave in and ended up using it that way, but I tried not to do it very often.*' The reporter explained, '*If we have biases, reporters are usually very careful not to let that creep out. And that's guarded and held quite close to the chest. Because if you let it creep out, and it creeps in your copy, you lose your integrity. And if you lose your integrity – that's the only commodity that I have, and you don't want to lose that. I've long given up the concept that I am an unbiased person. I have biases. We all have them. Now, the question is, can you be fair in the stories that you write? And that was the important thing here.*' One journalist recalled an awareness of how language was being used to sensationalize the camp: '*We heard all of these stories that the people in the camp were connected to U.S. militia groups. I flipped off –* "*oh, c'mon – these people are just a bunch of rag tags, they are not organized, they are not militant, they are just people!*"' (interviews with journalists).

Many of the journalists found the labels convenient, and they saved time. All members of the media covering the standoff faced the pressure of deadlines, '*so, you have a tendency as a reporter to fall into a shorthand – in choosing words and things like that.*' For journalists filing more than one story per day, labels eliminated having to spend time on composition. The use of computers was particularly helpful: '*When you do two or three stories a day on your laptop, you're storing them all the time on a disk, so if you're doing any story – I would ... I think everybody would do this – call up a previous story, so you don't have to keep repunching the background ... I guess some of the stock adjectives, phrases were there* [too]' (interviews with journalists). Timesaving strategies were especially important for Canadian Press reporters, who faced a hypothetical deadline-every-minute by having to feed news stories to several time zones. On occasion, this meant that there was no time to compose the story on a computer, and the reporter had to dictate the breaking-news over the telephone to the editor in Vancouver to top up the basic story.

In the media discourse analysis of the newspaper stories, occasionally I found labels in direct quotations of media sources. More often, I found labels inserted into indirect quotations in newspaper stories. The inclusion of these terms appeared inconsistent when media sources who were sympathetic towards the camp were paraphrased. The bias imposed through journalists' use of labels in indirect quotations was particularly obvious when the media sources were either supporters of the people in the camp or spokespersons unlikely to use inflammatory language in media communications. The following examples are taken from the *Globe and Mail*; I have italicized the invective labels in the news story quotations.

> Nathan Matthew, a spokesman for the so-called liaison group between the *rebels* and the RCMP said earlier that the *squatters* were looking for reassurance. ('Three Natives Shot in Firefight,' *Globe and Mail*; taken from *Victoria Times Colonist*, 12 September 1995 a1 [CP])

> Shuswap spokesman Tom Dennis said earlier that negotiators have asked the UN to send observers before the *renegades* surrender. He said it's the only way the *rebels*, mistrustful of the police, will lay down their arms and walk out of the remote camp on a piece of private ranchland along Gustafsen Lake in southcentral British Columbia. Aboriginal negotiators need three days to comply with demands from inside the camp to involve the international community and set up a procedure that will guarantee the *rebels*' safety, said Dennis. ('Maverick lawyer kept from *rebels*,' *Globe and Mail*; taken from *Victoria Times Colonist* 15 September 1995, a3 [CP])

As demonstrated by these examples, the labels appear to be an imposition of the journalist's perception of the people in the camp. The reporters whom I interviewed for this study agreed that the imposition of labels was an '*inappropriate*' journalistic practice.

The label *rebel* frequently appeared in newspaper headlines. Headlines traditionally economize language for minimal space, which is how one journalist explained the frequent appearance of *rebel* during the Gustafsen Lake standoff. Headlines are authored by editors, who also face deadlines and are disengaged from the scene of the story: '*And we complain about headlines all the time – reporters do – like, you know, "Why did you put that headline on my story for?" kind of thing*' (interviews with journalists). One example of a headline misrepresenting a news story during the Gustafsen Lake standoff was an account of a traditional sweatlodge ceremony that took place at Alkali Lake. In the news story the activities were respectfully described, but the headline composed by an editor in Vancouver was entitled, 'Natives Steamed,' reflecting the *Vancouver Province*'s penchant for the sensational. A culturally sensitive audience might interpret the headline as ridiculing the traditional spiritual practice, thus further inflaming the situation.[1]

How appropriate were these terms? *Rebel, renegade,* and *squatter* had aspects of meaning that seemed to accurately describe the situation and the people involved. Camp members defied the RCMP, and some of them denigrated the legal system, distinguishing themselves from the mainstream and signifying themselves as *rebels*. Some of the people in the camp were filmed carrying illegal weapons and shooting at a helicopter. There were witnessed shooting incidents, at least one of which could have been fatal to police officers. Furthermore, some of the people in the camp dressed in a manner that suggested guerilla warfare. These behaviours could define the people in the camp as *renegades*. The people occupied land that was part of Lyle James's ranch, and they refused to leave, much like *squatters*. In this light, the terms of reference used to describe the camp seem appropriate.

However, the *fetter* of language is that meanings associated with a concept cover a broad spectrum, but once they are committed to a word, many of the nuances are lost.[2] The articulation of words is the result of information processing, and words are necessary for categorization and labelling. *Rebels, renegades,* and *squatters* classified everyone at the camp into rigid characterizations. The associated behaviours implied in the meanings of the labels were ultimately questions for the court to decide. Yet during the standoff these terms implied that a judgment had already been made. Reconsidered in this way, I propose that *rebels, renegades,* and *squatters* were extreme characterizations and overgeneralized the complex composition of the camp. The imprecise labels could not convey exceptions and limitations: they offered an all-or-nothing proposition. I argue that the media's employment of these labels was an example of media stereotyping. Thus, if journalists set for themselves the goal of objectivity (defined as avoiding evaluative representations), their choice of terminology to describe the camp would be one indicator of how committed they were to this goal.

Stereotype Labels in Newspaper Stories

Table 6.1 presents a quantitative analysis of the use of the labels *rebels, renegades*, and *squatters* in 17 newspapers across Canada. I added *100 Mile House Free Press* to the sample during the fieldwork. The table provides the tallies of usage within the news narratives and indirect quotations for each of the newspapers. Labels used in direct quotations by the media sources have been excluded. Where applicable, footnotes for individual newspapers break down the news stories written by staff reporters from news stories authored by Canadian Press.

The newspaper stories regularly described the people inside the camp in terms that conveyed an imagery of volatility and lawlessness. While news stories used 'militant' on occasion, the terms most frequently employed in all of the newspapers to describe the occupants of the camp were *rebels*, *renegades* and *squatters*. Media sources occasionally incorporated these words to refer to the people in the camp, but the labels were found mostly in headlines, story narratives, or in indirect quotations of media sources.[3] Newspaper stories about the conflict at Gustafsen Lake contained few of these three terms in the news stories in mid-August. Within a week of the press conference at Williams Lake, however, the labelling became prevalent. At first, these terms were used as collective nouns: 'the *rebels*,' 'the *renegades*,' 'the *squatters*.' Very quickly, the label *rebel* became linguistically productive in news stories, expanding the descriptive possibilities and extending the terms from the people in the camp to the lawyer Bruce Clark, who claimed to represent them. Subsequent news stories began referring to '*rebel* natives,' 'aboriginal *rebels*,' '*rebel* camp,' '*rebel* demands,' '*rebel* crossfire,' '*rebel* protesters,' '*rebel* truck,' an 'armed *rebel* standoff,' and a '*rebel* lawyer.' To a lesser extent, there were allusions to '*renegades*,' 'native *renegades*,' '*renegade* leader,' and a '*renegade* lawyer.' '*Squatters*' was also used on occasion, but the label was not elaborated much beyond '*squatters*': 'about two dozen *squatters*,' '*squatters*' camp,' '*squatters*' armed camp,' and '*rebel squatters*.' The general ratio of the use of *rebel* compared with *renegade* and *squatter* was about 6:1.

In this study, repeated patterns of labelling allowed for a measurement of one example of stereotyping of the people in the camp. Some newspapers more than others relied on stereotype labels to characterize the protesters. However, this fact did not necessarily correlate with the number of stories published. The data show a disproportion between the ratio of total stories published and with the ratio of total labels, indicating fluctuations in reliance of label usage. Newspapers with the greatest difference in the ratios, indicating a greater proportional reliance on labels, include the *Victoria Times Colonist, London Free Press,*

TABLE 6.1
Labels in News Stories and Embedded in Indirect Quotations (IQs)

Newspaper	No. of Articles	% (x/529 stories)	Labels	IQs	Total	% (x/1689 labels)
Victoria Times Colonist[a]	30	5.6	84	23	107	6.3
Vancouver Province[b]	64	12.0	121	24	145	8.5
Vancouver Sun[c]	83	15.6	191	25	216	12.7
Calgary Herald[d]	37	7.0	96	14	110	6.5
Edmonton Journal[e]	46	8.6	136	17	153	9.0
Regina Leader Post	14	2.6	49	3	52	3.0
Saskatoon Star-Phoenix[f]	19	3.6	45	16	61	3.6
Winnipeg Free Press	28	5.2	74	7	81	4.8
London Free Press[g]	26	4.9	89	14	103	6.0
Toronto Star[h]	25	4.7	73	8	81	4.8
Globe and Mail[i]	80	15.1	250	58	308	18.2
Le Devoir	1	0.1	1 [rebelles]	0	1	0.05
Montreal Gazette[j]	22	4.1	70	11	81	4.8
Halifax Chronicle-Herald	6	1.1	21	6	27	1.6
Charlottetown Guardian	18	3.4	47	12	59	3.5
New Brunswick Telegraph Journal[k]	6	1.1	4	0	4	0.2
St. John's Evening Telegram	24	4.5	84	16	100	5.9
Subtotal	529		1435	254	1689	
100 Mile House Free Press[l]	32	5.7 (x/561)	7	0	7	0.4 (x/1696)
Total	561		1442	254	1696	

[a] Of the 30 stories published in the Victoria Times Colonist, 18 were written by CP, 10 stories were written by staff reporters (8 invectives, 0 IQs), and 2 stories combined authorship from staff reporters and CP (4 invectives, 3 IQs).

[b] Sixty-two out of the 64 stories taken from the Vancouver Province were written by staff reporters (116 invectives, 22 IQs). One story combined the Vancouver Province and CP (1 invective, 1 IQ); the other was from CP alone.

[c] Eighty-two out of the 83 Vancouver Sun stories were written by staff reporters (185 invectives, 25 IQs); 1 story was from CP alone.

[d] The 37 Calgary Herald stories were taken from a variety of sources: 24 from CP; 7 from the Vancouver Sun (10 invectives, 0 IQs); 1 story was from the Ottawa Citizen (3 invectives, 1 IQ); 1 was authored by a staff reporter (1 invective, 0 IQs); 4 stories combined CP, Vancouver Sun, and the Vancouver Province (12 invectives, 1 IQ).

[e] The 46 Edmonton Journal stories were taken from several sources: 30 from CP; 8 from the Vancouver Sun (21 invectives, 3 IQs); 2 from the Vancouver Province (4 invectives, 0 IQs); 1 story combined CP with the Vancouver Sun (0 invectives, 0 IQs); and the remaining 5 stories were from staff, Edmonton Journal Services, and Southam Press (11 invectives, 3 IQs).

f   Two stories from the *Saskatoon Star-Phoenix* were written by staff and freelance journalists (5 invectives, 0 IQs); the remaining 17 stories were from CP.

g   The *London Free Press* published 24 stories from CP, 1 story from the *Vancouver Province* (1 invective, 0 IQs); and 1 story from *Southam Services* (0 invectives, 0 IQs).

h   The *Toronto Star* stories were taken from several sources: 18 stories from CP; 1 story was from the *Vancouver Sun* (0 invectives, 0 IQs); 1 story combined CP with the *Toronto Star* staff (3 invectives, 1 IQ); and 5 stories were from staff (0 invectives, 0 IQs).

i   The *Globe and Mail* published 66 stories from CP, 12 stories from the *Victoria Times Colonist* (5 invectives, 0 IQs); 1 story from the *Winnipeg Free Press* (5 invectives, 0 IQs); and 1 story combined several sources (0 invectives, 2 IQs).

j   The *Montreal Gazette* published 18 stories from CP; 1 story from the *Ottawa Citizen* (3 invectives, 1 IQ); 1 story from the *Vancouver Sun* (8 invectives, 0 IQs); 1 story that combined staff and CP (3 invectives, 0 IQs); and 1 story was written by staff (0 invectives, 0 IQs).

k   The *New Brunswick Telegraph Journal* was the only newspaper (besides *100 Mile House Free Press*) in this sample that did not include stories from CP. Instead, 2 stories were from Southam Press (3 invectives, 0 IQs); 2 stories were from United Press International (1 invective, 0 IQs); 1 story was from Reuters (0 invectives, 0 IQs); and 1 story was written by staff (0 invectives, 0 IQs).

l   Because the *100 Mile House Free Press* publishes on a weekly basis, the final story date is 20 September 1995. Other newspaper stories are taken up to 19 September 1995 inclusive. All of the stories published by the *100 Mile House Free Press* were composed by staff journalists.

Globe and Mail, Montreal Gazette, and *St. John's Evening Telegram.* The *Vancouver Province, Vancouver Sun, Winnipeg Free Press,* and *New Brunswick Telegraph Journal* used proportionately fewer labels than other newspapers. The *Vancouver Sun* and the *Globe and Mail* published the greatest number of stories, and they also had the highest frequency of labelling. However, the *Vancouver Sun* used a significantly smaller proportion of labels (12.7%) compared with the *Globe and Mail* (18.2%), which used the highest proportion of labels in the Canada-wide sample.

By far, the lowest usage (relative to the number of stories published) is found in the *100 Mile House Free Press*, with seven occasions within the 32 news stories published during the standoff period. *Renegade* was found in two separate captions of photographs and once in the body of a news story. *Squatter* was used once in a headline. Three news stories published at the conclusion of the standoff incorporated *rebels*. Other occasions of labelling the camp (most often as *renegades*) were found in editorials, which I excluded (as I did editorials from other newspapers) from the tallies. One might argue, however, that the news stories in the *100 Mile House Free Press* were different from the daily news published by other outlets. The local news accounts combined synthesized episodes from the previous week with interviews, press conferences, and coverage from other media products. Still, the significantly lower total confirms the effectiveness of an editorial policy that sensitive to representing the conflict in a way that supported positive relations between the local Native and non-Native communities. Combined with other practices that minimized sensationalism and reduced the potential for conflict between local Native and non-Native communities, the editorial goals of the *100 Mile House Free Press* demonstrate similar restraint by avoiding language that could promote stereotypes.

Labelling in Canadian Press News Stories

Table 6.2 identifies the number of labels in news stories, including those embedded in indirect quotations (IQs) in stories entirely written by Canadian Press. None of the news stories that were a composite of Canadian Press accounts and other media sources have been included because of the difficulty in determining the source of the labelling. For comparative purposes, I put the Canadian Press data in the numerator, in a ratio form, with total Canadian Press and non-Canadian Press data in the denominator for each of the newspapers.

Table 6.2 distinguishes the labelling found in Canadian Press news stories. During the period of the standoff, Canadian Press produced 58% of the news stories that yielded 71% of the labels in the cross-Canada sample. Canadian Press also authored 75% of the labels embedded in indirect quotes. Newspapers such as the *Calgary Herald* and the *Edmonton Journal*, which drew from a variety of sources or combined various stories, were more likely to minimize the labels in the editing process. If newspapers were generally reliant on Canadian Press for news accounts, however, the labels remained, unless they were edited at the local level. This appears to be the most likely explanation for variances in the newspapers east of Alberta that relied on Canadian Press. The *Toronto Star* data also support the heavy usage of invective labelling by Canadian Press. The significant reduction of labels in staff-authored accounts corresponds with the period in which the newspaper sent in its own reporter to cover the story. The quantitative results of the *Toronto Star* are consistent with the newspaper's reputation for moderate representations of minorities. A contrast in the Maritimes newspapers is found between the *New Brunswick Telegraph*

TABLE 6.2
Labels in News Stories Written by Canadian Press

Newspaper	CP Articles/ Total	CP Labels/ Total	CP IQs/ Total	Total CP Labels/ Total	CP Articles %	CP Labels %
Victoria Times Colonist	18/30	71/84	20/23	91/107	60	85
Vancouver Province	1/64	4/121	1/24	5/145	1.6	3.4
Vancouver Sun	1/83	6/191	0/25	6/216	1.2	2.7
Calgary Herald	24/37	70/96	12/14	82/110	65	75
Edmonton Journal	30/46	100/136	11/17	111/153	65	73
Regina Leader-Post	14	49	3	52	100	100
Saskatoon Star-Phoenix	17/19	40/45	16/16	56/61	89	92
Winnipeg Free Press	28	74	7	81	100	100
London Free Press	24/26	88/89	14/14	102/103	92	99
Toronto Star	18/25	63/73	7/8	70/81	72	86
Globe and Mail	66/80	240/250	56/58	296/308	83	96
Le Devoir	1	1	0	1	100	100
Montreal Gazette	18/22	56/70	11/11	67/81	82	82
Halifax Chronicle-Herald	6	21	6	27	100	100
Charlottetown Guardian	18	47	12	59	100	100
New Brunswick Telegraph Journal	0/6	0/4	0	0/4	0	0
St. John's Evening Telegram	24	84	16	100	100	100
Total	308/529	1015/1435	192/254 (75%)	1207/1689	58	71

Journal, which did not publish any Canadian Press accounts and had few labels,[4] and in other Maritimes newspapers, which relied entirely on Canadian Press and featured significant labelling. Last, the case of the *Globe and Mail* demonstrates the compounded effect of labels in the publication of multiple news stories from Canadian Press. The potential impact of stereotype labelling is increased because the *Globe and Mail* is distributed throughout Canada as a national newspaper.

Further comparisons of news stories authored by staff from individual outlets and by Canadian Press reveal several news production contexts that may have influenced the use of labels. One trend was an increased rate of use during periods of high activity, such as important developments in the police operation, the arrival of an important authority news source (such as Grand Chief Ovide Mercredi or Bruce Clark), and when tensions were high (especially after outbreaks of violence or foiled attempts at resolution). During these *peak* periods more stories were written, thus increasing the likelihood that the labels would be incorporated. Conversely, as the tension decreased and resolution seemed imminent, the number of labels was reduced. Another pattern is that if only one story was produced, covering several incidents and developments, a complex story with multiple sources and themes was provided, often featuring an increased reliance on labels. Stories about peripheral activities and incidents, stories that featured less authoritative sources, and human interest stories tended to have fewer labels. These patterns of representation were confirmed with the newspapers in the cross-Canada sample. Another trend was that if more than one reporter from the same outlet was covering or writing stories about the event, the likelihood of the appearance of labelling was greater. Increased staff usually meant that more stories were published per day, and both journalists would have been influenced by the tension of the situation (although not necessarily to the same extent).

The data imply that some outlets either had an editorial policy or made a decision regarding the language incorporated in news accounts. This point was confirmed by interviews with *Vancouver Sun* and Canadian Press journalists. Similarly, the quantitative data and interviews with the editor of the *100 Mile House Free Press* reflect a decision to curtail the use of these terms. This also appears to be the case with the *Toronto Star*, which stopped labelling during the time that its own journalist was covering the standoff. Yet within the group of newspapers that employed Canadian Press stories there was some evidence of editing at the local level: identical stories were published in several newspapers, showing some variation on the incorporation of labels. Similarly, when news stories were the product of a synthesis of newspaper sources, evidence of editing labels (both insertion and deletion) was found. I learned from the interviews with the journalists that individual journalistic style (which was evident in newspapers that rotated reporters) and editorial policies or newspaper traditions also influenced the frequency of negatively charged language. The *Globe and Mail*'s record of label usage demonstrates the impact of their publication of primarily Canadian Press stories, which ran concurrently, resulting in a pattern of high but stable use of labels during the month-long standoff.

The quantitative patterns of stereotype labels and the journalistic contexts suggest multiple reasons for their occurrence, but in spite of the debates over the appropriateness of using these terms to describe the camp, the print media samples in this research demonstrate that few outlets restrained this language for any sustained length of time. For several print journalists (at least), the use of these terms became part of their news production routines. The data also point to the effectiveness of editorial policies compared with occasional editorial attempts to neutralize the language, which suggests that prohibitive policies and conventions are also not as susceptible to external influences and news production pressures to engage in stereotypical representations. At the same time, it is important to note that the quantification of labels is only one measure of stereotyping in news stories. Headlines, story themes, rhetorical strategies, and grammatical structures used within the news narratives may contain other indications of stereotyping within media discourse. As previously discussed, damaging stereotype characterizations also were brought about by the RCMP labelling the people in the camp as *terrorists*, as well as by unverified and exaggerated details from the RCMP media sources. Therefore, it was possible for newspapers that seldom used labels to exhibit other features that contributed to stereotyping. Still, a more likely case (demonstrated by the contrast presented by *100 Mile House Free Press* and Canadian Press) is that the absence or prevalence of such labels is an indication of the potential of other stereotyping features.

Audience Responses to the Media Characterizations

How media audiences evaluated the news *performances* is an indicator of some of the outcomes and a validity check for the analysis of the context and products of the news. In this case study, *audience* is considered in two ways. Audience evaluation is regarded from the perspectives of leaders of those who were *on stage* during the event or involved in the reconstruction of the event for trial purposes. Chief Nathan Matthew, lawyer George Wool, and District Superintendent Len Olfert expressed concerns regarding the potential harm to the public identities of the people (or institution) that they represented due to audiences' reacting to sensationalist media coverage. The audience also included people who lived in the vicinity of the standoff. Audience interpretation of media messages requires each individual to evaluate the media messages within a frame of prior experiences, of attitudes and beliefs, and of what is perceived about the players and the situation portrayed in the news. In this way, multiple interpretations of the situation are possible. Large audiences may reach a consensus opinion, but there is always potential for segments of the audience to evaluate media messages much differently from the majority of people. What set apart the media audiences surveyed in this study were their differing resources and abilities to evaluate the news stories. Some audiences were close enough to the situation that they became peripheral players in the media coverage. This increased their interest in how the press characterized them or their group. Some of the people in the Native and non-Native communities in the area were concerned that the behaviours and beliefs of a few people might be interpreted as being representative of the whole group. In this situation, there were few options to control or correct the information that was transmitted to the media.

I begin this discussion with three individuals, who, because of their leadership roles in relation to the specific players in the conflict, were particularly concerned about how unfavourable audience impressions from the media coverage might damage the reputations and credibility of the groups that they represented.

Chief Nathan Matthew

Chief Nathan Matthew of the North Thompson Band was sceptical of the media coverage. Indeed, one of his primary functions as a media liaison for the Native intermediaries was to counter the RCMP portrayals to the media. **How would you characterize the RCMP portrayal of the dispute to the media?** *'I felt the RCMP put a deliberate negative spin on this for their own purposes. They really overplayed their hand. I felt that if they would have come to us in the beginning – a resolution would have been possible. There are also problems on our side – traditional chiefs versus elected chiefs – I'm elected – this creates a tension among us.'* Chief Matthew expressed concern about the lack of RCMP regard for the safety of the elders who were waiting for clearance to enter the camp area just as the firefight took place: *'This was a place where we really felt a lot of betrayal by the RCMP. We had put a group of our own people at risk. They [the RCMP] didn't tell us everything was booby-trapped.'* The characterizations that the RCMP gave the media concerning the camp may have strained relations even further between Native groups. At the same time, Chief Matthew found that Natives were also stereotyped. *'The RCMP really put a negative slant [on the protesters] – the old stereotype "vicious Indian."'* Chief Matthew also questioned the necessity of the manpower and equipment, since they also lent to the sensationalism in the media: *'Why did they need so many troops and armoured carriers?'* He found that *'the media were all out for the excitement – the blood, the guts, the drama –*

that's what I was really upset about. The media played up the violence' (interview with Chief Matthew, 17 February 1998).

Defence Counsel, George Wool

Defence lawyer George Wool was concerned about the media coverage and the potential impact on a fair trial for the defendants. This became one of the essential areas towards which he directed his defence research and strategy. Wool used television and newspaper stories from the Vancouver area to compare the facts with the media coverage. He said that he had formed his initial personal opinion of the conflict since the Williams Lake press conference, when the RCMP *'paint*[ed] *the Natives, if you will – as terrorists.'*[5] He said that once he was acting as counsel to some of the defendants, he learned that *'the RCMP withdrew that internally, because we found notes of the RCMP command to tell Montague to quit using the word "terrorists."'* According to Wool, the RCMP media strategy was so effective that *'when we went into the trial – we had our hands – one hand behind our backs, in the sense of a fight, because – it had already been decided – by the vast majority of people, that you had here – "bad people," "good people" ... And so – you start with this case – the media coverage was, I think, excessive, and I think it was very effective.'* Wool talked about establishing the media coverage as a primary concern during the trial *'to try to set out the point that the RCMP created the media, the publicity. And I wanted to get that out very quickly, so that the jury would understand that the police didn't go into this thing as an impartial group, attempting to gather evidence of a crime. They went in as a large media campaign, to first create these people as "bad" or "terrorists" and then, later, gather the evidence. So, my strategy was to get that point out rather quickly. Because I felt that the trial – the further it went on, the jury should have that point, and fast.'*

Wool had several concerns over the RCMP's release of inaccurate information to the media and failures to make corrections: *'What frightens me is the RCMP – and the media – they never checked out alibis, or attempted to verify accounts. The RCMP were more interested in getting news releases than verifying authenticity. Police lost sight of their role in the justice system.'*[6] In his estimation, the Gustafsen Lake standoff was a *'police constructed event ... I would say probably – 100%. 100%.'* In his estimation, the Williams Lake press conference was *'a self-created crisis'* that prevented a pre-arranged settlement meeting, which would have taken place a few days later.

As a former RCMP staff sergeant, Wool considered Gustafsen Lake *'an embarrassment'* and a departure from the values that he believed were the foundation of the RCMP's role. He confirmed that the negotiation tactics used by the RCMP during the Gustafsen Lake standoff were based on an American policing model for conflict negotiations. Wool assessed this model, as used at the Gustafsen Lake standoff, as counterproductive. He thought that it actually incited violent responses from the camp and was particularly unsuitable for negotiations involving Native people. Overall, he did not find the American police framework appropriate for a Canadian context. Nor was he impressed with the RCMP's media strategies employed during the Gustafsen Lake standoff: *'The most important thing you learn* [as an RCMP member] *is that you are the eyes and ears of the court – you have no responsibility to the media. There is an honest professional deference* [between the two institutions]; *the media is to provide a check on the RCMP, the RCMP is to represent the law.'* He raised the question: *'How close should the press be to the RCMP?'* In Wool's estimation, the Gustafsen Lake standoff was a situation in which the press and the RCMP became too close (interview with George Wool 26 May 1997).

RCMP District Superintendent Len Olfert

According to RCMP District Superintendent Len Olfert, the RCMP faced the dilemma of conducting a criminal investigation of serious weapons offences without access to a crime scene and scant physical evidence. As a result, *'we might have had trouble with convictions.'* Abandoning the standoff was not an option, and the RCMP were committed to ensure that the weapons and the offending parties were removed from the camp: *'So – you know – that was an extremely unusual situation, calling for some unorthodox methods that – you could throw out the rule book. And we threw out the rule book on* everything *– not just media. On every-*thing. *Like, we did things that – heretofore would have violated probably operational manuals in all kinds of respects.'* With regard to the *RCMP Operational Manual II.16 Media/RCMP Relations* protocols, District Superintendent Olfert stated, *'I didn't read that* [document] *at all.'* Another concern was the impression that the RCMP had discriminated against the Native people involved in the standoff. According to Olfert, *'There's two levels of policing – like, one for whites and one for Natives. And I think that the cultural impact on Native policing is on a much higher plane than it is for whites. Like, you have to be very sensitive and careful. And – there will be the exception – but it's a rare exception when members don't realize that – "you* *best be on your best behaviour because – you're just opening the door to too many things here.'* He received feedback reports about the effects of the standoff and the media coverage on the RCMP members: *'I don't know of how many on the other side, but a lot of members' lives have been affected forever. And some actually had to leave the force because of their involvement in this – in this situation'* (interview with District Superintendent Olfert, 17 February 1998). This is corroborated in Janice Switlo's *Under Siege*, an earlier work on the 1995 Gustafsen Lake standoff, in which she states: 'RCMP Emergency Response Team members disclose that prior to being dispatched, they were told to make sure that they had their Wills in order and to take care of any personal business necessary in the event that they would not return. These members were working long hours, sleeping as little as three hours at a time, with no days off. They were exhausted and edgy and as a result very volatile. These men were subjected to psychological manipulation designed to facilitate their cooperation in the slaughter of those at the Sundance site. It was intended that it not take much to set them off' (1997:24).

Olfert learned that after the standoff some of the officers had to seek counselling for sleeplessness and other stress-related conditions, all attributed to the Gustafsen Lake crisis. He described the logistics of containing the area with significantly fewer personnel than a military operation would ordinarily require. This was information that could not be relayed to the media at the time, *'Because – usually in an investigation where we involve our tactical teams, we have total control – isolate an area, contain it, set up perimeters, no one goes in, no one goes out here.'* Gustafsen Lake is a rural area that was difficult to contain without massive manpower. *'One military consultant told us that for them to contain the area, they'd need two battalions – and we were trying to do something with about – you know – 300 or 400 members, and not all of them deployed at any given time.'*

Aside from insufficient personnel, there were concerns for safety: *'So they're out there in the bush, not knowing if they're going to be hunted or not, you know. And that sort of thing played on the members' minds under pretty tough climatic conditions too.'* The stress, temperature fluctuations, length of shifts, and logistics of accommodations created the most difficult working conditions ever experienced by the RCMP.

In addition to the above circumstances, the media coverage was the only source of information about the standoff for many of the families of RCMP officers. In many instances, it was impossible for the officers to contact their families to advise them of what was happening: *'The family at home – sees the media coverage, and those members that have been shot at and the vests protected them, and information is not getting back to the families – where their loved ones are, and what they're involved with.'* According to District Superintendent Olfert, several members of the RCMP were pressured by their families to leave the force because of perceptions that the conditions were so dangerous. At least one officer left for this reason. *'So – those sorts of things were really, really tough on the members. And it – just never came out – you know – that sort of story.'* Olfert referred to the Gustafsen Lake operation as a *'logistical nightmare.'* Internal communications were insufficient to update families on what was happening: *'In an ideal world, what we would have probably is at least on each shift, one information person that does nothing but – you know, contact families and make sure that the whole unit knows what's going on. But because things escalated so quickly, and we just extended our resources to the max, right? These sorts of things weren't done. In retrospect, we're looking back now and saying, "Well, you know, that's probably an area that – " We didn't realize the impact of this thing, really, until it's over'* (interview with District Superintendent Olfert, 17 February 1998).

Summary

Although the above reflections represent perspectives of only three important players in the standoff and the trial, there is a sense of the diverse negative, immediate, and long-term effects of the media coverage. The co-construction, by both the RCMP and the media, of the characterizations of the camp had the potential of stereotyping and generating a public outcry for retaliation against the camp and Native people in general. The RCMP's lack of ethical judgment in the release of investigative information in advance of the trial, characterizing the people inside the camp as terrorists and criminals, and failing to immediately issue corrections to erroneous press releases that furthered these portrayals, potentially threatened the defendants' rights to a fair trial. Yet provision of corrected information for the jury would affect only a fraction of the people who potentially were misled by the media coverage.[7] Distortion of the event in the media also conveyed an unrealistic sense of fear and danger to the families of RCMP officers, who had no other sources of information. This circumstance revealed a recursion between the RCMP press releases, the media coverage, and police families as a hidden media audience.[8] The feedback responses to the

RCMP district superintendent about the RCMP families suggests that similar stress might have been experienced by families of the people in the camp, who also depended upon the media for developments of the situation. Thus, the sensational media coverage that promoted vilified stereotypes, accentuated violence and danger, and generated public outcries for police reprisals were potentially harmful to the people at the Gustafsen Lake camp. In addition, the above narratives point towards wider, socially disruptive impacts for Native and non-Native relations, RCMP morale, and public trust in Canadian law enforcement and the media.

Local Audiences

100 Mile House and the surrounding Native communities were the closest centres to the standoff, and how it was resolved would influence local Native and non-Native relations, as well as a collective historical memory, for years to come. In terms of the impact of the media coverage, one could surmise that they were standing on *ground zero*. If the situation did not end peacefully, this would be the region most closely associated with the standoff[9] and most likely the epicentre of any damage to social relations between communities after the police and the media had left.

Chief Antoine Archie

According to Chief Antoine Archie of the Canim Lake Band, many of the people living on the reserve were embarrassed and angry about the conflict, the potential repercussions, and the way associations of the conflict were being tied erroneously to their community. The media coverage increased the amount of attention given to the dispute and the aims of the camp, which most Native people in the area dismissed as lacking legitimacy. He described the *media circus* that occurred when the journalists arrived at 100 Mile House en masse. '[They] *were so excited when things were happening. When things got quiet, they* [the media] *started interviewing one another. We'd pick up the* Vancouver Sun *and these people they were interviewing were* [other] *reporters! They were interviewing one another for a while, for a couple of days'* [we both laughed]. '*But Steve* [Frasher, of the *100 Mile House Free Press*] *kept an eye on things.*' Subsequent to the standoff, Chief Archie and other local chiefs were pressured by various Native groups to make public statements in support of the Gustafsen Lake camp. Much of the rationale for joining their ranks was based on the way the camp was treated by the RCMP and the RCMP's use of the media. Chief Archie refused to make such statements, because *'they're not heroes,'* and there were many instances when those in the camp were disrespectful towards the local elders: *'I have to cut through the bullshit before I give anybody my support, and I don't think that a lot of people* [did] *that.'*

He found that his media celebrity was most evident when he went to 100 Mile House. *'The publicity? It was hard for me to live with for a while, there, right? Going to town – like, if I wanted to eat out – it was tough to walk into a restaurant – people, oh – you know – "Gustafsen Lake this, Gustafsen Lake that." All of this, eh? – People I didn't even know.'* Chief Archie recalled that one of the primary concerns during the standoff was the possibility that somebody would die, especially evident after the shooting death of Dudley George at Ipperwash, Ontario: *'We didn't want anybody to get killed. We didn't want any RCMP to get killed. We didn't want anyone of that group to get killed – because they would've. Because there are groups who would have made it some of their agenda – a later agenda. We wouldn't have had control over what happened after that'* (interview with Chief Archie, 25 July 1997).

Ranch Owners Lyle and Mary James

For Lyle and Mary James, the media coverage was not an important issue. During the standoff, they relied mostly on local newspapers and to a much lesser extent on Vancouver newspapers. They did not own a television. Lyle James did not feel bombarded by media attention during the standoff, although he did grant some interviews. Since the couple did not follow the media coverage very closely, they were unable to evaluate how close it came to their understanding of the situation. James knew that the RCMP had since been criticized for their handling of the standoff, and he acknowledged that *'probably they did make some mistakes.'* At the same time, *'I sure would not discredit the RCMP in any way. And – the RCMP handled it very well in the way it was done – that there was no loss of life whatsoever.'* He recalled that *'there was an* awful *lot of tension in 100 Mile House at the time.'* Despite the furore of the standoff, they described the way they made positive connections with Native people: *'Some, we wouldn't have met otherwise'* (interview with Lyle and Mary James, 27 July 1997).

Media Audience from 100 Mile House

The local people I talked to consisted mostly of people in the hospitality industry and shopkeepers – non-Native people who had lived at 100 Mile House between 5 and 20 years. 100 Mile House was in the media spotlight for almost a month during the standoff, which constituted the talk in coffee shops, barbershops, and generally everywhere in town where people gathered: *'We sold out of newspapers daily – no matter how many we brought in. And everybody –* everybody *was buying newspapers.'* Only a few residents attended the press conferences. *'You could sense – you would have one group there, one group there, and the media in the middle. There was a lot of tension. And you could see the potential that, if things got out of hand here and in the community, that you would have a very serious situation. So, one has to acknowledge and admire the players – whatever segment they represent, for maintaining a certain control in that sense.'* According to some of the people I talked to, local people were not approached by the media, unless the journalists *'thought there was a story'* (interviews with local some residents of 100 Mile House, July 1997). A local souvenir shop did a brisk business making commemorative 'Camp Overtime' tee-shirts for several of the members of the media as well as the visiting RCMP.[10] At the conclusion of the standoff, Staff Sergeant Martin Sarich of the 100 Mile House RCMP detachment placed a full-page thank-you notice in the *100 Mile House Free Press* to the residents of 100 Mile House and local communities.

The local schools attended by Native and non-Native students addressed the conflict by discussing the issues with the students and providing them with various perspectives. According to one teacher, this approach was important because her 'students came into class knowing only the picture painted by the media' and this caused tension between Native and non-Native students.[11] Chief Archie said that the people living on the Canim Lake reserve were embarrassed that their children, attending school in town, would have to endure potential taunts and criticisms from the other students. In addition, he recalled that some of the Native students attending the school located across the street from the RCMP Gustafsen Lake Operation Command Centre overheard operations personnel making racist comments: *'They could talk any way they wanted, and nobody could stop them'* (interview with Chief Archie, 25 July 1997).[12]

Yet many that lived in the vicinity felt disconnected from the standoff. The majority of the people inside the camp were not from the area, and the only significant change in town was the visibility of the RCMP and the media. The news accounts sometimes differed from information the local people heard on the scanners or from occasional veiled comments made by the RCMP officers, who were guests. There were periods during which the news accounts over the television and in the newspapers held little information: '*Actually, we would get a real chuckle out of – you know – like the reports that nothing was happening – desperate attempt to try and make something happen on the media! You know – through innuendo – or something like that – so that it made good copy.*' Television coverage, using visual shots of the town as a backdrop, provided a limited perspective. Many of the people considered that seeing their town on the television news was '*weird.*' '*Especially they did a lot over the top – they parked at Exeter – at Exeter Road there, over top of the fields. So, you see the field all the time, instead of the town, really ... It was like – there wasn't that much really of the town. They parked where the golf course is, and they looked out over the field, and, "this is 100 Mile!"*' (interviews with some local residents of 100 Mile House, July 1997).

It was common knowledge in the town that some of the people in the camp were slipping out after the barricades went up, and a few of the town folk mentioned this fact to the RCMP. But the residents did not seem especially concerned. Other than for an occasional fishing trip, few people travelled down the forestry road that led to Gustafsen Lake. Another reason was that the people most likely to escape were local and would be familiar with the area. Nobody regarded these individuals as particularly threatening. The large number of police staying in town also contributed to the sense of security. I found that the most frequent reason given for the local community's lack of fear was that Gustafsen Lake is 35 kilometres from town. Thus, the issue of public safety was raised by the RCMP during the standoff, based on their evaluation of the situation and not likely informed by reactions of people in the town.

Several people considered the police involvement and the media coverage of the standoff as '*overkill.*' '*We got a lot of misinformation, and they were telling people – the police were making up stories about what was going on – a lot of it. Mind you – we heard – we were listening on – like, through the scanner.*' Local residents heard many conversations over the scanners, including some in which they heard Wolverine cursing at the police negotiators. '*I think that the police did a good job in a lot of ways.*' Not everyone agreed with the RCMP's restraint towards the camp. One comment I heard during the fieldwork was '*I don't care if it's the Natives or whites – I don't care who it is – if something like that happens – I'd go in and blow them away. I mean – I wouldn't be playing games like they do. And it was a big game*'[13] (interviews with some local residents of 100 Mile House, July 1997).

It did not make sense to several of the people that it took 400 RCMP personnel to contain and defuse a situation involving 21 people. The people I spoke with considered that the money spent on the standoff and the trial did not reflect the kinds of criminal charges and jail sentences laid against the people who stood trial for the standoff. There was a perception that something was seriously out of proportion: '*And – I mean, the money that was spent was stupid. And – when it's all coming around now – well, a lot of them have been charged with mischief, and none – and a lot of not really serious things.*' One of the residents thought that the large media presence may have delayed the resolution: '*You take a situation like that – and if you took the media out of it – and say that – it just happened here, and it didn't hit all the news, or gained the notoriety – it would've been gone in two days*' (interviews with some local residents of 100 Mile House, July 1997).

Local residents were probably the best civilian audience to critically assess the media coverage of the standoff. These people were familiar with the area, and if they had been keeping up with the local news, they would have had prior knowledge of the Sundance and some of the incidents that had taken place in previous years. But the factor that most distinguished this audience from others was that many were listening to police communications from radio-scanners. In addition, a few people employed in the hospitality industry heard hints of information from RCMP officers with whom they had regular contact as clients; these unauthorized sources provided the residents with a comparative basis to judge what they were obtaining from the media. All of the people that I spoke with concluded that the *outside* media exaggerated the situation. They, unlike other audiences, noticed the efforts made by the media to fill news gaps when there were no developments in the dispute. However, only a few identified that the RCMP press releases contributed to the way the news accounts dramatized the event.

Local Media

The *100 Mile House Free Press* journalists had several advantages over the other media who gathered to cover the standoff. Aside from having reported on the Sundance since 1993, the newspaper staff were familiar with the seeds of the conflict and watched it escalate. They were aware of the sources who knew the background and the sources who made themselves available for interviews but who interpreted the conflict in terms of contentious issues or political agendas. The local newspaper did not use unauthorized police telecommunications because the staff knew it was illegal. According to editor Steven Frasher, *'We had the ability and stand back and refuse to be spoon fed – and take a week's worth of what was there and choose what was the most pertinent, or what was missed by others.'* They monitored the accounts from other outlets, but tailored their account according to specific editorial objectives. *'We felt for the long-term – more than the day-to-day, play-by-play sort of thing – it was more important for us to explain "what's happening – why," and try to put it in a context of – what is this going to mean for us as a community – both Native and non-Native, and working together after this is all over.'* Frasher explained that, for the *100 Mile House Free Press*, any one of the events, such as Grand Chief Mercredi's visit or the shooting incidents, would have been front-page stories. But during the standoff there were times when a week's worth of stories occurred on a single day: *'We had a real challenge to try to be fresh when* we *hit the streets – our once-a-week shot – on Wednesday morning.'*

Because the *100 Mile House Free Press* was a weekly newspaper, news stories of specific shooting incidents and developments were up to six days old. Its coverage of the dispute drew on a wider net of local sources than other media and, occasionally, comments from the attorney general. The newspaper provided more interviews with the Native chiefs in the vicinity than other newspaper outlets in this research. The accompanying photographs of the camp were published only during the time that media access was available, and they were not included later in the standoff as file photographs. Other pictures included scenes from Checkpoint 17, media sources, the bullet-riddled RCMP vehicle, the spectators at the 11 September firefight press conference, and the surrender scene with the helicopter containing Wolverine flying overhead. In contrast to the presentation of the firefight story by other newspapers in the sample, the *100 Mile House Free Press* headline was 'Bullets shatter peace prospects.'[14] However, the large accompanying photograph had nothing to do with the standoff. It was a scenic picture of a rainbow over rustic log buildings at the 108 (Ranch) Heritage Site. Frasher said that the choice of picture was deliberate: *'We did this because the local people were choking on what was happening – we wanted to lighten it up.'* The local newspaper's coverage of the standoff differed significantly from other newspapers, partly because it was not as dependent upon RCMP press conferences as the other outlets. In addition, the editor set specific objectives early in the conflict to cover the event without disrupting the relations between the local communities.

One aspect of the RCMP media operation that struck Frasher as being unusual was the RCMP's display of evidence that incriminated the camp for engaging in illegal activities: *'They hadn't gone to trial yet, and yet they're publicly exposing all the evidence against them – the police argued it was a public safety issue – but again, you see how far out* [the camp] *was.'* Frasher mentioned that, at 100 Mile House, the local RCMP detachment and the newspaper consider themselves responsible for ensuring that trial evidence or investigations are not compromised by the release or publication of inappropriate information: *'How are we better serving our community by doing that?'* Frasher did not have difficulty with being asked to withhold publication for security reasons, *'but it's another thing to lie to me.'*

Frasher considered the standoff *'a story that we're going to be watched for.'* It was going to be part of the provincial and national history, and the town's media coverage would be part of the historic record: *'We've got to get it right – we can't afford to get it wrong. We don't want to come across looking like "Mayberry RFD." And – at first bite, a lot of the big media tended to look at us that way.'* Frasher believed that the story had deeper implications that went beyond 100 Mile House. He reflected, *'Many people in town – to this day – can't appreciate that kind of pressure that the RCMP was under – that even if one of those people were seriously hurt or died out there – that would be a cloud that would affect that operation, affect the Native communities here, that had nothing to do with the people that were in that camp. And it would have put a cloud over this community that we'd never get rid of. And to that end, I think it's really admirable that – whatever forces were in play that kept that kind of conflagration from happening – are to be applauded, from whatever side they're from'* (interview with Steven Frasher, 23 July 1997).

Image Management by Local Native and Non-Native Communities

Local Native and non-Native communities shared the concern that the media coverage would stereotype them. In both cases, people were worried that the media would focus on extreme perspectives of those associated with their group, and audiences outside the vicinity would assume that these individuals were representative of their group. Most often, the select few who expressed extreme attitudes to the media were marginal in the community or from outside the community. False impressions would most likely occur because media outlets from outside the community lacked familiarity with the local people and local values.

The people in 100 Mile House could not escape the media spotlight – anything and anyone in town that might be connected to the conflict was a potential news story. The media covered street demonstrations protesting the standoff, which in turn attracted people from other parts of the province where there had been Native blockades. The presence of Native supporters and families of people in the camp, congregated across the street at the Red Coach Inn parking lot, heightened the sense of drama in these news clips. The spectacle of non-Native people carrying signs and placards and making comments to the media was an embarrassment for those who did not share these views. At the time of the standoff some local residents were worried that the media coverage would give the impression that the demonstrators were townspeople and that the town was racist: *'I didn't recognize one single face! And nobody else I talked to recognized a face.'* Some people said that there weren't any locals at the demonstrations, but others commented that a few townspeople with intemperate views were seen there. One person said, *'We know all of the Native leaders and the band and that – I mean, they get along with everybody. Nobody has ever had a problem, and they still don't have a problem. But the way the media was written up, and the radio – you'd swear 100 Mile was against the Natives. And none of these people – like you looked on the news – like – do you know anybody?'* The people who came from out of town to protest the standoff were not necessarily appreciated: *'Because it put us too much on the map. I mean, we got to be known!* It wasn't a good name! [laughs] *And it wasn't really something that we really – it's not a – noisy town'* (interviews with some residents of 100 Mile House, July 1997). To the media and the supporters (from various perspectives) who came to the town because of the standoff, the standoff might have appeared to be a Native versus non-Native, or a Native versus police, conflict. But most people from local Native communities, as well as from the town, recognized that such interpretations were simplistic.

Relatives and business associates from outside the vicinity contacted some of the residents to clarify the impressions left by the media coverage. There were questions as to whether the residents were wearing flak jackets, whether the standoff was disrupting the schools, and whether the town was barricaded. Some of the local businesses were directly affected: '*I had salesmen phoning up to see if they could get into town – because they were afraid the roads were all blocked, and they wouldn't be able to get near. I mean – the media coverage made it sound like it was right in the middle of town!*' There were a few hotel cancellations from Europe because of the perception (from the news) that the volatile situation was so close to the town (interviews with some residents of 100 Mile House, July 1997). Despite some journalists' attempts to avoid presenting the town as the site of the standoff, several people found, from outside contacts, that the media (particularly television) were giving the impression that 100 Mile House was under siege. The residents were left to smooth over the misunderstandings with extended families, hotel guests, and business associates living outside the area.

One person told me that the news coverage was so extensive that '*out-of-towners were telling us what was happening here!*' Nevertheless, this resident did not agree with, or appreciate, the outsiders' perspectives. One of the outcomes of the standoff is that some of the local people now are more conscious of media representation: '*Because, I mean, before you took it at face-value – what it was – you know – that they were reporting, what was happening. But now – it's sort of – you know – it's this – it's still the same – you know – from out-of-towners doing this, or is this the locals, or – you don't really know if what you're reading is what's happening*' (interviews with some residents of 100 Mile House, July 1997). If they had never reflected on them before, the local audience learned about the power and authority of the media during the standoff. The people I spoke with seemed to be jaded from the experience, and most viewed the media more critically than they did before the standoff.

For the Native communities, the potential source of stereotyping was the camp itself. The chiefs of the Canim Lake and Canoe Creek bands consistently presented their communities' political aims and values to the media as separate from those expressed by spokespersons at the Gustafsen Lake camp. Chief Antoine Archie was one of the first Native leaders to speak with the media during the beginning of the dispute: '*I talked to those reporters outside – with no backing or anything like that, and I gave them my side of the story – where I stood. I wouldn't back down, with these guys* [at the camp].' Overall, despite the rhetoric used by the camp with the media, which denigrated the British Columbia treaty process, Chief Archie did not consider the media coverage to have hurt the treaty process. He believed that one of the reasons was that he and Chief Agnes Snow of Canoe Creek were consistent in their comments to the media: '*Anytime we got interviewed by anybody there, they'd ask us what our stand was, we'd said, "We're going to negotiate. We're in the treaty process, and we're going to negotiate." We kept on repeating that all through that – all through that standoff.*' But he also felt that he had been unfairly '*criticized by some of the media that I had looked up to and respected,*' concerning his use of the Shuswap language in the CBC Radio message. '*And – You want to talk? I won't even talk to them*' (interview with Chief Archie, 25 July 1997).

A Question of Harm

The Gustafsen Lake standoff prompted the eruption of some of the most vilifying stereotype schemas between groups during Canadian peacetime. When the media became oblivious to their repeated use of negative stereotypes, the line between objective reporting and editorializing was blurred. The media's reliance on such depictions underscores the power of news production practices and editorial policies to transmit stereotypes of a minority group in a conflict situation. Unless they identified themselves as Native or were particularly sensitive to how their stories would be received by their audiences, journalists would have no idea about how their characterizations might inflame Native people. It is also doubtful whether they considered that the media portrayals, for the most part, fulfilled the negative side of a thematic dichotomy promoted by the RCMP: *law-and-order versus criminals.*

In this chapter we have seen that a variety of stereotype images found within the media characterizations of the standoff were damaging to the people at the Gustafsen Lake camp, RCMP members' families, and local Native and non-Native communities. These groups represent those who may have been compelled to take news accounts at face value because there were no other options, as well as those who had insider information about the conflict to discern the extent of the distortions. The audience responses affirm that news stories that include stereotypical images and language spanning several weeks at a time take on a life of their own, well beyond the event. The impact statements reveal a consensus that the media characterizations had been so internalized that they affected these people – personally, socially, and professionally.

In the larger picture, it is Native people across Canada who are most likely to experience long-term effects from the damaging stereotypes. Vilifying portrayals of volatile Aboriginal protesters connoted a social positioning of the camp, reducing people to fixed characterizations, rendering them justifiably disposable if the situation warranted. Yet the associated connotations of these characterizations are not so clear-cut that they would differentiate the people in the Gustafsen Lake camp from other members of Native communities where blockades or other protests have been held. The early references to the 1990 Oka standoff during the media coverage of the 1995 standoffs at Ipperwash and Gustafsen Lake established a coherence that linked these events. The Oka schema was transmitted through a media file photograph of a Mohawk warrior face to face with a Canadian soldier. The linkages between previous and current situations are also accomplished through the visual images and language used to portray the people involved. The association of these portrayals with a few Native people engaged in a contentious dispute might be offensive to some; nevertheless, they encouraged intolerance towards Native people in general. In my assessment, based on this study, the media's reliance on representations that promote stereotyping is pernicious, because once their characterizations are disseminated, it is impossible for media to control the impact on behaviours and attitudes in the future.

CHAPTER SEVEN

Wartime Images, Peacetime Wounds

In hindsight – we got used tremendously – like a cheap hooker – thoroughly manipulated.

Interview with journalist

The Gustafsen Lake standoff was an anomaly among other Native conflicts in Canada. Unlike the 1990 Oka and 1995 Ipperwash standoffs, there were no changes in ownership of contested land. Instead, those people from the camp whom the RCMP arrested were tried in a criminal court and convicted of a variety of offences. In retrospect, the dispute itself was insignificant. The ideological beliefs and the radical demands for terms of settlement by the camp spokespersons, the massive police operation launched to contain the situation, and the extensive media coverage inflated the conflict's importance in the press. In many ways, the event was like a small-scale war. However, the implications of the struggle over media representation of the event may prove to be more important than the *war* itself.

The media's involvement in the Gustafsen Lake standoff has been likened by some to a *media circus*. But dismissing the event as a media circus disregards the harm done to Native and non-Native relations, to RCMP morale, to the media's confidence in the RCMP, and to the public's trust in the media and the RCMP.[1] It avoids addressing the systemic aspects within media and the RCMP that contributed to the harm. When the standoff is judged insignificant, institutional practices and policies that contributed to the media coverage remain unquestioned, and the segment of society that gave the cues that allowed the characterizations to occur remains unchallenged.

The most influential institution in contemporary society is the media, a consideration that figures into the conduct of other social institutions. We live in an era in which institutions take greater control over their information, employing media specialists for the purpose of image management, which inevitably influences the news media. As Hackett and Zhao (1998) state, 'More and more of what passes for news is, in effect, commercial and institutional propaganda' (1998:178). This recognition does not diminish the fact that we continue to depend on the news in order to interpret the world in relation to our personal and social identities. Truth has social and cultural relevance and is central to the trust that news media establish with their audiences. The contradiction between the prevalence of image management and the dependence of the media on institutions providing them with reliable information has serious ramifications for current media research.

A Structural Approach to the Study of Media

Not all media research methodologies account for the real world of news production, despite the knowledge within the media profession that context plays a vital role in media outcomes. Text-based media analyses are limited in the data to be evaluated, which in turn curtails the appreciation of the contexts that underlie media representations. In these approaches media contexts are dismissed as either irrelevant, or generic in terms of the event, media outlet, and journalists involved. Findings tend to characterize media as either entirely responsible for media representations or having little or no agency against political and commercial entities that influence media characterizations. When news production practices are identified as the probable cause of particular representations in the news, hypotheses cannot be tested from within the same data collection. Any proposed explanations ignore the complexity of the circumstances and the lived experiences of the news producers that may be at play.

News discourse methodologies that discredit or ignore the truth-value of news also neglect a component of the discourse tied to the norms of journalists in western democratic society. Text analyses that interpret media products as fiction remove accountability from media and their sources because, in this paradigm, factual accounts are unimportant. This works in favour of powerful media sources, because in such research perspectives the evaluation of news, in terms of truth, accuracy, and representational adequacy, is considered irrelevant in the post-modern era. Although critical approaches detect bias, ideology, and racism – if the analyses are limited to examining lexical or grammatical features – they would still be unable to identify that the media message itself may be patently false. Furthermore, traditional discourse-centred news methodologies cannot deal with important social realities that the media fail to report in the news. Ultimately, research based entirely on textual data restricts contributions to public policy decisions.

Media theorists have long since identified that high-ranking sources usually carry the greatest influence in representations in the news. They tend to accept this as an inevitable outcome of the hierarchy of media sources, synonymous with *the way things are*. Consequently, media research recommendations often suggest that audiences be educated in critical media literacy as a countermeasure. Nevertheless, critical literacy skills have their limitations. Critical literacy still hinges on textual skills and constrains any appreciation of actual media contexts. More important, placing the locus for social transformation on the media audience is another way of accepting the status quo within the media industry; it shifts the responsibility away from the media organizations and their influential media sources to the consumers of their products. In this way, research approaches that are limited to news discourse and in which media contexts are glossed over inadvertently become accomplices with regimes and agendas to contain public knowledge, to limit investigations, and to minimize the potential for social transformation.

This case study shows the importance of the milieu of journalists, their routines, their negotiations with sources, and the influence of the unfolding event on the media outcomes. The unification of media texts and contexts in a comprehensive research approach makes it possible to discern underlying causal factors that otherwise might have remained unnoticed. These factors, in turn, offer greater specificity to inform public policy and to facilitate change at systemic levels.

Structural elements are at the heart of institutional relations, practices, and policies that underpin the media products. Because of their hidden nature (media and their sources rarely advise the public how they negotiate information) these elements are prone to reproduce over time. In the preceding six chapters, we have seen how the dispute was transformed from a local news story to a national news event. News production processes, routines, and adaptations to the situation were examined to show how they influenced the news characterizations. The details of the event and the perspectives of journalists and their sources allowed for several strategic analyses of specific episodes at a micro level. These analyses identify how the media and their sources competed and struggled for the controlling frame of the news accounts and how institutional factors subdued competition and promoted the near-hegemonic dominance of the news narrative by the RCMP. In chapter 5 the underlying processes of stereotype construction and the dissemination of stereotypes to a national audience were considered, and several groups adversely affected by the media coverage were documented.

In this final chapter, we will look at several of the macro-level structural elements that influenced the overall media coverage of the 1995 Gustafsen Lake standoff. The chapter concludes with a discussion of public policy with regards to the media, the RCMP Media Relations Program, and an update on the Gustafsen Lake standoff.

Macro-Level Structural Elements Influencing the Media Coverage

Tension of the Situation and Media Proximity to the Police

The identification by some of the journalists with the tension experienced by the police was a contributing factor in the media representations. The trial testimonies of several RCMP (including ERT) members revealed that they were unable to remain emotionally detached from the conflict. One journalist stated that the RCMP conveyed this tension in their press releases before they set up the barricades: '*I had a real concern that this would lead to bloodshed. And so the tension grew through this thing. You had the sense (certainly through Montague) that it seemed a point of pride – that they* [RCMP] *couldn't be seen to be backing down from this challenge to their authority ... It became a bit of a concern that you could have some sort of state-sanctioned slaughter.*' One of the reporters had been to Croatia, and he said that Gustafsen Lake was much more volatile. Everyone I interviewed considered Gustafsen Lake an extreme in terms of journalistic coverage, conflicting perspectives, logistics, and representations of people and events. The combination of sustained attention to one story, exhaustion, and response to the stress of the situation likely accentuated the importance of the developments in the news accounts: '*People became really obsessed with this whole little world around 100 Mile House. There were other things happening in the world*' (interviews with journalists). Of all of the media, only the local newspaper staff covered a variety of news events that were not related to the standoff. The other journalists were focused entirely on the standoff story, and, for those who were not rotating shifts with colleagues in Vancouver, there were few opportunities to take a day off.

The RCMP's scheduling and pacing of their press conferences contributed to the hold that the police had on the media, and the reporters' exhaustion kept them from seeking other sources outside the immediate area. Journalists were afraid that they would miss an important breaking-news announcement. Some reporters were aware that the RCMP media personnel were reining in the media: '*Keep'em all at one place at one time. And that's where you get the information – is the press conference – where everybody has to be there, you know*' (interview with journalist).

Information management meant that, on most occasions, the RCMP carefully doled out sketchy information to the media, and rumours and details from unauthorized sources were seldom, if ever, validated by the RCMP media liaison. On the other hand, the RCMP's pattern was to report shooting incidents initiated by the camp and then to have their media personnel supply journalists with detailed accounts. Through media pools, the police controlled media's movements, and minimized the potential of alternative interpretive frames. Since pool arrangements were intended to provide audio and video materials to the larger group, the journalists were obliged to take powerful sources at their word.

The RCMP barricades and the loss of access to the camp increased the media's dependence on the police, but decreased the opportunities for critical or investigative journalism. Media had to trust that the RCMP would provide accurate details about the developments in the conflict and the conditions facing the people inside the camp. Similarly, RCMP threats of legal action ensured that most of the journalists would refrain from using unauthorized radiotelephone transmissions in news accounts, and thus the supremacy of the RCMP press releases for police information was preserved.

The incorporation of the media into the RCMP investigation and operational strategies also blurred professional boundaries between the two groups. Such situations included the complimentary transportation; the confiscation of media materials; and the involvement of journalists in police strategies such as the 'smear campaign,' the media tours, and the display of evidence under investigation. The confiscation of CBC video-recordings of the camp calls into question the RCMP's actual motives for risking the safety of journalists, who were allowed to enter the camp in spite of the RCMP's declaration that the protesters had engaged in acts of terrorism. The interactions between the media and the RCMP media personnel point to the various ways in which the media and the police helped each other. However, police-arranged news-gathering opportunities made it difficult, even for outlets that normally avoid close identification with sources, to remain impartial.

For the most part, those Vancouver journalists already sensitized to exploitation by RCMP media personnel believed that during the stand-off the exploitation simply became more blatant. However, several less critical journalists experienced a shift during the standoff, and certainly during the trial: they no longer hold their former degree of trust in RCMP media personnel.

Media Cooperation and Competition

Both cooperation and competition were evident in the relations be-tween different media throughout the standoff. Often during major news stories media observe what competitors select for their top sto-ries, the type of information that is conveyed, and the angles of the various news accounts. Since the electronic media face frequent dead-lines throughout the day, newspaper journalists keenly attend to the coverage given by television and radio. The uniqueness of the Gustafsen Lake coverage, however, did allow journalists to develop closer friend-ships with colleagues and to share the media material in a manner that had seldom occurred during previous news events.

Yet competition was a primary structural element that drove the media during the standoff and it was manifested in several ways. Competition was one of the main reasons why several outlets remained committed to covering the standoff until the end, despite growing disenchantment that they were being manipulated and their exorbitant expenditures on equipment and labour.[2] This competition ensured that none of the outlets would abandon a story that rivals were providing to an eager audience. Jockeying among the media for favourable status with the police media personnel also perpetuated perceptions of an inner circle of *media favourites*. At the same time, journalists faced a dilemma: '*If you try to get too chummy with the cops, you have this tendency to get yourself into a position of conflict ... And, of course, you're relying on the police for all of your information by this time, right? So, are you going to burn your source?*' (interview with journalist).

Some journalists ignored this aspect of competition and remained at a distance from the RCMP media personnel. It was difficult for them to accept that other members of the media openly fraternized with a powerful media source during such a conflict. *'I don't like getting buddy-buddy with authority figures – I have distant relationships. He* [Sergeant Montague] *didn't like it – that I didn't suck up to him, I didn't chit-chat with him'* (interview with journalist). Nevertheless, journalists' efforts to distance themselves from the RCMP media personnel did little to alter their dependence on the RCMP for information or to increase the reliability of the information that the RCMP media personnel relayed to them.

Yet there were occasions when attempts were made to respond as a cohesive unit for the common good. Some of the reporters considered staging a media boycott of the camp when the camp leaders refused them access but scrapped the idea when they realized that those journalists already granted access to the camp would not relinquish their competitive advantage over other outlets. They were more successful later, when the journalists excluded from the television media tour of Camp Zulu pressed for a similar news opportunity. However, competition between journalists may have prevented them from developing a sustained, unified front to counter strategies employed by the RCMP media personnel to control the media. There was never a hint that some of the other journalists might join the *Vancouver Sun* in its bid to resist the RCMP's media domination. To some extent, friction within the media (which is mildly present under ordinary circumstances) may have been encouraged by the RCMP media personnel: *'Towards the end, I think it was almost a divide and conquer attitude among the RCMP with the media. By picking their favourites they could do it that way'* (interview with journalist).

Media Bias

The journalists recognized that their own biases and editorial policies also shaped the way that they cast their stories: *'Some media threw their objectivity out the window. Once you stop trying ... subjectivity lets loose.'* Although the RCMP controlled much of the information, individual outlets could choose how they represented police information and how they presented the news story. Media outlets that had a policy or a plan to regulate the type and presentation of news were less likely to conform to the pressures of publishing information in the manner conveyed by the RCMP. Yet even the most persistent efforts of the media outlets (including the *100 Mile House Free Press*) could not have verified the accuracy of the details of the shooting incidents as they were provided by the RCMP media personnel. Therefore, all media outlets regularly covering the event contributed in some way to presenting a bias that favoured the RCMP.

Media Resistance

Most journalists attempted to balance the story with other perspectives. The *Vancouver Sun* offered the greatest contest to the RCMP official interpretations, but this approach initially involved testing, if not breaking, the law. The *Vancouver Sun* was also the most forthright in printing editorials relating to the circumstances of the RCMP operation, which circumvented media witnessing and greater investigative coverage. One *Vancouver Sun* reporter concluded: *'If I was able to go in today ... I would be far, far more aggressive with the police. And I don't think any police officer's life was put in danger by what we did. As a matter of fact, I think if we had done a better reporting job, there probably would have been less danger to the lives of the police officers. I think they sort of got – I think the RCMP got kind of out of control there, with their big macho plans to stop things. And you know, had we been able to portray that at the time in the media, maybe somebody would have yanked their chains a bit, and have them back off sooner'* (interview with journalist).

   Vancouver Sun editor, Gary Mason, interpreted the threats he received for publishing radiotelephone conversations as another means to level the competition between the media and to prevent important information about the camp from getting out to the public: *'My biggest ... concern I had about the coverage in general was that we were only getting one side of the story. That was really the crux of our concern. Everything that we knew, heard, anything about that – was all coming through the RCMP.'* According to Mason, the *Vancouver Sun*'s coverage of the Gustafsen Lake standoff provided a sense of excitement, energy, and resourcefulness that is rarely sustained over the course of one event: *'It did wonders for the morale of the newsroom. To see us going out there, way out in front of everyone else, and just saying, "Yes!" That's just great!'* (interview with Gary Mason, editor of the *Vancouver Sun*, 6 November 1996). Mason maintained that there was little or no real risk to lives and that the public should have access to alternative perceptions of the situation, rather than those based on the police interpretations alone. Yet outside British Columbia the *Vancouver Sun*'s reach did not extend to the majority of the Canadian media audience (see chap. 4, n.16).

Media also resisted the RCMP by publicly commenting on the situation after the standoff. However, few outlets broached the topic of police media strategies with their audiences. A few days after the CBC sent a letter of complaint to the RCMP (19 September 1995),[3] CBC Television broadcast 'The Standoff at Gustafsen Lake' during *The National*.[4] The documentary made an oblique reference to the RCMP involving the unwitting media in their operational strategy. It characterized the conclusion of the standoff as a successful collaboration between local Native communities and the RCMP. There was no mention of the contentious CBC Radio message, the RCMP confiscation of CBC materials, or errors in RCMP press releases (which would have surfaced by this time) in the CBC's review of the event. Indeed, the most critical evaluation of the RCMP operation came from interviews with Chief Nathan Matthew. The *Vancouver Sun* and *Vancouver Province* published critical news stories, commentaries, and editorials when the standoff ended and when questionable RCMP media strategies were examined at trial.[5] Yet these disclosures of manipulation failed to grasp the breadth and variety of incidents in which the RCMP compromised media ethics in the implementation of their media plan.

Media Empowerment

Few of the journalists believed that they could have prevented the RCMP from manipulating them during the Gustafsen Lake standoff story. Once committed to covering the event, journalists had to accommodate their coverage to the overriding circumstances of the RCMP instituting their operational plan. Press conferences, though usually weak on content, became important news events in themselves, rather than one source of news. Although journalists realized that the conflict was more complex than the RCMP were presenting it, for the most part they accepted the police version at face value: '*There was still a belief that what the RCMP told you – if they – even if they weren't telling you a lot, what they did tell you had to be the truth. That there was a reliance upon them – since they weren't giving you anything anyway. If they did give you something, there was no point in giving it to you unless it was true.*' For most of the journalists interviewed, taking the RCMP perspective at the time was common sense.

Yet during this research, many of the journalists criticized the police manipulation, identifying themselves as unwitting victims: '*In hindsight – we got used tremendously – like a cheap hooker – thoroughly manipu-*

lated.' A few directed blame on the fallibility of the media itself: '*I don't believe everything I read in the newspaper, you know, so I have no – and I work for newspapers, so I hope people don't.*' Others took a more philosophical approach, saying that the manipulation of the media by the police is a normal situation: '*The cops always have the media as their plan. I mean, that's a given ... you shouldn't be a reporter if you believe otherwise.*' According to another reporter, awareness of the manipulative situation did not provide any strategies for resistance: '*But it doesn't mean you can do anything about it.*' This reporter hedged his accounts with '"*RCMP said" ... but it doesn't do much – it's gospel once you say it.*' Other reporters said that, if they had been more open with their audiences about the questionable accuracy of some of this information, they would have felt more credible. Several journalists stated that the most offensive part of the experience was the way the RCMP media personnel had blatantly lied to them and betrayed a trust that the media must have in law enforcement sources: '*Probably the most glowering thing is the fact that – while they're talking about sanctity of life and a desire not to have violence, that they go ahead and try to kill somebody. I find that beneath their integrity, probably ... But, in retrospect, I think they should have levelled with us, and said so ... I think that they should have said – "In the midst of all this, with the pressure, we made a mistake, and we did this. ..."*' (interviews with journalists).

Time Factor

Nobody – police, media, or media sources – could have foretold from the early days of the conflict that a resolution would take so long to achieve. The duration of the standoff, deadline demands, and the tension of the situation wore the media down. Some journalists were concerned that, over time, their stories might have conveyed a bias favouring the police because of their prolonged dependence on the RCMP for news stories. This dependence was not one-sided: the longer the conflict dragged on, the more the police put the media's resources to use for their operational plan. Over time, the RCMP's ability to convey accurate information to the media appeared to have decreased proportionately, culminating in their silence concerning the shooting incident with the person walking near the lake. Conversely, the success of several RCMP media strategies (to involve the media in their operational plan) depended upon restricting time, which forced journalists to make hasty decisions. Thus, the element of time contributed to the dramatization and police bias in the media portrayals and lent itself to the RCMP co-opting the media resources for their operational plan.

Eclipse of Insider Definitions by Outsiders

The distinction between insider and outsider law enforcement and media helps to explain why the adjacent Native and non-Native communities felt disengaged from the RCMP's operation and the mass media coverage of the standoff. The police and media who lived in the vicinity were connected in the social network by professional as well as personal ties. As members of the community, they had a personal stake in events that affected the region, and they were cognizant of how their professional roles fit into the functioning of the neighbouring communities. In the early days of the conflict at Gustafsen Lake, their assessment of the situation incorporated professional as well as local frames of reference. The shift from insider to outsider perspectives occurred when the 100 Mile House RCMP detachment called for additional assistance, which positioned the local police (by choice) and the local media (by circumstance) at the periphery of the event. Thus, community policing and media values associated with the region became subsumed in the arrival of outside police and media, who took their lead from outside the local sphere.

Both the police and the media outsiders were in a transient relationship to the town. The RCMP gathered to conduct the standoff operation and to create an organization and a planning structure separate from those of the local RCMP detachment. The journalists from outside the area were, for the most part, reporting to Vancouver or head offices in eastern Canada; they were focused on the tasks required for their assignments, which were independent of local awareness or sensitivities. Faced with demands for involvement in assigned work duties, they had little time to develop connections at the local level. The size of the police and media contingencies, the equipment brought in to facilitate their assignments, and their identification as members of their institutions who were performing specific functions during the conflict created near-separate perceptual universes from the local community. Thus, it is not surprising that the identities and values of the local communities became peripheral during the standoff. The Gustafsen Lake standoff truly became a situation of 'outsiders telling locals what was happening,' leaving the local communities to recover in the aftermath. This issue will be revisited, later, in the discussion of public policy.

Cultural Misperceptions

Several underlying cultural misperceptions, involving the media as well as the RCMP, emerge in the examination of the event and the media coverage. The journalists were not equally at ease dealing with Native people and showed a wide range of experience and knowledge about Native culture and issues. Covering this hectic news story did not allow many occasions for media and Aboriginal people to develop relationships beyond a superficial level. One opportunity for cross-cultural sharing took place at the Alkali Lake meeting, when people from the Shuswap community invited journalists to participate in the sweatlodge ceremonies. On another occasion they met Arvol Looking Horse, Keeper of the Sacred Pipe, whom many of the Native people venerate, and the media characterized him as the Aboriginal 'Pope.'

Yet research interviews and the newspaper accounts give evidence of journalists' cultural misunderstandings about Native people and their traditions. There were news stories that implied that a *spiritual vision* to hold the Sundance at Gustafsen Lake prompted the standoff.[6] The cross-section of newspaper stories represented a theme of conflict between Aboriginal spirituality and western understandings of property ownership.[7] Several journalists incorporated the perspectives of Sundance practitioners and academic sources to explain the Sundance ritual, including news stories that emphasized the secret and violent aspects of the ritual.[8] However, some accounts associated the recent introduction of the Sundance at Gustafsen Lake (and its origins outside the Shuswap tradition) with the questionable authenticity of the demands of the camp. This created an air of suspicion about the introduction of the ritual into the Cariboo region. The Vancouver-based media characterizations overlooked the fact that most of the local Sundance practitioners did not support the people inside the camp. Even with this appreciation, a group of local Native elders and leaders felt compelled to destroy the remnants of the arbour to discourage future Sundances at Gustafsen Lake and to distance themselves from the notoriety of what had transpired there. Language barriers also fed into the mistrust, as exemplified by the concerns raised about the appropriateness of the Shuswap message broadcast over the CBC Radio. It is reasonable to expect that none of the media understood the Shuswap language, yet familiarity with the local chief who provided the message was likely within their control.[9] These representations of the conflict went beyond the media's support of the RCMP's interpretive frame of the Gustafsen Lake standoff, which, according to District Superintendent Len Olfert, was concerned with weapons and shooting offences. The commanding officer was emphatic that the operation had nothing to do with religious practices or the dispute over land ownership.

There also were examples of RCMP officers acting on misperceptions about Native people. Throughout the region, RCMP stopped Aboriginal people going about their business on suspicion of being involved with the protest. Native students in town complained that they overheard RCMP officers using racial epithets. According to trial records, some ERT members stated that they feared sleeping at night in the bush lest they be 'scalped' (Switlo 1997: 24). The RCMP who led the media tour of the Gustafsen Lake camp represented *all* of the dugouts as being constructed for strategic defence, although some were, in fact, traditional Shuswap pit houses built in previous years. We will examine the RCMP misperceptions in the discussion of public policy, below.

News accounts that associated Native spirituality with contributing to or causing the conflict augmented the already apparent suspicion, fear, and lack of empathy between Native and non-Native people, as did law enforcement characterizations of physical evidence at the camp to the media before confirming the facts or, for that matter, before a trial. There is little doubt that these misunderstandings led to misrepresentations in the media that could encourage intolerance of Aboriginal people.

Wartime Images, Peacetime Wounds

The conditions that permeated the Gustafsen Lake news coverage parallel media and military institutions during wartime situations. A few journalists recognized the tactics as being similar to those used by the American military during the 1991 Persian Gulf War: '*Basically, the more this thing dragged on, the more we really felt – it was – almost like the B.C. version of the Kuwait War. Where the ... Pentagon and the U.S. government did such an unbelievable job of controlling the message. And the RCMP – it was a mini-version of that – that they were doing exactly the same thing, employing exactly the same strategy, in terms of controlling where the media could go, exactly the information that they were going to get on a daily basis, making sure that they didn't have access to the opposing forces. So, I mean, that's why – the more we thought in those terms, the more that I got fired up*' (interview with Gary Mason, editor of the *Vancouver Sun*, 6 November 1996). Another reporter stated, '[Montague] *just does not understand the role of media in a democratic society. Media acts as a check on the police – pestering the police is a good thing. Montague doesn't understand this – doesn't think it's a problem to take over access to sources. He just doesn't get it, and that scares me.'* There was a sense that, at the Gustafsen Lake standoff, the RCMP were not compelled to be accountable to the public and could legitimately *'write their rules as they went along.'* Consequently, those journalists who were frustrated by this situation had no one with whom they could lodge complaints: *'This goes back to the fundamental concern most people have – who polices the police? ... Who are you gonna phone? The mayor? The premier? The attorney general?'* (interviews with journalists).

A short time after the Gustafsen Lake standoff, RCMP media personnel held a media debriefing in Vancouver for select media that the police advised was off-the-record. During this meeting, RCMP media personnel confirmed that they employed some of the same media strategies used during the 1991 Persian Gulf War. One journalist described the RCMP debriefing: *'The RCMP referred to the incident as an example of how media and the RCMP cooperated. I'm not so sure. We knew we were getting a controlled version of reality – but no other reality was legally possible.'* Another journalist recalled that, at this meeting, the RCMP acknowledged that they disregarded their media protocols. They justified their actions with the 'end-justifies-the-means' principle that the standoff had ended without injury or death. Their argument was similar to the idea, *'We pulled it off, didn't we?'* He left the meeting *'wondering if I was given the straight goods, or if I'm getting the stage-managed version'* (interviews with journalists). It seemed that the debriefing was an attempt to placate the media and characterize the RCMP's media relations at Gustafsen Lake as a success. The RCMP rationale at the time did not consider that their media strategies undermined media and police ethics and, in a broader sense, the principles of a pluralist democratic society.

Public Policy and the Media

There were several news production and other contextual factors that led to the media's stereotyping of Aboriginal people and to the journalists' being manipulated by the RCMP media personnel. An appreciation of these factors can provide the basis for Canadian media to set their own guidelines in anticipation of future occasions when they will encounter these issues.

Outlets that had established guidelines and conventions concerning the representation of the conflict and the players, as well as their responsibility for future social relations, were less susceptible to external influences. Consequently, they were less likely to engage in inflammatory stereotypical representations. Conversely, those outlets that did not have guidelines regarding these issues were more easily swayed by the RCMP information management strategies. Further, even when individual journalists *were* sensitive in their representations, their superiors or peers did not always support them. This emphasizes the importance of media's establishing their own guidelines in anticipation of such news-gathering contexts. This case study identifies several areas for policy development.

Stereotyping in media products was, in part, the result of journalists' (and their superiors') remoteness from the context of the local community and their own diverse audiences. Most journalists wrote for their editors and within the interpretive frames and traditions of their employers. Consequently, their sensitivity to the social consequences of their characterizations was diminished. In addition, many journalists from the large media outlets seemed to be perceptually unaware of their engagement in the process of building and transmitting stereotypes. Policy alternatives should include making greater efforts to connect with local media and local audiences for news stories and becoming more self-critical of representations and consequences of representations.

Journalists who lacked an understanding and an appreciation of Native cultural traditions were more susceptible to sensationalizing unfamiliar religious practices, making simplistic inferences, and insensitively representing Native traditions. This finding identifies the need for journalists to become better informed about Native cultural values and practices, including those journalists and editors who compose the headlines. Media personnel need to increase their awareness of the tendency to create false dichotomies that perpetuate an *us against them* theme that surfaces particularly during social conflicts involving Native people. These false dichotomies (such as contrasting Native spirituality or religious practices against non-Native values) offer symbolic representations over which media have no control once they are published or broadcast. News practices that minimize the construction and transference of stereotypes of Native people should encompass language and visual representations as well as sensitivity to the diversity of media audiences.

The coercive relations between the media and the RCMP were more apt to occur because of news reporting traditions that withheld contextual details of how media negotiated and interacted with their powerful sources. The level of reality that media traditionally make available to the public is composed of the media products of the news gathering. When the underlying news production circumstances of a news event become public information, previously unknown levels of reality are revealed: the structural relations between the media and their sources in their negotiations and struggles to construct a definition of the situation in the construction of the news. When media include this contextual information in the news products, they integrate different layers of reality, bringing hidden aspects of the news to the surface. On such occasions, a traditional news schema is breached. Instead of observing and interpreting, the journalists identify themselves to their audiences as active players in the news event.

During the Gustafsen Lake standoff and the trial, a few journalists and media outlets, on occasion, did adapt to the situation by reporting on the context of the news gathering. This point was demonstrated in the CBC Radio program, *Now the Details*, in which the ethical conflict that developed between CBC Radio and the RCMP was discussed. In addition, news stories and editorials in the *Vancouver Sun* and the *Vancouver Province* critically examined the use of the media in the RCMP operational plan.[10] These findings support media outlets' experimenting with news communication formats that allow journalists to emerge as active players in the event that they are reporting, an approach that would provide openings for media to examine their ethical issues in the public arena and to generate public debate. Such a development would be radical. It would shift the relations of power between media and important sources, but force both to become more accountable to the public. Innovative news practices that reveal more about how news is negotiated with sources would promote an empowered, democratized journalism and a more open society.

Public Policy and RCMP Media Relations

This case study uncovers a fundamental contradiction between RCMP practice and policy during the Gustafsen Lake standoff. In spite of the organization's rhetoric concerning community policing, non-discriminatory practices, and professionalism, the case study reveals the fallibility of systemic components that are supposed to ensure the functioning and integrity of the force. The RCMP's need for security while carrying out their operation curtailed their mandate of being more transparent to the public. Nevertheless, even after it was no longer an issue, the

RCMP's transparency was confounded by their reluctance to admit to the public that they had made mistakes and that these mistakes had resulted in serious public harm.[11]

The RCMP offered several rationales to explain their conduct with the media during the Gustafsen Lake standoff. Police personnel implied that their extreme interpretation of the situation justified their lack of compliance with established media guidelines. The RCMP's trial testimony and interviews with them suggest that the hectic pace of the police operation might have contributed to poor communication channels to the RCMP media section.[12] During the trial, the police claimed that because the standoff was a life-and-death situation, several departures from standard police procedures were necessary.[13] District Superintendent Olfert testified that unverified information was released to the media to 'prevent reporters from talking to people on the street.'[14]

Yet in the United States recent criticisms of the Federal Bureau of Investigation (FBI) show that the RCMP are not the only law enforcement agency caught up in image management and 'spin control.' The trend for law enforcement agencies to adopt a corporate culture accentuates the importance of both public relations and media influence. Critics believe that this emphasis risks subverting the role of law enforcement within the framework of a democratic society.[15] Furthermore, in Janet Chan's study of racism within the police culture in New South Wales, Australia, it is shown that law enforcement's commitment to openness and accountability does not necessarily lead to a positive police image. Instead, it has the potential to open the proverbial Pandora's box, with law enforcement agencies becoming increasingly defensive and protective of their internal operations. Adverse publicity threatens to expose weaknesses and systematic abuses, compelling law enforcement organizations to find scapegoats and to minimize the issue by disclaiming embarrassing revelations as aberrations (1997:185). Ironically, the media most often act as both the cause of and the remedy for public humiliation of law enforcement agencies. Current criticisms of the FBI, along with the RCMP media relations concerning the Gustafsen Lake standoff, support this finding. These three examples also illustrate that in spite of managerial initiatives and policies to promote transparency, there is an offsetting response by the law enforcement agencies to expend resources and energies to engage in 'damage control' with the media. This circular response is a serious obstacle to identifying systemic discrimination and to instituting sustainable policing reform.

A comparison of the media outcomes in light of the *RCMP Opera-*

tional Manual II.16 Media/RCMP Relations (see appendix 7 for pertinent excerpts) reveals that this crisis would have benefited from these established guidelines. Many of the errors of misinformation and breaches of ethics that jeopardized a fair trial could have been avoided. The protocols might have prevented press releases and their delivery from being influenced by the emotion and stress of the situation, and adherence to the protocols might have mitigated the damage to the RCMP's reputation when allegations of media manipulation were made public during the trial.

Subsequent revisions in 1997, 1998, 1999, 2000, and 2001 to the *RCMP Operational Manual* provided further support for this sort of crisis.[16] This includes referring to the federal level the media coordination of incidents that might gain national attention. 'Divisions are to notify the National Communications Services Branch of any local incidents/occurrences which might be of a sensitive nature and are likely to be the focus of national/international interest. The coordination for any RCMP response to such incidents will be the responsibility of the National Communication Services Branch, Public Affairs and Information Directorate' (M/R C.5 and M/R F.8). Other provisions are more specific to conduct with the media. 'RCMP employees will provide the media with prompt, courteous and impartial service' (M/R C.3). 'Confirm the obvious by covering the 'who,' 'what,' 'when,' 'where,' 'why,' and 'how' of situations (5Ws and H) without identifying individuals' (M/R E.1.a). 'Never release the name of a suspect. Once charges have been laid the accused's name may be released as public information. This information is also available from the court docket' (M/R E.1.b); 'Do not speculate or offer your opinion. Report only the facts' (M/R E.1.c.); 'Always protect the integrity of the criminal investigation. Do not discuss or comment on ongoing investigations' (M/R E.I.e). RCMP officers currently have as a reference a media handbook, *RCMP and the Media: A Spokesperson's Guide* (1998). In particular, they are advised that all RCMP officers potentially will deal with the media, and therefore the information contained in the handbook is relevant to all members. Outlined are methods of building successful media relations, dealing with crisis situations, and responding when corrections are required. Officers also are cautioned to consider how information may affect the 'general public' before releasing it to the press. Still, the current media/RCMP relations manual does not address some of the other sensitive issues discussed in this case study,[17] Future public policy reviews should consider changes in the following areas.

Neither the *RCMP Operational Manual II.16 Media/RCMP Relations* protocols nor *RCMP and the Media* acknowledges the diversity in Canadian society nor identifies the need for press releases to reflect this consideration. Policy revisions must identify the importance of greater sensitivities towards Aboriginal people under investigation, including language guidelines for descriptions of people under investigation during press releases and provision of specific examples of appropriate use of language that does not offend minority groups, inflame the situation, or adversely affect public opinion. Such inclusions would be in keeping with Canada's multicultural policy and the 1996 *Report of the Royal Commission on Aboriginal Peoples*, which called for media representations of Native peoples that avoid harmful stereotyping. They are also supported by recommendations in the 2000 RCMP *Aboriginal Policing Review Final Report* for improved communications when dealing with various segments of Aboriginal society.

Current guidelines do not distinguish specific audiences that are affected by RCMP press releases. A policy review should account for 'hidden audiences,' such as the families of RCMP officers and members of various minorities.

Current media/RCMP protocols recognize the usefulness of the media to the RCMP. 'Good communication with the media can often assist the RCMP in a police investigation, e.g. allowing an investigator to solicit information concerning suspects, victims or witnesses and educate or reassure the public' (M/R D.2.). However, there is no mention of ethical considerations or professional boundaries between the law enforcers and the media. There is no discussion of the RCMP confiscating media products. There are no distinctions regarding the RCMP's relations with the CBC, the public broadcaster as opposed to private broadcasters. Evidence of the RCMP overstepping its role as a law enforcement agency in its relations with the media (in Vancouver as well as in the context of previous Native blockades, such as the one at Douglas Lake) indicates that the roots of the problem are systemic and are not limited to the case of the 1995 Gustafsen Lake standoff. A policy review should address the professional and ethical considerations in the value of media in law enforcement contexts, including the ethical responsibility of the RCMP to obtain informed consent prior to engaging members of the media in police investigations.

This case study brings to light the ease with which the RCMP disregarded existing media policies and their reluctance to acknowledge publicly their culpability for the consequences. Yet the RCMP's concern

about public approval implies that, had there been greater public awareness of and accessibility to the media/RCMP relations policies, the
police would have been under greater pressure to comply. A public
policy review could respond to the issue of public education by making
copies of RCMP media protocols more accessible to the media outlets
with whom they have dealings and to all the communities that they
serve. The increased availability of this information would be consistent with community-based policing and the RCMP's commitment to
openness and trust with the media and the public.

The instances of the RCMP acting on cultural misperceptions and
stereotyping of Aboriginal people during the Gustafsen Lake standoff
demonstrate the need for increased and continuing education of RCMP
personnel in the areas of Aboriginal issues, history, and culture. This is
also a central finding in the 2000 RCMP *Aboriginal Policing Review, Final
Report.* In the report cross-cultural training is found to be an efficacious
strategy to improve communications between officers dealing with
Aboriginal people and those discussing Aboriginal people in the media. Such training is consistent with the goals of community-based
policing, and it may break down barriers between law enforcement and
Native people. One point on which this case study and the 2000 RCMP
Aboriginal Policing Review Final Report differ is policy development.
RCMP personnel polled for the report objected to additional policies
and stated their preferences for practical information, training, and
education. However, the findings of this case study point to the fact that
this approach would not result in consistent, sustainable improvements.
Officer education should be grounded in formalized policies that specify
behavioural expectations in the provision as well as the application of
officer training. Such structural supports are more likely to promote
standardized treatment of Aboriginal people and to improve public
accountability.

Epilogue: Since the Gustafsen Lake Standoff

The Gustafsen Lake standoff occurred when a group of Native people
chose violence as a strategy for social transformation. The RCMP met
them with a show of force and a threat of counter-violence. In the end,
both sides claimed victory. The intervention of Native elders visibly
contributed to the end of the standoff, and the RCMP were able to point
to their having defused the situation without loss of life. However, the
cessation of overt conflict has not provided a satisfying closure. Local

Native communities are still trying to distance themselves from the notoriety of the conflict. During and after the Gustafsen Lake trial, supporters of the defendants sought alliances with local Native communities and the National Assembly of First Nations in order to demand an inquiry on the RCMP's excessive use of force during the standoff. At the time of this writing, no inquiry has yet been initiated. Other than sporadic guest articles and RCMP responses to allegations of police misconduct in British Columbia newspapers, the media focus has shifted to treaty and land settlements and continuing Native protests. In November 2000 a U.S. court judge refused to extradite one of the Gustafsen Lake defendants, who had fled to the United States while serving a parole connected to charges laid from the Gustafsen Lake standoff trial. Canadian authorities sought to have the U.S. court extradite the individual to serve the 702 days remaining on his sentence. After a review of the Gustafsen Lake trial, the judge concluded that the 'defendant's crimes were "of a political character" and therefore may not provide the basis for extradition of [the] defendant to Canada.'[18]

Contrary to predictions at the time, the Gustafsen Lake standoff did not derail the treaty process. Indeed, some people believe that it was the impetus for negotiations with more than 40 Aboriginal councils and nations and allowed for a smoother passage of the Nisga'a treaty, which was ratified in April 2000. Nevertheless, disputes over land and resources continue to fuel Native blockades in British Columbia. In 2002 the potential for conflicts and the derailment of treaty negotiations was exacerbated by the provincial government's referendum to gauge the public mandate for treaty talks. This referendum exposed the vulnerability of Native people in British Columbia to the whim of political agendas despite treaty rights protected by the constitution.[19]

It is inevitable that conflicts involving non-Natives and Natives over resources draw media, and the Burnt Church, New Brunswick, blockade (2000) is the most recent clash. But has the media tenor substantively changed since Oka, Ipperwash, or Gustafsen Lake? A review of the coverage of several Native conflicts since Gustafsen Lake finds that media continue to rely on wartime characterizations. Such rhetoric has multiple influences. It reinforces the social dichotomy of *us against them* that has persisted since the colonial era. It provides subtle models of behaviour for conflicting sides. It encourages media audiences to lump all Native protests into a generalized, but restrictive schema. It undermines a mandate for governments at various levels to seek equitable resolutions at the negotiating table. The prevalence of wartime themes during Oka, Ipperwash, and Gustafsen Lake has had a cumulative effect. Members of the dominant society – who do not understand the historic contexts of disputes, are otherwise ambivalent, or have already come to negative conclusions about Native protests – will be less open to considering any Native protest as a valid demonstration by valued Canadian citizens.[20] Even if only some members of the media resort to wartime themes in the coverage of Native protests, the foundation has been laid to maintain the association of negative stereotypes in the public's perceptions.[21] The pattern has taken on a life of its own.

Poverty, limited life chances, institutional discrimination, and struggles over land and resource issues continue to marginalize Aboriginal peoples in Canada. A growing population of disaffected Native youth drawn to urban gangs does not bode well for Native people, already overrepresented in the criminal justice system.[22] According to recent government reports, Native militant groups are amassing illegal weapons and are continuing to be a serious threat to national stability, in spite of denials from Native leaders. Such reports anticipate future violent engagements with Native people and, perversely, make them perceptibly more probable.

Yet the greatest threat to Canadian society may not reside with Native militancy and the violent response it engenders in state agencies. It is more conceivably the lack of a commitment to change the institutional processes and social practices that affect the inequalities in the social system. Media and law enforcement are only two components of a larger system.

Concluding Remarks

Underpinning this case study is the recognition that the RCMP Media Relations Program and news production policies and practices are forms of social practice. Policies and practices manifest the ways that these institutions situate themselves in the society that they serve. Both law enforcement and media are powerful influences in the construction of social identities, including the naming of society's enemies. But neither institution can control the processes that symbolically link a typology, or the labelling of a few, to members of an entire group. Therefore, these institutions need to be more aware of this phenomenon and its potential consequences in a democratic pluralist society.

In a democratic society, transparency of police information enhances public trust in the law enforcement agency. Such transparency cannot exist without the media. Media must also maintain a trust with their audiences that the information they supply is accurate. At this level, it appears that the relations between law enforcement and the media are symbiotic. In an ideal world, there would not be a conflict between these two institutions, because they appear to have complementary goals. Yet within a democratic framework, the aspect of disproportionate, but distinctive, power is recognized in the functions that police and media serve in relation to each other in society. Police engage in law enforcement, but media serve as a check on police use (and abuse) of power. In the end, media may provide the primary impetus for law enforcement reforms.

This study of the 1995 Gustafsen Lake standoff chronicles a historical event that has social implications that extend well beyond the event. It models a methodology for tracking the underlying structural elements that influence extreme media characterizations. It may also serve as a warning of the precarious state of Canada's pluralist democracy when the distinctions between *law enforcement* and *media* become obscured during a serious conflict involving Native people.

Chronology of the 1995 Gustafsen Lake Standoff

1989	Percy Rosette asks Lyle James if he may hold a Sundance at Gustafsen Lake.
1989–95	The years that the Sundance took place at Gustafsen Lake.
June 1995	Unconfirmed reports of shots fired at forestry workers.
17 June 1995	A meeting takes place between representatives of the ranch owner (Lyle James), people at the Gustafsen Lake camp, and the Cariboo Tribal Council.
2–12 July 1995	The Sundance is held at Gustafsen Lake.
11 August 1995	Forestry officers arrest two men for illegal fishing practices. The officers discover illegal weapons during a search of the vehicle. The men are taken into RCMP custody.
18 August 1995	Shots are fired at an RCMP Emergency Response Team (ERT) near the Gustafsen Lake camp.
19 August 1995	The RCMP hold a press conference at Williams Lake.
24 August 1995	Shots are fired by camp members at an RCMP helicopter.
25 August 1995	Grand Chief Ovide Mercredi visits the Gustafsen Lake camp. A gunshot is fired shortly after he departs. A few hours later, the RCMP set up barricades, preventing further media access to the camp.
26 August 1995	Grand Chief Mercredi makes a final visit to the Gustafsen Lake camp.

27 August 1995   Shots are fired at two RCMP officers and their vehicle. They are saved from serious injury because they are wearing flak-jackets.

29 August 1995   The RCMP media relations officer holds an off-the-record meeting with the media.

4 September 1995   The RCMP report a shooting attack on RCMP officers and their vehicle to the media.

5 September 1995   A few members of the media witness and document the arrival of armoured personnel carriers. (APCs)

6 September 1995   The RCMP confiscate CBC Television videotapes.

7 September 1995   A meeting between leaders of 17 bands of the Shuswap Nation and RCMP officials is held at Alkali Lake.

7 September 1995   The RCMP report that some people in the camp shot at an RCMP helicopter.

8 September 1995   Shuswap intermediaries begin visiting the Gustafsen Lake camp; they bring food for the people.

11 September 1995   Twenty-five Aboriginal bands hold a meeting at Merritt, British Columbia.

11 September 1995   A firefight takes place between the Emergency Response Team and the people at the Gustafsen Lake camp.

12 September 1995   The Emergency Response Team fires on a lone male walking near Gustafsen Lake.

13 September 1995   Native spiritual leader Arvol Looking Horse visits the Gustafsen Lake camp.

13 September 1995   Chief Antoine Archie sends a message to the Gustafsen Lake camp in the Shuswap language and in English over CBC Radio.

15 September 1995   Television crews tour RCMP Camp Zulu.

16 September 1995   A media pool tours RCMP Camp Zulu.

17 September 1995   The Gustafsen Lake standoff ends and the camp occupants are taken into RCMP custody.

24 September 1995   Several members of the media attend the RCMP tour of the Gustafsen Lake camp.

8 July 1996–
20 May 1997   Trial of the Gustafsen Lake defendants in a high-security courthouse convenes in Surrey, British Columbia. The trial ends with 39 acquittals and 21 convictions.

APPENDIX 2

Abbreviations

AIM   American Indian Movement
APCs   Armoured personnel carriers
CBC   Canadian Broadcasting Corporation
CP   Canadian Press
DIA   Department of Indian Affairs
ERT   Emergency Response Team
FBI   Federal Bureau of Investigation (U.S.)
IQs   Indirect quotations
NDP   New Democratic Party
RCAP   Royal Commission on Aboriginal Peoples
RCMP   Royal Canadian Mounted Police

History of Aboriginal Disputes in Canada

Native resistance in Canada can be traced back to the reserve era, which began in the 1830s (Wilson and Urion 1995).[1] The federal government passed a series of Indian Acts, beginning in 1868. Direct appeals from Aboriginal groups to the federal government began as early as 1874, when delegations of Native leaders travelled to Ottawa to make appeals for land allocations for reserves (Long 1992). The federal government's response was to proceed with more Indian Acts. The 1880 Indian Act protected reserves by redefining them as Crown lands, and by prohibiting taxation of reserve land or property on the land. It imposed a chief-and-council band structure that paralleled local government and was similarly subordinate to central authorities. The Indian Act also gave the federal minister of Indian affairs and his officials the authority to regulate reserves and Native bands (Tennant 1990:45).

During the 1930s and 1940s Aboriginal groups became more organized and began to form networks across Canada and to pressure provincial and federal governments for reform. In 1951 Ottawa's response to these overtures was to amend the Indian Act, although paternalism and colonialism were still perpetuated in more subtle forms. In 1969 the federal government produced the *White Paper on Indian Policy*. It recommended that the special status of Native Indians be gradually eliminated through policy mechanisms. The White Paper served as a catalyst for large-scale organization of Native interests (Long 1992:120). Natives opposed the proposed changes to their status and considered the White Paper proposals another imposition of white law to define Natives' lives. In 1970 Native political and spiritual leaders agreed to adopt the position paper *Citizens Plus*, from the Indian Association of Alberta.[2] In this report the White Paper was rejected because it did not recognize the symbolic importance of treaties to status Indians. It was felt that without treaties, Native people would lose their traditional cultures and way of life. They believed that their last hope for these to survive rested on official recognition of their special status (Weaver 1981; Long 1992:121).

The response to the White Paper signified the emergence of the modern period of Native politicization, which persisted throughout the 1970s and 1980s (Long 1992:121). In this movement, arguments for self-government and original sovereignty and for an expanded sense of Aboriginal rights were formulated. By 1981 concerns about land rights had been redefined to include the right to Aboriginal self-government. During this time, Native people utilized the courts to have their arguments heard. In 1973 the Nisga'a tribe of British Columbia lost the *Calder* case against the federal government for recognition of their ownership of traditional lands. Yet this outcome held promise. Although the Supreme Court's split decision regarding the current existence of Aboriginal title favoured the federal government, it also affirmed pre-existing Aboriginal title before the arrival of the Europeans. This encouraged Native groups to proceed with their attempts to have their inherent Aboriginal rights recognized. The treaty process in British Columbia evolved from that 1973 ruling. In 1997 the Supreme Court decision on the *Delgamuukw* case affirmed Indian ownership of traditional land[3] and acknowledged the validity of oral history in a court of law. The Supreme Court has subsequently identified the need to evaluate oral history evidence similar to other facts before the court.

In the 1960s, when Native leaders were honing their skills in political and legal lobbying, a *strategic militancy* emerged from the Native Indian movement. Its function was to provide a second line of defence if the legal and political avenues were hindered at the federal government level. The American Indian Movement (AIM), as well as black militant resistance in the United States, influenced Canadian Native militancy as far as using similar tactics to draw public and official attention to specific concerns. Strategic militancy motivated protests staged by various Aboriginal groups in Canada, including the Lubicon Cree in Northern Alberta (1980s), the Haida in British Columbia (1980s, 1990s), the Peigus Indian Band in Manitoba (1989), the Algonquins at Golden Lake in Ontario (1988), and the Mohawks at Kanasetake at Oka, Quebec (1990) (Long 1992:127). Protests targeted logging companies, the military, and the Canadian public. However, the adversary was ultimately the Canadian state (Long 1992:127). As early as 1974 the RCMP described the Indian movement 'as the single greatest threat to national security,' though pockets of unrest were dismissed by politicians '"as socially insignificant actions by a small and desperate group of Indian extremists"' (Long 1992:127, quoting York 1989:251). Natives came to recognize the power of media during these incidents of strategic militancy and that it could be used to their advantage to gain national and international attention for their discontent and to increase support for their cause. Strategic militancy continues to motivate the majority of Aboriginal protests after Gustafsen Lake.

APPENDIX 4

Excerpts from
RCMP Operational Manual II.16 Media/RCMP Relations

The following protocols are taken from the *RCMP Operational Manual II.16 Media/RCMP Relations*. These protocols were in effect at the time of the Gusafsen Lake standoff:

Section C. 3: A free flow of information between the RCMP and the media shall be carried out through a formal dialogue that is continuous, open, relevant, timely and reliable.

Section C. 4: The RCMP shall provide the media with prompt, courteous and impartial services in consideration of their needs, sensitivity to public demands, and protection of public and individual rights.

Section F. 1 c: Keep a record of information given to the media to protect against misquotation, exaggeration or sensationalism.

Section F. 1 d: Ensure that any information released to the media does not: result in injury, injustice or embarrassment to anyone, either innocent or accused; result in publicity that could affect the course of a trial; and contravene the provisions of the Privacy Act, Access to Information Act, or the Canadian Charter of Rights and Freedoms.

Section G. 1. c: Do not prejudice future trials by: discussing evidence; referring to the character or reputation of the accused; discussing any previous record the accused might have.

Section G 1. d: Do not release the name of a young offender.

Section G 1. f: If deemed appropriate, display seized contraband ... or other items to provide the media with photo opportunities, provided: 1. Continuity is maintained; 2. It does not violate an individual's rights under the Privacy Act; and it does not give the impression that an accused is being subjected to a trial by media.

APPENDIX 5

Toronto Globe and Mail Account of the 11 September 1995 Firefight

Invective labels are highlighted in bold type by S. Lambertus.

The Toronto Globe and Mail

The following story is reprinted from:
Times Colonist, Tuesday September 12, 1995   a1

Three natives shot in firefight – Nobody is leaving the camp, Mounties

Newswire
told, after battle with armored carriers – By Steve Mertl 100 MILE HOUSE, B.C. (CP) –

Three natives were shot during a firefight Monday with RCMP using armored personnel carriers outside an armed camp in the B.C. Interior.

It was not known how serious their injuries were.

Rebel leader William Ignace, known as Wolverine, 'advised our negotiators that three people were injured as a result of the gun battle,' RCMP Sgt. Peter Montague told a news conference.

When RCMP suggested helping the wounded leave the camp, 'his response was that nobody was leaving the camp and the conversation ended.'

Monty Sam, a Shuswap native, went into the camp after the gun battle, said Sam's wife Jeannette Armstrong.

Montague identified some of the camp's leaders, saying that 'for reasons of public interest, the RCMP is now compelled to inform the public as to whom we are dealing with at the camp.' 'There's a criminal agenda which is continually being advanced by the criminal element in that community,' he said. 'They have usurped any legitimate goal and objectives of the local people with their own self-serving criminal agenda.'

The gun battle began when a pickup truck tried to go outside a 'no-go zone' around the camp, he said.

But an aboriginal negotiator said police knew the pickup truck was coming out of the camp to meet native elders. 'The RCMP were well aware that these people come out of the camp, come up to the road and sit awaiting the arrival of the delegation,' said Gordon Sebastian.

The truck was disabled when it drove over an 'early warning device' police had put in a logging road in the zone, Montague said.

The two or three people in the truck then grabbed weapons and ran into the bush, he said. A Bison armored personnel carrier on loan from the Canadian Forces then joined the fray but experienced mechanical difficulties when it was hit by fire from an AK–47 assault rifle, Montague said.

A second Bison was called in but both vehicles 'came under heavy fire' so police started shooting back, he said.

He said police recovered an AK–47 and a hunting rifle from the truck.

It was the seventh time police have been fired on.

Nathan Matthew, a spokesman for the so-called liaison group between the **rebels** and the RCMP said earlier that the **squatters** were looking for reassurance they won't be harmed if they give up and won't be abandoned when they face the justice system. 'They must have some kind of safety provided to them,' said Matthew, a member of the Shuswap Nation and chief of the North Thompson band. 'There must be some reassurance that due process will be had for them.'

The standoff entered its fourth week Monday in the confrontation between the armed aboriginals and police surrounding the remote piece of ranchland the natives claim as sacred aboriginal territory.

The liaison group went into the encampment Sunday and met with its leaders for several hours.

Matthew said the issues on the table are the safety and security of camp members, exactly how guns in the camp will be turned over and a guarantee of adequate legal counsel. Meanwhile, B.C. aboriginal leaders were called to a meeting in Merritt on Monday to discuss the standoffs at Gustafsen Lake and Ipperwash park in Ontario.

Chief Scotty Holmes of the Upper Nicola band said the native leaders would discuss ways of assisting in peaceful resolutions of both disputes.

Matthew made no mention of the **rebels'** core demands – that the Queen and British Privy Council review the traditionalists' claim to the site because they don't recognize the jurisdiction of Canadian governments and courts.

Matthew also tried to clarify his weekend comments referring to the occupation as a 'peace camp,' despite the shooting incidents.

He said the term was meant to hark back to the site's previous use as a venue for sacred sundance ceremonies.

LENGTH: Medium
CLASS: News

ACCESSION NUMBER: 00006049
DOCUMENT NUMBER: 950912TC001

Vancouver Sun Account of the 11 September 1995 Firefight

Invective labels are highlighted in bold type by S. Lambertus.

The Vancouver Sun – Final C
Tuesday September 12, 1995   A1
News
GUSTAFSEN LAKE STANDOFF

Three Rebels feared hurt in wild shootout
PETE McMARTIN; JEFF LEE
VANSUN
100 MILE HOUSE
STORY TYPE: NEWS; CRIME
LENGTH: Long (> 700)
SUBJECT: INDIANS; DEMONSTRATIONS; TRESPASSING; SHOOTINGS;
CRIME; BC; RCMP

100 MILE HOUSE – Police and native Indian leaders presented starkly different versions Monday night of a shootout that may have left three of the **rebels** at Gustafsen Lake injured.

The gunfight erupted about 2 p.m. as a negotiating committee from a native Indian liaison group approached the RCMP's final checkpoint into the camp – a log barricade across the road.

Several hours after the gun battle, two **rebels** were arrested outside the armed camp and another man was reported missing.

Glenn Deneault and Edward Dick were taken into custody by police emergency response team members about 9:30 p.m., said RCMP Sgt. Peter Montague.

'They came out of their own accord; they wanted to come out and they did,' he said.

The two men were escorted out of the camp area in a convoy of police cars to the RCMP detachment at 100 Mile House, where they were interrogated.

Montague also said that an unidentified woman involved in the afternoon firefight – which earlier conjecture had as being mortally wounded – had been hit in the arm and was receiving medical attention from **rebels** inside the camp. He said medical assistance offered by the RCMP was refused.

Deneault has previous criminal convictions for fraud and theft, Montague said.

Montague also said late Monday that another **rebel** went missing during the afternoon firefight. The man may have been hit by rifle fire of 'unknown origin,' he said.

The shootout was triggered when native Indians drove a red pickup truck beyond a perimeter police had warned them not to cross, Montague said.

'Yesterday, the occupants of the camp had been advised to stay within a confined area and that area was well described to them. The RCMP had tightened their security net, and they were well aware of that,' Montague said.

'When the Shuswap representatives were approximately three kilometers from the camp, the same red pickup from the camp whose occupants had previously fired upon the RCMP helicopter, departed the camp and drove outside the restricted perimeter.'

'Quite a ways' outside the perimeter, Montague said, the red pickup drove over an RCMP early-warning device 'and was disabled.'

Montague confirmed it was an explosive device.

He said the two occupants, or possibly three, jumped out of the truck and ran into the woods with their weapons.

'The RCMP pursued the individuals but discontinued the pursuit when the two individuals commenced firing upon our members. A search of the vehicle resulted in the recovery of two weapons, an AK–47 and a hunting rifle.'

Montague said AK–47 fire from the native Indians disabled a Bison armored vehicle manned by RCMP emergency response team members. He said the number of rounds exchanged were in 'the thousands.'

Montague was asked why RCMP forced the issue with the **rebels** by tightening the perimeter on Sunday if negotiations were so close to reaching a peaceful conclusion.

'It was a very simple thing; they want beyond the perimeter and were told not to,' he said.

'We drew a map for them. We showed them exactly where the perimeter was.'

After the gunfight, Montague said, RCMP contacted the camp and spoke to Jonesy Ignace, who goes by the name of Wolverine. Ignace told the RCMP that three people were injured, including an unarmed woman. When RCMP asked Ignace to return everyone to the camp so the injured could be removed, Montague said Ignace told them 'nobody was going to leave the camp.'

Wolverine let fly a string of expletives and accused police of betraying their promise not to hurt the campers.

'You murdered one of our women, you bastards,' he screamed over the phone. 'It's payback time, you motherf—ers.'

(Ignace later referred to three people being injured – not killed – in the firefight.)

Police asked if anyone in the camp wanted to come out, but Wolverine said no one would leave.

Later, Percy Rosette, one of the spiritual leaders in the camp, accused police of double-crossing the campers.

'Everything went wrong with your people. It was a bomb,' he said. 'You people started firing first again. Your people sent bombs.'

He said no one would come out now because they believed the police would kill them.

Still later, another person in the camp, who refused to identify himself, picked up the phone and told police to back off or they would be killed.

'I'll tell you something before you tell us. You are going to listen. That wasn't very nice what you done, and you better expect we are going to engage you. We are not going to back down. All you f—ing people get out of here now or we're going out now and you'll be answering for a lot of shit, and this will spark the fire worldwide.'

Shortly after the exchange of gunfire, an ambulance entered the outer perimeter, but returned minutes later without any of the injured.

Police responded to the firefight by bringing in a large number of officers from the emergency response team.

The firefight came as the four native negotiators reached the inner perimeter at 2 p.m. One of the negotiators, Gordon Sebastian, said police were aware that a greeting party from the camp came every day to meet negotiators.

But when the Shuswap elders reached the meeting point, no one was there. Shortly after, 'there was a large discharge and we felt the wind on our faces and clothes,' Sebastian said. 'And then there was small calibre fire – about 11 or 12 shots.'

He said they did not hear gunfire again until 2:15 p.m., 'at the most, 60 rounds were fired.' He disputed the RCMP's estimate of thousands of rounds being fired.

Police later yielded to demands from the camp to allow one of the negotiators, Sam Marleau, to return unescorted to determine what happened and who was injured. Marleau had not emerged from the camp late Monday.

Marleau's wife, Jeanette Alexander, another of the negotiators who had entered the perimeter, said the main objective of today's aborted negotiations was the placement of the perimeter.

She said the camp was cut off from water and firewood, and the people inside had wanted the border extended.

Montague refused to discuss the issue of the perimeter.

Rather, in a dramatic move, he read off a litany of charges and convictions against at least half a dozen of the main players in the camp, including Jones (Jonesy) Paul Ignace, Joseph Adams Ignace and John Hill, known as Splitting The Sky.

But Sebastian, a lawyer, publicly rebuked Montague and the RCMP for what he said was a public relations 'game' in talking about charges against the individuals.

ILLUSTRATION

BILL KEAY/ Vancouver Sun/ ROARING PAST ROADBLOCK: ambulance speeds by RMCP at checkpoint on road to Gustafsen Lake **rebel** camp after gunbattle
WOLVERINE

CP

NOTE

Native leaders fear rise in violence, A2 Dosanjh sees peaceful end dimming, A3 Standoff preceded by a vision, A3

ID NUMBER: 9509120006

DOC. #: 950912VS00

Excerpt from RCMP (Unclassified Memo) 1 September 1995

To: Supt. OLFERT
From: Sgt. MONTAGUE

Issue Two: Wolverine and His Band of Thugs
Wolverine (IGNACE) is an advocate of violence in order to advance his political agenda. By definition, he is a terrorist. He attempted to promote violence at Adams Lake and was shunned by the local Natives. [Reference to another camp member is deleted.][1]

STRATEGY:

The RCMP should send out a clear and concise message which will bring the proper focus to this issue. The agenda being promoted is one of violence engineered by Wolverine and his thugs. The public knows nothing about Wolverine et al and their criminal background. Before the Force makes any physical move the public should be made aware that our actions are being precipitated by the criminal actions of proven criminals.

ACTION:

At a media conference, profile the criminal backgrounds of the occupants.

Issue Three:

The RCMP has put an enormous effort into this operation. Remarkable restraint has been demonstrated. Considerable tax dollars are being spent.

STRATEGY:

The public should be made aware of this effort. The public must see that the RCMP is capable of flexing its muscle but will only do so if absolutely necessary. Presently, the public might be getting the idea that we are not capable of dealing with this impasse, thus their confidence in the Force could possibly be diminished.

ACTION:

Full media coverage of our resources. Not the operational plan itself, but just the resources. Manpower, ERT., PSD's, FLIRS, Helicopters, Communication Experts, Financial Support, Psychologist, Weaponry, Gas, etc. Provide the media the opportunity to see our new warehouse headquarters.

Notes

Introduction

1 A female member of the camp was shot in the arm during a skirmish with the police, and a soldier from the Canadian Armed Forces (part of a group that was brought in to drive and service the armored personnel carriers) was injured while handling a stun grenade.

2 This information is taken from the transcripts of the *Proceedings at Challenge for Cause Application*, No. X043738, New Westminster Registry, New Westminster, B.C., 7 May 1996.

3 I consider 'players' to be synonymous with 'social actors.'

4 Van Dijk is one of the most authoritative international scholars of media characterizations of minorities.

5 The guidelines that I followed are consistent with the (1997) University of Alberta Standards for the Protection of Human Research Participants, the Tri-Council Policy on Ethical Conduct for Research Involving Humans (17 June 1999), and the ethics standards set out by the (2001) Social Science and Humanities Research Council of Canada.

6 Several journalists volunteered to drop their anonymity for this research and for any subsequent publications. To maintain consistency, I declined these offers.

7 Some of the journalists found these painstaking measures amusing.

8 'Wescam' is the name consistently used in media and court references to the RCMP's aerial video recordings.

1. Serious Red Alert

1 I am including this discussion of the RCMP's deviation from their media

plan at the Gustafsen Lake standoff here in order to differentiate the ideal from the real. Without this explanation, it would appear that the preceding narrative of the media event is a form of entrapment of the RCMP, which was not the purpose of the research.

2 Staff Sergeant Sarich confirmed that his detachment is cautious when supplying the media with any information regarding an investigation because of the risks of tainting a subsequent trial.

3 This statement was confirmed by journalists from CBC Radio, CBC-TV, and the *Vancouver Sun*.

4 It is not unusual in the interior of British Columbia for Native people to marry into non-Native families that own ranches.

5 The Sundance is a sacred rite that originated with the Oglala Sioux of the South Dakota plains in the nineteenth century, and it has since spread to other regions and (to some extent) has been adopted by members of different tribal traditions. It is a ritual of sacrifice to the Creator and a means of personal renewal that requires the preparation of a sacred arbour and other sacred symbols, as well as fasting, praying, and dancing. Several variations of the ritual have developed among different groups. The formal ceremony may exclude the participation of non-Native people. It may involve (as did the 1995 Sundance at Gustafsen Lake) the male dancers piercing their chests. Thus, the notion of Sundance 'tradition' is variable and relative.

6 Four years later during the trial, the defence counsel demonstrated to the court that the RCMP could not identify who was responsible for the shooting.

7 Clark included the Gustafsen Lake case with other Native land submissions to the Queen at Buckingham Palace on 27 March 1995.

8 The Emissaries of the Divine Light is a spiritual movement that was brought to 100 Mile House by Michael Exeter, a descendant of one of the founding settler families in the area. In 1912 the Exeters, a socially prominent family in England, had purchased a large tract of ranchland near 100 Mile House, and Michael Exeter's father was sent to the region to operate the ranch. Michael Exeter himself became involved with the Emissaries of the Divine Light in the 1940s or 1950s; when the founder died, he became the spiritual leader of this worldwide movement. He also inherited the title 8th Marquess of Exeter when his father died. At the time of the standoff, Michael Exeter owned the Red Coach Inn and the adjacent property that became the hub for the media covering the standoff.

9 Although Hill did not mention this during the interview, another source inside the camp alleged that Hill, as the leader of the Sundance, was not

physically present for this confrontation. At the time the eviction notice was presented, Hill was praying in the distance. This source also stated that one of the ranch hands brought a video camera and filmed Hill as he prayed. This filming was said to have breached the sacred protocols of the Sundance.

10 According to Lyle James, cattle require a stable route from year to year; otherwise, they become lost, and the size of the property makes it difficult for ranch staff to locate them. He advised me that this is a common understanding among cattle ranchers.

11 This incident was well documented in the media and during the trial. One of the ranch hands, apparently after consuming alcohol, allegedly had ridden to the camp late one night on horseback, yelling and making a commotion that woke everybody. He claimed that the ranch hands and the police were going to raid the camp and burn it down. This scene was witnessed by non-Native people camping nearby, who later testified in court that the incident did occur.

12 Lyle James was unable to attend this meeting because he was in the hospital.

13 According to Palmer (1994) there is no legal survey for the Alkali Lake Reserve No. 1. All existing documents post-date the establishment of the reserve.

14 *100 Mile House Free Press* editor Steven Frasher was the only journalist at the Sundance camp who took a picture of the Sundance arbour, which turned out to be the only picture in the roll of film that was overexposed.

15 This excerpt is taken from the news story, 'Sundancers denounce militant action,' *100 Mile House Free Press*, 5 July 1995, 3.

16 Although the elder's name is used in the newspaper article. I have not disclosed it in order to protect the elder's personal security.

17 Excerpts taken from 'Sundancers denounce militant action,' 3.

18 Lac La Hache is a community north of 100 Mile House.

19 At the 18 August Williams Lake press conference, Sergeant Peter Montague identified the Lac La Hache incident as one of the justifications for considering the activities in the camp 'terrorist' in nature.

20 This quotation is taken from the newspaper story by Elizabeth Aird, 'English aristocrat and Gustafsen Lake militant have close spiritual beliefs,' *Vancouver Sun*, 14 September 1995, B1.

21 *100 Mile House Free Press* editor Steven Frasher recalled that Percy Rosette showed the media where the burial grounds were located during their tour of the Sundance camp in June 1995. However, Chief Antoine Archie was later quoted in the local newspaper: 'The elders do not know of any burial

sites in this area,' and Chief Agnes Snow supported him by adding, 'All the community members, elders, chiefs and councillors of all the Northern Shuswap stand together on this.' These statements were included in the news story, 'Chiefs condemn radical action of "outsiders" at Gustafsen Lake,' *100 Mile House Free Press*, 23 August 1995, a3. The authorized survey map of the Gustafsen Lake area (District Lot 114, Lillooet District File 3615, Drawing No. 9615SKE/69) prepared by British Columbia land surveyors Kidston and Hemingway on 29 August 1996 was introduced as court evidence. The map did not indicate the presence of a Native burial site.

22 The correct spelling is Pena, but this is how the name was spelled in the published account.

23 The actual date on this chronology published in the *Vancouver Sun* was 17 August 1995. I have confirmed with other sources that the incident occurred on 18 August 1995. This detail was corrected in the lengthier chronology published the following day, 'Standoff at Gustafsen Lake preceded by a vision,' *Vancouver Sun*, 12 September 1995, A3.

24 According to the *RCMP Report to Crown Counsel* (Kamloops Sub/Division File 95KL-334), one of the Native constables (unnamed here to protect his anonymity) reported that while visiting the camp on 18 July 1995, he talked to 'unknown males' about a tree-cutting incident. At that time, he saw a red dot of light, which moved across the centre of his chest and then disappeared. The following day at the camp, the same constable observed, on another Native RCMP officer who had accompanied him, a red dot of light move across the chest and disappear. A senior ERT officer interpreted this light as an infrared sighting device associated with a firearm. Switlo's (1996) account of the Gustafsen Lake standoff describes how Sundance camp occupants Percy Rosette and his wife also witnessed red circles of light appearing on their foreheads from high-powered weaponry. They associated this occurrence with low-flying helicopters hovering over the farm where they stayed after the standoff. They feared that they were going to be assassinated by the RCMP before the trial (Switlo 1997:132).

25 Defence counsel George Wool argued during the Gustafsen Lake trial that firearms are part of the rugged Cariboo culture. He asserted that the RCMP's lack of understanding of this cultural element led to their over-reaction to the 11 August 1995 seizure of weapons and that only a few of the weapons were illegal or considered out of the ordinary for the region. During my interview with Staff Sergeant Sarich of the 100 Mile House RCMP detachment, I asked about the prevalence of weapons and the implications on policing in the area. He confirmed that one of the distinctive factors of law enforcement in the interior of British Columbia is that

civilians possess a large number of firearms (compared with those in urban areas). In his experience, the RCMP can expect to confiscate six to twelve firearms from one residence during a domestic dispute. This appreciation has increased concerns for the safety of RCMP officers and was one of the factors that guided his calls for ERT assistance on six occasions in 1995. Staff Sergeant Sarich said that in the case of developments at Gustafsen Lake, his decision to involve the ERT to defuse the situation was consistent with previous practices.

26 The RCMP admitted during the trial that they did not have a search warrant for the camp prior to this reconnaissance mission. This information is taken from the news story, 'Police wanted 4,000 troops at Gustafsen,' *Vancouver Province*, 8 January 1997, A4.

27 During the trial, the RCMP testified that they had assumed that the people inside the camp knew that the camouflaged men were ERT officers. The officers did not consider that they might have been mistaken for vigilantes.

28 In a news interview the three Native RCMP officers spoke publicly about their involvement. One of the Native RCMP officers, Bob Wood, told the reporter that he had resigned from the force because of the way the RCMP had dealt with the dispute at Gustafsen Lake. He felt as though his advice was being ignored, and the resolution meeting, which was to have been held between 18 and 21 August 1995, 'would have settled the matter.' After the ERT was compromised on 18 August, he and the other Native RCMP officers were asked not to go into the camp. Staff Sergeant Martin Sarich and Sergeant Peter Montague defended this decision because of the rising danger to their officers. Constable Charlie Andrew was quoted as saying that he was 'upset and frustrated by his treatment during the standoff' and, in hindsight, should not have become involved. Constable Geordie Findlay said that originally he believed that the RCMP were not interested in his input. (Findlay submitted a report to his superiors on 12 July 1995, which traced the history of the Gustafsen Lake area. He recommended that the RCMP not take action, reasoning that if the RCMP used force against the camp, the current lack of local support might be reversed and would make the police 'look bad'). After he testified in court, however, Findlay learned of other incidents that pointed to escalated tension at the camp and the possibility that somebody might be killed. Findlay's final assessment was that, rightly or wrongly, the RCMP had to 'take action,' and he was thankful that nobody had died. This information is taken from the news story 'Botched siege prompts native Mountie to quit,' *Vancouver Sun*, 11 July 1997, B4.

29 Percy Rosette telephoned the 100 Mile House RCMP, but because of the

early hour, the call was transferred to the Williams Lake RCMP detachment.

2. Media Circus

1 The quotation from Superintendent Olfert is taken from '"Terrorism" will end, RCMP warns,' *Calgary Herald*, 20 August 1995, A12 (CP).
2 Bill Chelsea was chief of the Alkali Lake (Esket) Band, which is Northern Shuswap culturally but is not part of the Cariboo Tribal Council.
3 According to defence lawyer George Wool, the prosecution was never able to connect the shooting incident at Lac La Hache or the confiscation of weapons at the Fraser River with the Gustafsen Lake Sundance camp. Wool argues that, by assuming these linkages and making them known to reporters, the RCMP were providing the media with details that had yet to be proved in court.
4 During the Williams Lake press conference, the RCMP displayed an AK–47 assault rifle, a loaded 9-mm semi-automatic pistol, as well as another rifle; martial-arts weapons; a garrote, which is used to strangle; two machetes and an axe. This information is taken from the news story, '"Terrorism" will end, RCMP warns,' *Calgary Herald*, 20 August 1995, A12 (CP).
5 At the time of the standoff, the media referred to the group of Native elders and chiefs who were invited by the RCMP to go into the camp as 'Shuswap negotiators.' Steven Frasher pointed out to me that this was an oversimplification, because the intermediaries belonged to the Gitksan, Okanagan, and Shuswap First Nations. For this reason, I have used 'Native intermediaries' or 'intermediaries' in order to avoid misidentifying group affiliation. Dr Mike Webster from the RCMP negotiating team also advised me that 'intermediaries' is a more appropriate term to describe the role of the Native elders and leaders who comprised this group. The RCMP had trained negotiators, who continued to work behind the scenes, and their roles were distinct from those of people who went into the camp.
6 Many of the incoming RCMP also stayed at the Red Coach Inn. At a midpoint in the standoff, Sergeant Montague requested that the police take over the whole hotel, but the manager declined.
7 News stories and commentaries that exemplify this point include 'Sundance ritual "new to B.C.,"' *Vancouver Sun*, 23 August 1995, B3; Mike Roberts, 'Cast from Good, Bad and Ugly,' *Vancouver Province*, 31 August 1995 A13; and Joey Thompson, 'Since when do natives have the only patent on visions?' *Vancouver Province*, 30 August 1995, A14.
8 Grand Chief Ovide Mercredi also noted that there seemed to be two

different perspectives in the dispute. He identified the 'hawks,' who had a militant perspective, with Wolverine as the primary exponent; and the 'doves,' who had a spiritual perspective, with Percy Rosette as the faithkeeper and most frequently identified spokesperson for the spiritual aspects of the camp. This information is taken from the news story, 'Indian camp "split" over leaders,' *Vancouver Sun*, 31 August 1995, A3.

9 The phrase 'come out in body bags' appeared in several news stories, including 'If we go in body bags, we win, defiant B.C. natives say,' *Edmonton Journal*, 23 August 1995, A1.

10 One of the people at the camp told reporters that the shooting incident with the forestry workers and the shot fired at the ERT officer (18 August 1995) were misrepresented and that the shot was a warning shot fired into the air. This information is taken from the news story, 'Indian rebels plan to "leave in body bags,"' *Vancouver Sun*, 22 August 1995, A1. A subsequent news story included information from a camp source, who admitted that there were 'a couple of .22-calibre rifles, but none of the heavy weaponry, such as an AK–47, that police found at the Fraser River.' This quotation of the news text is taken from the news story, 'RCMP conducts wide probe into militant Indian group,' *Vancouver Sun*, 24 August 1995, B6.

11 The episode was discussed on a website and referenced in the news story, 'Rebel saga rides the Internet,' *Vancouver Province*, 27 August 1995, A5. Other newspaper accounts of the helicopter shooting include: 'Mercredi given 2 days to end Indian standoff,' *Vancouver Sun*, 25 August 1995, A1; and the RCMP press release of the incident is found in the *Globe and Mail* (reprinted from the *Winnipeg Free Press*), 'Shots ring out at rebel camp RCMP chopper observes native gunfire,' 25 August 1995 (CP).

12 Chief Antoine Archie confirmed in our interview on 25 July 1997 that the Cariboo Tribal Council invited Ovide Mercredi to Gustafsen Lake. Several people (including media and police) assumed that either the RCMP had invited the Grand Chief of the Assembly of First Nations or he came on his own initiative. These speculations fuelled distortions that presented both the RCMP and the grand chief in a negative light.

13 This information is taken from the news story, 'Mercredi given 2 days to end Indian standoff,' *Vancouver Sun*, 25 August 1995, A1.

14 Grand Chief Mercredi's description of his relationship with the people at the camp is found in the news story, 'The Standoff,' *Vancouver Sun*, 28 August 1995, A3.

15 This quotation is taken from the news story, 'Mercredi, rebels clash over ways to seek justice,' *Vancouver Sun*, 26 August 1995, A1.

16 This quotation is taken from the news story, 'Behind the barricades of defiance,' *Vancouver Province*, 27 August 1995, A28.

17 This information is taken from the news story, 'Mercredi: Rebels risk death,' *Victoria Times Colonist*, 26 August 1995, A1 (CP).

18 The news stories in the *Globe and Mail* were reprinted from: '-Natives-Weapons Drop the guns, Mercredi tells rebel natives,' *Winnipeg Free Press* 26 August 1995, a2 (CP); 'Tension rises with native groups Shot fired after the Assembly of First Nations national chief Ovide Mercredi met with rebels,' *Charlottetown Guardian*, 26 August 1995, 1, section A; and 'Mercredi meets with rebel natives,' in the *St. John's Evening Telegram*, 26 August 1995, 7.

19 During the standoff, 'fail' and 'failure' were the most frequent descriptors of Grand Chief Mercredi's negotiations at the camp used in the *Vancouver Sun* (2: 1 in a headline, and 1 in a chronology) and the *Vancouver Province* (5: 1 in a lead-in, 2 in chronologies, 1 under a photographic illustration, 1 in the news narrative). These words employed in the headline, lead-in, chronologies, and the statement following a photographic illustration would have a greater influence than their usage in other parts of a news narrative because of the summarizing functions. The *Victoria Times Colonist* and the *Globe and Mail* printed stories originating from Canadian Press that did not use 'fail,' but presented the negotiations as confrontational, ending in a stalemate, with no sense of progress.

20 Wolverine commented about the pending meeting with Grand Chief Mercredi, 'He can put on fatigues, then he's welcome to come on this side of the fence.' See 'Mercredi given 2 days to end Indian standoff,' *Vancouver Sun*, 25 August 1995, A1.

21 The photograph was taken by Jonathan Green, a former reporter for the *100 Mile House Free Press*.

22 The RCMP barricades also caught another journalist by surprise. Allegedly, this reporter had set up a tent in the bush, a few kilometres from the camp, and when the RCMP erected the barricade, he was on the wrong side of the line. He hid inside the tent, hoping the police would not find him, but they discovered him the day after the barricades went up. He was taken into town by the RCMP, who seized his film, processed the pictures, and asked him to identify who was in the pictures. The journalist subsequently left 100 Mile House.

23 A *Vancouver Sun* news story outlines Grand Chief Mercredi's complaints about the RCMP's interference with his second (and final) negotiation meeting at the camp. Mercredi accused the police of 'sandbagging his mediation efforts.' He described the mood in the camp as 'extremely angry and hostile,' and he predicted violence between the camp and the RCMP if the police did not stop the pressure tactics. He said that low-flying helicop-

ters were buzzing the camp and increasing the level of tension. According to the news story, Mercredi disclosed that the RCMP were 'advancing plans to invade an illegal camp of armed native Indians because of white public opinion ... They told me that they have to go ahead for two reasons – one, they don't want to set a precedent. And two, they are saying white public opinion demands it. That still doesn't make it right.' Mercredi is quoted again: 'The greatest presumption in law is innocence. Everyone is entitled to that. These individuals, whether you agree with them or not, are entitled to that.' These excerpts are taken from the news story, 'RCMP actions anger Mercredi,' *Vancouver Sun*, 28 August 1995, A3.

24 Clark's constitutional argument was based on an application of the 1763 Royal Proclamation; he identifies that the queen's Privy Council is a more appropriate institution than the Canadian judiciary for negotiations involving Canadian Native people and their rights.

25 The RCMP did seize weapons from a vehicle headed to the camp on 25 August 1995, the same day as the first meeting between Grand Chief Mercredi and the camp. They included a 12–gauge shotgun and ammunition, two illegal high-capacity magazines for a .308–calibre assault rifle, 200 rounds of .308 ammunition, and a bow. This information is taken from the news story, 'Cops, natives on brink of violence,' *Vancouver Province*, 27 August 1995, A5.

26 An unclassified RCMP memorandum to Superintendent Olfert from Sergeant Montague dated 1 September 1995 identifies a concern that 'There is a potential danger that members might express views not consistent with our official messaging.' The recommended strategy is that 'The Force should never allow such a negative message to leak out. If we can prevent internal turmoil from becoming a story, we should' (1–2).

3. Show of Force

1 This excerpt was overheard on the radiotelephone link between the camp and the RCMP negotiators and published in the news story, 'Hopes rise for ending armed standoff,' Vancouver Sun, 31 August 1995, A1. It was published days after the RCMP advised the media to cease publishing from this source.

2 The persuasive cues bear a striking resemblance to several of the situations that evolved between the RCMP media relations personnel and the media during the Gustafsen Lake standoff. One cue is an appeal to a sense of reciprocity – where a party is compelled to reciprocate a favour. Another cue is to encourage a commitment; this could begin with a small request,

subsequently enlarged to a greater one (or the reverse). Automatic responses of obedience may be fostered with authority as a cue. A similar cue is the imitation of others for appropriate behaviour, especially when there are uncertainties of appropriate behaviour. Compliance is also encouraged when requests are from those we know and like. Last is the principle of scarcity: we desire and value entities that are perceived to be recently scarce and for which there may be competition. This information is taken from the 'Influence in Crisis Management,' *RCMP Gazette* 58:2 1996: 8–14; and 'The Use of Force and the Gustafsen Lake Barricade' *RCMP Gazette* 58:2, 1996: 16–19. These articles are not available from a public library.

3 One of the details of this episode missed by the large media outlets was that the forestry workers were Aboriginal men, working for a Native-operated forestry crew. There were rumours among the Gustafsen Lake supporters that this shooting incident was fabricated by the RCMP. It was established during the trial and confirmed during the research by defence counsel George Wool that the incident did occur and that the shooting originated from certain unnamed members of the camp.

4 The shooting episode involving the two RCMP officers contributed to a series of near-panic situations and confrontations. A group of four RCMP officers in a police vehicle on an adjacent forestry road became lost when they were instructed to clear the area. They eventually abandoned their vehicle and were flown out by helicopter. The vehicle was retrieved three weeks later. A few hours after the shooting incident, German tourists (one of whom the police thought resembled someone in the camp) unwittingly drove into the area that the RCMP were still in the process of securing. RCMP officers jumped out at the vehicle in a full 'take-down,' with police weapons aimed at the vehicle, much to the confusion of the tourists who could barely speak English. There were several RCMP car searches during the standoff. On one occasion two vehicles with several Native passengers (including a baby) were stopped on the forestry road leading to the checkpoint. According to the news account, one the occupants of the vehicles commented, '"It's not a shock to be treated like this because my people are always treated like this."' The last incident is taken from the news story, 'Hopes rise for ending armed standoff,' *Vancouver Sun*, 31 August 1995, A1.

5 I confirmed that the flak-jacket shooting episode was a pivotal event for the RCMP at Gustafsen Lake with Sergeant Montague and Staff Sergeant Sarich.

6 Over the past few years, it has become common for the RCMP to monitor news stories in high-profile RCMP investigations. In the case of the

Gustafsen Lake standoff, the RCMP also conducted public opinion polls to gage their pubic approval rating.

7 Journalists from small or independent newspapers were not allowed to attend, nor were any of the spectators.

8 'Reports gained by phone anger RCMP,' *Vancouver Sun*, 30 August 1995, A3.

9 Most of the insertions of unauthorized radio-telecommunications were so subtle that an analysis of the media texts could not pick them out with any certainty.

10 By the time I interviewed the journalists, a few of them said that they had reversed their original judgment of the *Vancouver Sun*'s decision to continue incorporating police radio-telecommunications. Reflecting back on the situation and the issues that had come up in court, they said that they wished that their news organizations had also published from the radio-telecommunications.

11 I found out during my fieldwork that the dispute between the RCMP and the *Vancouver Sun* was not resolved during the standoff, although months afterwards, the editor received a letter from Sergeant Montague. The letter advised the editor that the British Columbia Department of Justice had found that the newspaper was accountable under Section 9(2) of the Radiocommunication Act for intercepting and divulging radiocommunications without permission from the originator (the RCMP). The conclusions of the RCMP were that the *Vancouver Sun* had 'acted contrary to public interest.' The letter anticipated that if similar circumstances arose in the future, 'we will be able to mutually agree on what constitutes legitimate public interests without compromising the objectives of our respective organizations' (letter dated 8 December 1995). The matter has not been pursued in court at the time of this writing.

12 At the time of this writing, Bruce Clark's argument remains unsupported by the Supreme Court of Canada.

13 The shift in the media's and the RCMP's presentations of Clark are tracked in the following *Vancouver Sun* news stories. Just as Bruce Clark became known in the Gustafsen Lake media coverage, the *Vancouver Sun* identified Clark as the lawyer who formerly had represented the Lil'Wat Peoples Movement in British Columbia, which was charged with obstructing and assaulting police during a blockade. Clark's arrest after refusing to leave a courtroom was mentioned in the same news story. This information is taken from the news story, 'Indians fear police assault,' *Vancouver Sun*, 21 August 1995, A1. RCMP and media support of Clark is found in 'Lawyer allowed to talk to rebels in bid to end standoff,' *Vancouver Sun*, 30 August 1995, A1. The transition period, during which the RCMP and the media

provided a minor degree of affirmation (but no outward signs of negativity), occurred with Clark's press release after his visit to the camp. This fact appeared in the news story, 'Lawyer says police shot at Indians first,' *Vancouver Sun*, 1 September 1995, A1. Clark's 'official' role in the RCMP strategy is provided in the news story, 'Standoff lawyer parries with police' *Vancouver Sun*, 2 September 1995, A1. The signal of Clark's fall from grace came when the British Columbia attorney general renounced Clark's resolution proposal in 'Lawyer accused of "criminal extortion,"' *Vancouver Sun*, 2 September 1995, A4. The full reversal of the RCMP on their assessment of Clark is identified in the news story, 'Gustafsen Lake standoff: RCMP find bullet-ridden vehicle,' *Vancouver Sun*, 5 September 1995, A3.

14 One of the most personal attacks on Clark in the media is found in a newspaper column entitled, 'A face only an alien mother could love.' The columnist links Clark's personal appearance with his association with the people inside the Gustafsen Lake camp. It is stated in the article, 'It is disturbing to see their legal advice is coming from someone who looks almost exactly like an alien who crash landed in the Nevada desert in 1947 ... If all this is not compelling enough there is one final piece of evidence that proves beyond any doubt that this is an alien from outer space. Look again at the picture. Notice the peculiar eyeglasses. So far as I can determine, eyeglasses like this are not available anywhere in our solar system.' This excerpt is taken from the *Saskatoon Star Phoenix*, 31 August 1995, A2.

15 The topic of labelling in the newspaper stories will be discussed in chapter 6.

16 The RCMP psychologist, Dr Webster, said that the negotiations with the camp improved when Ovide Mercredi visited the camp. 'The next breakthrough was when Bruce Clark shot himself in the foot,' he added. 'We believed that if we didn't give him an opportunity that his name would be haunting us for the rest of this thing. So we inserted him and we believed that he would shoot himself in the foot. And sure enough, he did it. So that was good. We eliminated him there. He destroyed his own credibility.' This news story excerpt is taken from 'Patience "key" to peaceful outcome,' *Vancouver Sun*, 19 September 1995, B2.

17 According to this research, the errors in the characterization of the 4 September 1995 shooting episode were noted in the *Petition* for release from custody, 12 April 1996.

18 The RCMP press releases at 100 Mile House implied that the shooting incident caused the APCs to be brought in. The twinning in the news accounts of this detail and the precautionary cancellation of Native inter-

mediaries' being allowed into the camp added to the sense of danger and to the volatility of the people in the camp. In another news story published in the *Victoria Times Colonist* at about the same time (6 September 1995) British Columbia premier Harcourt is quoted as advising that the police had ordered the APCs two weeks earlier, around 23 August 1995. These details are taken from the news story, 'Harcourt calls for patience as key to Gustafsen peace,' *Victoria Times Colonist*, 6 September 1995, a3.

19 At this point during the conflict, Sergeant Montague had taken a five-day rest leave and was replaced by his assistant, Corporal Ward.

20 The research data confirm that BCTV included a short video clip and a voice-over referencing a shooting episode at Checkpoint 17 that bears a strong resemblance to this incident.

21 In his court testimony, Superintendent Olfert acknowledged the risks of a media leak about the RCMP's acquiring armoured personnel carriers. During a strategy meeting held on August 1995 he stated his concerns that the news would lead to a racial firestorm. The meeting was videotaped and later played during the trial. This information is taken from the news story, 'RCMP feared a "war,"' *Vancouver Province*, 9 January 1997, A8.

22 Because the hotel management recognized that communications between media personnel and informing media of RCMP press conferences would be problematic, two message boards were set up. One of these boards became an information centre for supporters of the protest, who posted faxes from other supporting groups; it became a source of contention at the time of the standoff because the hotel management received complaints from guests that the messages in the faxes were offensive. Near the conclusion of the standoff, these faxes were removed by the hotel staff. Some of the protest supporters believed that the directive came from the RCMP, but this contention was firmly denied by the hotel management.

23 Both the Red Coach Inn and the service station are owned by the Emissaries of the Divine Light (see chap. 1, n.8).

24 The attorney general was available for interviews in Victoria and Vancouver for the television outlets, and these were incorporated in the Gustafsen Lake television news stories.

25 Newspaper and television news accounts show that some of the spectators spoke with the RCMP media liaison after the press conferences. On one such occasion, a parent of a teenaged individual inside the camp confronted Sergeant Montague; she is quoted as saying, 'I want her to come home and I want her to come home safe. I want to let you know my daughter is not a terrorist. She attended the sundance ceremony on those grounds. I want to see her babies being born.' This excerpt is taken from

the news story, 'Indians offered gifts for freedom after talks fail,' *Vancouver Sun*, 29 August 1995, A1.

26 These tactics were confirmed by Sergeant Montague during my interview with him on 27 May 1997.

27 References to the lack of media witnessing include 'Selected media get look at Zulu; RCMP allow trips into forward base of operations,' *Vancouver Sun*, 18 September 1995, A3; and the editorial, 'All the news that's fit to ... be manipulated,' *Vancouver Sun*, 22 September 1995, A18.

28 Permission for media to film is implied with the understanding that the sources know the camera is in their presence. As a rule, subjects do not preview raw footage; media frown upon this practice because it might invite news sources to attempt editorial control, which the media outlet wants to avoid. Nor would it be appropriate for the journalists to warn the sources to conduct themselves any differently because they are being filmed, since it would be considered media tampering with the news event. This information and the policies and practices of television news production were confirmed with CBC-TV producer Sue Rideout in a telephone interview, 7 June 1999.

29 CBC-TV had purchased this video recording from a freelance photographer from the Gustafsen Lake camp.

30 According to CBC-TV producer Sue Rideout, there have been a few cases of law enforcement agencies' demanding their media materials. The CBC does not relinquish them unless a subpoena has been served, and it consults with its legal department to ensure that there is no alternative recourse. Ms Rideout also stated that, in recent years, the courts most often side with law enforcement on the issue of confiscating media materials for investigations. Under similar circumstances in an unrelated case, the CBC attempted to withhold the release of the media materials, but failed. The public response supported the CBC's passing over materials without contest. Ms Rideout stated that the issue is a sensitive one: at stake is the CBC's need to maintain its integrity as a public broadcaster, which does not include becoming an extension of law enforcement (telephone interview, 7 June 1999).

31 According to Superintendent Olfert, this initiative was particular to the Gustafsen Lake standoff, because the RCMP barricaded situation model advises against allowing any third party to enter the barricaded area. Such a practice is discouraged because of the risks that the third party might becoming the victim of a hostage-taking.

32 Chief Nathan Matthew corrected this information, saying that he was the chairperson, not the president.

33 Normally, the RCMP do not allow anybody to go beyond barricaded perimeters because of the potential for hostage-taking. Another measure that broke with the barricaded situation model was that the intermediaries also brought grocery staples (such as flour and potatoes) into the camp. According to a few of the journalists (and news reports at the time), the RCMP interpreted the supply of food as diminishing the incentive for the people in the camp to surrender.

34 By sophisticated, I am referring to the social status and structural and tactical power to orchestrate and control events, in addition to the technology, training, and a shared linguistic code system between the RCMP media personnel and the journalists.

35 The information integrated in the above narrative about the meeting at Merritt is taken from the interview with Chief Nathan Matthew and elder Bill Lightbown and from the newspaper story, 'Three rebels feared hurt in wild shootout,' *Vancouver Sun*, 12 September 1995, A1.

4. Out of Control

1 In this dialogue with RCMP Sergeant Montague, I am referring to the RCMP wescam video that shows the camp truck explosion. Sergeant Montague is basing his assessment on the RCMP simulation of the explosive device on another vehicle after the actual firefight. Ours were not the only contrasts in the interpretation of this blast. In the *Reasons for Judgement* the Honourable Mr Justice Josephson describes the outcome of the detonated explosive on the vehicle as 'a large cloud of dust' (Docket: X043738, New Wesminster Registry). On the other hand, in the *Petition* for the release of custody of Joseph Adam Ignace, the defence counsel describes the explosion as causing 'a great deal of smoke.' On the same page, the statement by Staff Sergeant Debolt, who was at the scene, also refers to 'a cloud of smoke' (*Petition*, p. 11, No. X043738, New Westminster Registry).

2 In the *Vancouver Sun* news story that ran during RCMP testimony at the trial it is stated: 'RCMP snipers using a laser-equipped rifle were given the green light to shoot-to-kill native Indians at Gustafsen Lake last year, according to court testimony. "It was my view that our members were in danger and they were to take whatever action they felt appropriate," said Vancouver RCMP Inspector Roger Kemble, the field commander at Gustafsen Lake. He testified at the trial of 14 native Indians and four non-Indians, who are charged with offences ranging from mischief to attempted murder, that he gave ERT members the authority on Sept. 10

to shoot any armed Indians' 'Snipers at Gustafsen able to "shoot to kill,"' *Vancouver Sun*, 12 October 1996, A17.

3 The following is from the transcript of my interview with RCMP Superintendant Olfert: **Tell me about this idea that there was a kill order that came out in court**. *'Yeah, it came out in court. Absolutely ludicrous! If there was a kill order, there would have been bodies all over the place. Because that could've been fulfilled just – immediately. Immediately. Absolutely. And I wasn't the front-line ERT commander. I – but that sort of command would've come from me. And it can't happen. There would be terms of engagement – and I don't know – in their briefings, like what their commanders, maybe to the members said, "if under these circumstances, this is where you're at, this is what the terms of engagement would be." But as a general kill order – sorry, non-starter. Can't happen'* (interview with Superintendent Olfert, 17 February 1998).

4 See Introduction, n.8.

5 I acquired excerpts of two shooting incidents recorded on RCMP wescam aerial videos. They were included in the Vancouver East Community 4 *Nitewatch* production entitled 'Gustafsen Lake,' which was broadcast in Vancouver in January 1997.

6 The Shuswap elder who suffered a heart attack was a brother of Percy Rosette. He did recover. This information is taken from the news story, 'Snipers at Gustafsen able to "shoot to kill,"' *Vancouver Sun*, 12 October 1996, A2.

7 I confirmed the height of the smoke with defence counsel George Wool.

8 Superintendent Olfert described the situation of the APC that was disabled as *'pandemonium.'* There was a barrage of bullets striking the metal exterior of the APC, resulting in a deafening racket. A police dog inside the APC was biting at the ERT members and attempting to bite the flying bullet casings as they were returning fire.

9 George Wool argued during the trial that much of the gunfire came from occupants of two APCs unwittingly firing at each other. Their positioning in the dense brush prevented the police inside the APCs from seeing each other.

10 According to District Superintendent Olfert, the shots fired by the RCMP were aimed high in the air to avoid casualties. This assertion can be substantiated by the fact that only one person was wounded, despite the firing of 'thousands of rounds.' During the fieldwork at Gustafsen Lake, I walked through the firefight area and saw what appeared to be a rust-coloured 'graze' mark, about four metres high, on the trunk of a tree. This was the only possible evidence of gunfire in the area found by *100 Mile House Free Press* editor Steven Frasher and me two years after the firefight.

11 The *Globe and Mail* news story was reprinted from 'Three natives shot in firefight,' which was published in the *Victoria Times Colonist*, 12 September 1995, A1. Similar Canadian Press versions of this story appeared on the same day in the *Edmonton Journal*, 'Natives wounded in firefight,' A1; *Saskatoon Star Phoenix*, 'Natives wounded in shootout,' A1; *Regina Leader Post*, 'Gunfire at BC native protest,' A1; *Winnipeg Free Press*, 'Natives hit in shootout,' A1; *London Free Press*, 'Three natives shot in BC, rebel leader tells police,' A9; *Toronto Star*, 'BC Indians, RCMP trade fire at camp,' A10; *Montreal Gazette*, 'Three Indians injured in shootout with Mounties outside B.C. camp,' A6; and (Newfoundland) *Evening Telegram*, 'Natives shot in gunfight,' A1. In 'Three natives shot, rebels say,' (*Calgary Herald*, A1) incorporated accounts from Canadian Press, the *Vancouver Province*, and the *Vancouver Sun* were incorporated.

12 The 'early warning device' referred to by the RCMP media liaison during this press conference was a misnomer. The 'early warning devices' that the Emergency Response Team actually employed comprised a vast network of fishing lines rigged to detect protesters sneaking out of the camp.

13 This is the number of newspapers that were part of the Canadian Press cooperative news service at the time of the Gustafsen Lake standoff.

14 This excerpt is taken from the news story, 'Three Rebels feared hurt in wild shootout,' *Vancouver Sun*, 12 September 1995, A1.

15 Probably the most famous example of the *Vancouver Sun*'s challenges to authority was its breaking story in May 1992 on what became known as 'Bingogate.' The newspaper published the first allegations that the British Columbia provincial New Democratic party, under the leadership of Premier Harcourt, diverted bingo profits from the Nanaimo Commonwealth Holding Society (which were meant for charity) to the political party. The Bingogate scandal contributed to Premier Harcourt's resignation from office in 1996.

16 On occasion, *Vancouver Sun* news stories are reprinted in other newspapers belonging to Southam Incorporated. I was told in my interviews with *Vancouver Sun* staff that the potential for sharing its news stories with other newspapers does not influence the *Sun*'s editorial decisions. The above-mentioned *Vancouver Sun* news story of the 11 September 1995 firefight was not reprinted (in whole, or in part) in any of the 17 newspapers in the cross-Canada sample incorporated for this research. I could not ascertain whether the *Vancouver Sun* had posted this story on their website. Even if this were the case, it is doubtful whether the readership of this website would have been significant on a national scale.

17 A *Vancouver Sun* news story printed two days after the firefight seemed to

both support and hedge on the notion that the APC had been disabled because of gunfire: 'the 13-tonne vehicle, which is armed with a 7.62-mm machinegun, has some parts that are vulnerable to small-arms fire. Police have not said how the APC was knocked out' ('Military hardware now RCMP tools as Mounties try to resolve siege: ERT: militants' camp reported to be heavily fortified,' *Vancouver Sun*, 13 September 1995, B1). A correction about the disabled APC was published in a news story after the standoff: 'It was earlier reported that one Bison was disabled by gunfire. But the vehicle's transmission box was likely disabled after the Bison drove over a tree, Montague said' ('A-G defends airing of records: Dosanjh says RCMP action spurred by public safety issue,' *Vancouver Sun*, 21 September 1995, A3).

18 A review of the media materials confirms that subsequent news stories did not include the same detailed description of the truck occupants leaving the truck armed and firing weapons. This change supports the RCMP media liaison's contention that corrections were made informally and the media immediately complied.

19 The inclusion of Sergeant Montague's correction is taken from the news story, 'Gunfire at BC native protest,' *Regina Leader Post*, 12 September 1995, A1 (CP).

20 The *Vancouver Sun* and the *Vancouver Province* named individuals and their criminal records as provided by Sergeant Montague at that press conference. The *Calgary Herald* named three individuals, but none of the criminal records.

21 This quotation is taken from the news story, 'Records exaggerated: Mountie admits making "mistake" in radio interview,' *Vancouver Province*, 12 February 1997, A11.

22 In *The Information and Privacy Handbook*, 2nd ed., published by the Ministry of Government Services, Province of British Columbia (January, 1995) it is stated in (25.1): 'Whether or not a request for access is made, the head of a public body must, without delay, disclose to the public, to an affected group of people or to an applicant, information (a) about a risk of significant harm to the environment or to the health or safety of the public or a group of people, or (b) the disclosure of which is, for any other reason clearly in the public interest.' It is also stated: 'Where the public interest requires that the head disclose information to the general public, the head ensures that the information is released in a manner designed to reach the public at large.' At the same time, (15.1) pertains to disclosures harmful to law enforcement: 'The head of a public body may refuse to disclose information to an applicant if the disclosure could reasonably be expected to ...

(g) deprive a person of the right to a fair trial or impartial adjudication.' *The Policy and Procedures Manual*, Section C.3.12, which cross-references Section 25, states that a 'test of significant harm or public interest' be made prior to the disclosure.

23 The juvenile record referred to was for breaking and entering, aggravated assault, possession of a weapon, and bestiality. This information was published in the news story, 'Criminal records detailed,' *Vancouver Sun*, 12 September 1995, A2. The journalists I spoke with said that the 'bestiality' charge was one of the most memorable of all of the convictions read out that day and became the source of many jokes within the RCMP and the media.

24 These individuals included Johnny Guitar, John Hill, and Arnold Williams. According to defence counsel George Wool, the announcement began with identifying Johnny Guitar and stating his criminal record, which was the most extensive and serious of the records released during that press conference. Guitar claimed that he had never been at the camp, although he had participated in other Native blockades. Johnny Guitar was not among those arrested for the standoff at Gustafsen Lake, nor was he ever charged with any offences relating to the standoff at Gustafsen Lake. In one news story this inconsistency was noted: 'One of those identified, John Guitar, appeared before reporters to refute Montague's suggestion he is involved in the standoff ... Guitar said he had never been to Gustafsen Lake and is considering legal action against the police for releasing his criminal record. Asked to explain the apparent contradiction, Montague said police intelligence had placed Guitar in the armed camp at Gustafsen Lake' ('3 more militants surrender to police: Soldier injured by stun grenade,' *Vancouver Sun*, 13 September 1995, A1.) Johnny Guitar was arrested at the end of September 1995 for possession of an AK–47 assault weapon, along with one of the Gustafsen Lake defendants who was released on bail. This information is taken from the news story, 'Gustafsen sundancer arrested again,' *Vancouver Sun*, 2 October 1995, B1. Defence counsel George Wool confirmed, for this research, that Arnold Williams, another individual whose criminal record was announced at the press conference, also was not in the camp at this time.

25 This information is taken from the news story, 'Native leaders fear rise in violence,' *Vancouver Sun*, 12 September 1995, A2.

26 Sergeant Montague's grouping of the Adams Lake and Douglas Lake blockades with the Gustafsen Lake standoff appears to contradict his comments made to reporters earlier in the standoff: 'Sgt. Peter Montague said the situation at Gustafsen Lake is different from other standoffs

involving B.C. natives earlier this summer at Douglas Lake Ranch and Adams Lake ... With Adams Lake and Douglas Lake, there are legitimate native concerns that were addressed under due process in the courts.' According to Montague, 'Those positions had the support of most of the native community. At Gustafsen Lake, they have no support whatsoever.' This excerpt is taken from the news story, 'Indian rebels plan to "leave in body bags,"' *Vancouver Sun*, 22 August 1995, A1.

27 Sergeant Montague's distinction between people inside and outside the camp during the press conference for the television coverage was not confirmed in 14 newspaper outlets or by any of the interviews with journalists (including television journalists) who described the 11 September 1995 press conference.

28 The *Vancouver Sun* and the *Vancouver Province* did not provide identical lists of names and criminal offences, although both identified seven individuals. After duplications were eliminated, nine names and associated records were published in the newspapers. The news stories of the criminal records include 'It's a rogues gallery, cops say,' *Vancouver Province*, 12 September 1995, A5; and 'Criminal records detailed,' *Vancouver Sun*, 12 September 1995, A2.

29 The individual who was reported to the media as having previous convictions for fraud and theft voluntarily came out of the camp on the night following the firefight. During his initial court appearance, he shouted that he did not have a criminal record or a tendency towards violence. This information is taken from the news story, 'Rebel natives charged,' *Winnipeg Free Press*, 13 September 1995, a2 (CP). The error in the RCMP identification of this individual and the associated criminal record was discussed in court. While on the witness stand, Sergeant Montague testified that 'he had no idea whether or not such a record existed.' This excerpt is taken from the news story, 'Story of the standoff at Gustafsen Lake,' *Vancouver Sun*, 21 May 1997, A6. The RCMP also identified the only person in the camp with a previous record that related to behaviour during the trial proceedings of an unrelated protest. This information is found in the news story, 'Criminal records detailed,' *Vancouver Sun*, 12 September 1995, A2.

30 Shortly after the conclusion of the standoff, the attorney general defended the release of the criminal record to the media. '"I think this is public information in the sense that the convictions occur in a public and open court," Dosanjh said Wednesday. "To that extent, the record is always public." The RCMP decided to release information on criminal records for public safety, he said, noting police were unable to contain the huge area

surrounding Gustafsen Lake until the final few days of the standoff.'
Sergeant Montague also justified the releasing of the criminal records, and
in the same news story he is quoted as stating, '"The RCMP stands by all
its public statements."' These comments are taken from the news story, 'A-
G defends airing of records: Dosanjh says RCMP action spurred by public
safety issue,' *Vancouver Sun*, 21 September 1995, A3.

31 The full quotation is 'Union of B.C. Indian Chiefs president Saul Terry said
chiefs from his organization have asked the Cariboo Tribal Council and the
RCMP if they can do anything to end the crisis. Terry argued native Indians
occupying part of the ranch should not be viewed as terrorists or extremists. "I do not think we are really squatters or trespassers on our own land,"
he said.' This excerpt is taken from the news story, 'Radicals to reap support in shootout, leaders warn,' *Vancouver Sun*, 29 August 1995, A3.

32 This excerpt is taken from the news story, 'RCMP accused of bid to smear
Indian rebels,' *Vancouver Sun*, 13 September 1995, B4.

33 This research confirmed with Superintendant Olfert that, at the time of his
request for a 'smear campaign,' he was unaware of the RCMP policy
manual's instructions regarding media releases. However, he was certain
that the release of the criminal records and the abrogation from the policies
were discussed by the strategy committee.

34 During the trial, evidence from the RCMP training tape was presented,
showing a six-minute portion of an RCMP strategy meeting. In the meeting, Sergeant Montague is heard making the comment, 'smear campaigns
are our specialty.' The *'smear campaign'* remark was widely reported in the
media during the trial. News stories that discussed the *'smear campaign'*
include: 'Mountie regrets "smear" remark,' *Vancouver Province*, 21 January
1997, A9; '2nd cop backs away from earlier words,' *Vancouver Province*,
23 January 1997, A11; and 'RCMP say talk of smear campaign "in jest,"'
Vancouver Sun, 23 January 1997, B2. According to lawyer George Wool, the
RCMP requested and obtained a court order forbidding the discussion of
the training tapes, which were viewed in court, and prohibiting public
viewing. In Wool's opinion, 'withholding this evidence is not appropriate
for a liberal, democratic society.' Furthermore, he considered that the
reasons behind the RCMP's request were that *'the public may look at the tape
and decide RCMP media relations is a fraud'* and *'the RCMP is afraid the
content is so persuasive that it is going to hurt them* (interview with George
Wool, 26 May 1997).

35 This information was confirmed by non-police sources.

36 According to Shelagh Franklin, one of the people inside the camp at the
time, the RCMP negotiators assured the people in the camp that they

would be safe to go to the lake to get water and to wash. This information is taken from 'Gustafsen Lake,' Vancouver East Community 4 program *Nitewatch*, broadcast in January 1997.

37 The shooting distance was confirmed in the *Vancouver Sun* editorial, 13 June 1997, A20.

38 During his trial testimony RCMP Inspector Kemble, field commander at Gustafsen Lake, acknowledged his authorization for ERT members to shoot at the individual walking towards the lake on 12 September 1995: 'It was my decision at that time, based on the events the day before, and the previous shooting of our members, I authorized the members across the lake to shoot at the individual walking' (excerpt of testimony presented during the Vancouver East Community 4 program, 'Gustafsen Lake,' *Nitewatch*, January, 1997).

39 The morale of the RCMP was also discussed in the coverage of the trial in the news story, 'RCMP considered asking military to take over at Gustafsen,' *Vancouver Sun*, 12 April 1996, A1, A18.

40 The 'criminal Indian' stereotype is particularly ubiquitous because of the over-representation of Aboriginal peoples' serving time in correctional facilities in Canada.

41 'Two-hour shootout likened to Vietnam: ERT officer describes gunbattle: Gustafsen Lake,' *Vancouver Province*, 19 September 1995, A10.

42 This supposition can be traced back to the method Mohawk warriors used at Oka in 1990 to dispose of their weapons before they emerged from their protest camp. During the media coverage of the Gustafsen Lake standoff, quotations from police and government sources in news stories frequently alluded to the protesters' arming themselves with an arsenal of AK–47s. Thus, the media sources conveyed to the public the seriousness of the conflict and the dangerous nature of the people involved in the protest. At the same time, the constant references to this weaponry gave the impression that there were several AK–47s in the camp, which authorities knew was not the case. The *RCMP Report to Crown Counsel* identifies that, before the barricades were set up, the RCMP investigation determined that there were two AK–47s in the camp, one of which was in the back of the truck that was blown up.

43 During the RCMP investigation fewer than 200 (I was unable to ascertain the exact figure) shell casings associated with weapons fired from the camp were found. Such a small quantity had not been anticipated by the RCMP. District Superintendent Olfert testified in court that between 10,000 and 20,000 rounds were fired by the RCMP during the 11 September 1995

firefight. This information was taken from the news story, 'Police wanted 4,000 troops at Gustafsen,' *Vancouver Province*, 8 January 1997, A4.

5. Surrender

1 It was confirmed that John Hill, the 1995 Sundance leader at Gustafsen Lake, and David Seals, another Native person, provided the RCMP (before the barricades were set up) with a list of individuals who, they believed, could act as intermediaries, including Arvol Looking Horse and John Stevens. The RCMP media liaison, Corporal Ward, stated that the RCMP were unable to contact John Stevens until the final week of the standoff. Native intermediaries contacted Arvol Looking Horse to provide spiritual guidance for the camp. This information is taken from the news story, 'RCMP told to send in medicine men 3 weeks ago, Indian says,' *Vancouver Sun*, 19 September 1995, B2.

2 I confirmed that an individual did come out of the camp early that afternoon.

3 The information and quotations regarding the airing of the CBC message are taken from the radio program, *Now the Details*, broadcast by CBC Radio, on 17 September 1995.

4 The following is the news story quote from which this information is taken: 'Chief Arvol Looking Horse, a man native spiritualists equate with the Pope, was in the camp yesterday and was aware of the broadcast. "You could say it was a co-ordinated effort," said Montague' 'B.C. standoff appears close to quiet end,' *Globe and Mail*, taken from the *Winnipeg Free Press*, 14 September 1995, a3 (CP).

5 The news stories include 'Standoff at critical point,' *Victoria Times Colonist*, 14 September 1995, A1; 'High hopes for end to standoff dashed as deal struck with rebels falls through,' *Vancouver Sun*, 14 September 1995, A1; 'Bloodless end appears close,' *Calgary Herald*, 14 September 1995, A1 (CP); 'B.C. natives agree to quit,' *London Free Press*, 14 September 1995, 1 (CP).

6 Gordon Sebastian's remark alluded to the increased risk of violence if the full visibility of the people in the camp and the arresting officers was not possible. The quotation is taken from the news story, 'Standoff at critical point,' *Victoria Times Colonist*, 14 September 1995 a1.

7 This is taken from the CBC Radio show, 'The cops, the natives, and the CBC,' aired during the program, *Now the Details*, 17 September 1995.

8 Fraser successfully challenged his superiors' decision to remove him from the story.

9 RCMP psychologist Dr Mike Webster recalled that Chief Antoine Archie was the closest chief they could find who spoke Shuswap.

10 This point was made by the CBC executives interviewed during the program *Now the Details*, CBC Radio, 17 September 1995.

11 This quotation is taken from 'RCMP told to send in medicine men 3 weeks ago, Indian says,' *Vancouver Sun*, 19 September 1995, B2. Arvol Looking Horse's account contradicts Sergeant Montague's explanation at the time of the CBC Radio announcement.

12 One of the news accounts of the ERT member's description of the firefight appears in 'Two-hour shootout likened to Vietnam: ERT officer describes gunbattle: Gustafsen Lake,' *Vancouver Province*, 19 September 1995, A10.

13 This news story excerpt was taken from 'Selected media get look at Zulu: RCMP allow trips into forward base of operations,' *Vancouver Sun*, 18 September 1995, A3.

14 This comment was made by the British Columbia attorney general during the media tour of the Gustafsen Lake camp at the end of the standoff.

15 The name of these structures is taken from Chinook Jargon, and has several orthographic representations.

6. Terms of Engagement

1 This headline was published by the *Vancouver Province*, 10 September 1995, A8.

2 The notion that language can be a 'fetter' for conveying meaning was noted by Sapir (1921).

3 During the first week after the Williams Lake press conference, the labels appeared in quotations from media sources, and these sources included some of the Native leaders in the province. In these references the Native media sources used the labels to distinguish the people at Gustafsen Lake from other Native people. After that initial week I found that, however, direct quotations of this sort had all but disappeared, and the media itself became the most prolific users of the labels.

4 None of the 6 stories appearing in the *New Brunswick Telegraph Journal* were from CP: 2 were from Southam Press; 2 were from United Press; 1 was from Reuters; and 1 was written by *Telegraph Journal* staff. The total number of invectives used by this newspaper during the standoff was 4.

5 Ironically, Wool was in the Cariboo area during the standoff; he noticed then how the media were portraying the event and the people involved and the responses of the community that he was visiting.

6 According to George Wool, the *RCMP Operational Manual* guidelines on

media relations were not brought up in court as a defence argument. He said that the RCMP would have counter-argued that the uniqueness of the Gustafsen Lake standoff precluded reliance on such protocols. According to Wool, '*the RCMP testimony – started with the – this was an unusual event" kind of approach. And this was a different situation – and they had to adapt. So there was sort of a rationalization developed by the RCMP*' (interview with George Wool, 28 May 1997).

7 The fact that there were no corrections of misinformation to the media was exacerbated by the lack of media attention to the trial proceedings.

8 By hidden audience, I am referring to the idea that this is an audience that might not ordinarily be singled out for special consideration.

9 This assertion is based on the association that people have made with the 1993 standoff at the Branch Davidian Compound, transferring the location and the tragedy to the closest urban centre, Waco, Texas.

10 The souvenir tee-shirts designed at this shop for the RCMP included the RCMP logo and identified the particular RCMP division. A generic version for the media featured a dollar sign ($) with an arrow struck through it, and a mock title, 'Gustafsen Lake Detachment.' Another tee-shirt that was for sale (but not at this shop) featured a picture of an Indian status card inscribed with the Monopoly board phrase, 'Get out of jail free.'

11 This excerpt is taken from the news story, 'Schools urge sensitivity over standoff,' *100 Mile House Free Press*, 13 September 1995, 4.

12 Students also heard racial epithets from people working out of a small facility established by the Canadian Armed Forces adjacent to the temporary RCMP Operations Command Centre at 100 Mile House. Both were located across the street from a local school.

13 Negative sentiments about the Gustafsen Lake camp were not confined to a few local non-Native people. The local chiefs appealed for calm among a few in their communities who were also irate.

14 This headline appeared *100 Mile House Free Press*, 13 September 1995, 1.

7. Wartime Images, Peacetime Wounds

1 I noted this point particularly during the media coverage of the trial (when the media did cover the trial with regularity) when testimony concerning media misinformation and the RCMP 'smear campaign' took place.

2 The media provided cost estimates for the RCMP Gustafsen Lake operation (about $5.5 million) and the eight-month trial (at least $1 million). However, journalists from television, radio, and print were reluctant to provide figures for the amount their outlets spent on the standoff news

coverage. Estimates were that the *Vancouver Sun* spent between $50,000 and $60,000 on overtime and expenses. This sum represents a fraction of labour costs for the 50 to 60 media personnel at 100 Mile House. In addition to labour, expenditures were made on hotels, meals, and vehicle rentals. Media equipment costs included television satellite dishes, estimated at $6,000 per hour. Journalists from several of the outlets acknowledged that the costs of covering the standoff had influenced their employers to cover the trial on only a sporadic basis.

3 I was unable to obtain a copy of this letter from the CBC, but it was cited in the response article 'The facts about Gustafsen' written by Murray Johnston, assistant commissioner of the RCMP and commanding officer of 'E' Division in Vancouver (*Vancouver Sun*, 1 March 2000, A13). In this article, Assistant Commissioner Johnston corrects inaccuracies concerning allegations made in a previously published opinion article, 'Don't bury the tragedy at Gustafsen' (21 January 2000). He responded to the supposed military assistance, the RCMP's use of land mines, as well as the unarmed status of the truck occupants during the firefight and the RCMP's 'disinformation and smear' campaign. He also addressed accusations of the RCMP lying to the CBC and ignoring the CBC's letter of complaint (see chap. 7, n. 11).

4 CBC-TV broadcast this news documentary during *The National* on 24 September 1995.

5 One commentary that addressed some of the circumstances of media manipulation and produced a range of responses is found in 'Media should apologize for gullibility on Gustafsen Lake,' 'Rest My Case' column by Joey Thompson, *Vancouver Province*, 26 September 1997, A12. Staff Sergeant Montague (by then promoted and transferred to the commercial crime section) submitted a letter of rebuttal (10 October 1997, A49) that refuted the columnist's suggestion that the RCMP had enacted staff changes as a consequence of the Gustafsen Lake standoff. Montague also argued that, contrary to the notion that 'there were only a handful of convictions,' 15 of the standoff defendants had been convicted of serious crimes, and the RCMP had 'acted within the scope of the law' when they announced the juvenile record of one of the camp occupants. Montague clarified details regarding camp weapons during the firefight and stated that 'the following day' the RCMP had issued a correction to the media regarding the unarmed status of the people exiting the truck.

6 According to one such news story, 'Rosette says he had a vision that the patch of lakeshore property, owned by rancher Lyle James, was sacred. He squatted on the site last winter.' This excerpt is taken from the *Winnipeg*

Free Press, 1 September 1995, a3 (CP) (reprinted in the *Globe and Mail*). Another news story that makes this connection is 'Standoff at Gustafsen Lake preceded by a vision,' *Vancouver Sun*, 12 September 1995, A3.

7   The following example was identified, above, as a recurring stock phrase in Canadian Press news stories: 'The standoff entered its fourth week Monday in the confrontation between the armed aboriginals and police surrounding *the remote piece of ranchland the natives claim as sacred aboriginal territory*' (I have italicized the phrase for emphasis). I argue that such phrasing pits western notions of property against Native spirituality. This example is taken from the newspaper story, 'Three natives shot in firefight,' *Victoria Times Colonist*, 12 September 1995, a1 (CP) (reprinted in the *Globe and Mail*).

8   In the lead-in to a Sundance news account it is stated, 'The mysterious Sundance ceremony being performed by a native Indian group occupying part of the James Ranch in the Cariboo is a ritual only recently imported to B.C.' The religious ceremony is explained by Gerry Conaty, senior ethnologist at Calgary's Glenbow Museum, but the emphasis in the story is on the body piercing, which is only one aspect of the ritual. According to the *Vancouver Sun* account, Conaty 'said he has witnessed one such Sundance and said he found the experience "disturbing"' from 'Sundance ritual "new to B.C.,"' *Vancouver Sun*, 23 August 1995, B3). Another news story explains: 'Local chiefs don't back their claims and the site has been used for sundances for only about five years' 'Blood spills in sacred circle - Sundance ceremony is at the heart of standoff at Gustafsen Lake,' *Victoria Times Colonist*, 31 August 1995, a1; reprinted *Globe and Mail*).

9   That Chief Antoine Archie was a frequent media source for the *100 Mile House Free Press* is an indicator that the journalists from larger media outlets missed an opportunity to develop a rapport with the chief. Greater familiarity with the local chief and local Aboriginal sentiments about the standoff may have alleviated the media's concerns about Chief Archie's Shuswap message.

10   These include 'Reports gained by phone anger RCMP,' *Vancouver Sun*, 30 August 1995, A3; 'Selected media get look at Zulu: RCMP allow trips into forward base of operations,' *Vancouver Sun*, 18 September 1995, A3; and the editorial, 'All the news that's fit to ... be manipulated,' *Vancouver Sun*, 22 September 1995, A18.

11   The denial of any wrong-doing or harmful consequences from the RCMP's handling of the Gustafsen Lake operation is evident in Murray J. Johnston's (RCMP assistant commissioner and commanding officer of E Division) rebuttal to the opinion article, 'Don't bury the tragedy at Gustafsen'

(*Vancouver Sun*, 21 January 2000, Forum). The opinion article criticized the RCMP's actions at the Gustafsen Lake standoff, citing several alleged improprieties. Although I do not dispute Assistant Commissioner Johnston's assertion that the 'RCMP did not use military land mines at Gustafsen Lake,' I do not concur with several other statements. These include the assistant commissioner's contention that the military contributed only in an advisory role – because of the known fact of the presence of 8 APCs and trained military staff to drive and maintain these vehicles, which the Canadian Armed Forces had loaned to the RCMP for this operation. The assistant commissioner also stated that the RCMP 'did not at any time embark on a "disinformation and smear" campaign during the police operation at Gustafsen Lake,' and that the records show that two occupants of the truck that was disabled by explosives 'were armed with AK47 assault rifles.' With regard to these assertions, the *RCMP Report to Crown Counsel*, my interview with Staff Sergeant Montague, the RCMP memorandum of 1 September 1995 (appendix 7, below), and the trial records confirm otherwise. The assistant commissioner concludes his response by stating his objective: 'to point out the inaccuracies in this opinion article' and that 'these inaccuracies distort the truth, inflame emotions and characterize the events at Gustafsen Lake in a way that erodes the healing process that has evolved from this episode' ('The Facts about Gustafsen,' *Vancouver Sun*, 1 March 2000, A13).

12 Sergeant Montague's testimony concerning his working conditions is found in the news story, 'Second cop backs away from earlier words,' *Vancouver Province*, 23 January 1997, A11.

13 This was discussed in the news story, 'RCMP feared a "war,"' *Vancouver Province*, 9 January 1997, A8.

14 This quote is taken from the news story, 'Mountie denies seeking deaths,' *Vancouver Province*, 7 January 1997, A10.

15 Various U.S. senators, including Senator Charles Grassley, criticized the Federal Bureau of Investigation's 'cowboy culture,' 'that puts image, public relations and headlines ahead of the fundamentals of the FBI.' The senators found this attitude particularly evident in what they called 'bungling a number of high-profile cases,' including the fatal standoffs at Ruby Ridge, Idaho, in 1992 and at Waco, Texas, in 1993. The most recent case cited is the FBI's failure to provide a significant number of documents to the lawyers of defendant Timothy J. McVeigh. This information is taken from 'Senators criticize F.B.I. on McVeigh papers,' *New York Times.com*, 14 May 2001.

16 There have been notable revisions to the *Operational Manual II.6 Media/*

RCMP Relations from 1997 to 2001 (2001 is current as of January 2003). Other significant changes that are relevant to this study include directives specific to press conferences and avoidance of media favouritism. 'Use a press conference to communicate new and important messages about a significant event or to reveal information about complex investigations, police operations and community partnerships and initiatives. A press conference will focus media attention, save time by reducing the number of individual interviews, get the information out to all media simultaneously, and avoid accusations of favoritism to certain reporters' (M/R G.1). Other changes since the Gustafsen Lake standoff regarding media and RCMP relations cite the following directives: 'Cooperation with the media can result in accurate, balanced media coverage' (M/R D.1); and 'When requested to facilitate media participation in special programs such as ride along, see I.1.I.d and I.1.I.2.a.2' (M/R E.2). At the time of this writing, the *RCMP Operational Manual II.16 Media/RCMP Relations, RCMP and the Media*, and *Operational Manual II.16 Media/RCMP Relations E Division (British Columbia)* are available only through the RCMP Access to Information and Privacy Branch, 1200 Vanier Parkway, Ottawa, Ont., K1A 0R2.

17 The *RCMP Operational Manual II.16 Media/RCMP Relations. E Division (British Columbia)* (which lists additional provisions to the general *RCMP Operational Manual*) has not been updated since 1993. It does not identify special provisions for dealing with visible minority groups, other than to respect and use the most current politically correct vernacular to address the group identity.

18 This quote is taken from the news story, 'U.S. court refuses to extradite Canadian native,' *National Post*, 23 November 2000, A4.

19 Reactions to the 2002 treaty referendum in British Columbia are discussed in 'Referendum inflammatory, B.C. natives say,' *National Post*, 23 June 2001, A10; 'B.C. churches blast treaty referendum,' *National Post*, 5 April 2002, A1; 'B.C.'s treaty referendum "amateurish" pollster says,' *National Post*, 6 April 2002, A4; and 'B.C. Jewish groups join boycott of referendum,' *National Post*, 9 April 2002, A8.

20 This was a central finding in the public opinion survey regarding responses to Aboriginal issues by Langford and Ponting (1992).

21 A front-page headline in large bold print regarding the *mixed* responses among Native people to the proposed changes to the Indian Act demonstrates my point: 'First Nations to fight changes,' *Edmonton Journal*, 15 June 2002, A1. Another example, published only a few days later, is a front-page advertisement of a story in the fashion section of the newspaper: 'Mohawk

Mania: rebel hair makes a comeback,' *Edmonton Journal*, 25 June 2002, A1. More recently, a front-page story with the headline 'Will Act Cautiously, Fears Another Oka: Premier condemns native shakedown' links Oka with a conflict between Native communities and oil companies in northern Alberta. The news story describes Oka in terms of the involvement of the RCMP, the killing of a police officer, and a conflict between 'soldiers and natives that dragged on for 10 weeks' (*Edmonton Journal*, 30 January 2003, A1). That the source of the Oka conflict was the appropriation of a Native cemetery for a golf course and that a Native elder was killed from a rock thrown by a non-Native were not mentioned.

22 At the time of the research, Chief Antoine Archie expressed his concerns about the potential for outsiders (Aboriginal) who do not support the treaty process recruiting young people in his community for violent confrontations. This conversation took place *after* informal discussions I had with several Aboriginal young people attending the Gustafsen Lake trial in Surrey, British Columbia. Their anger was evident in their comments about forming armed resistance groups, which, I found quite chilling. In a more general context, Aboriginal leaders and scholars have been speaking out about Native youth gangs for the last few years. Urban poverty leading to gang membership is discussed in Fournier and Crey (2000), who identify that 'In almost every large city or town in Canada, young urban Natives face a crisis of rootlessness' and that 'gangs in Winnipeg attract "disadvantaged angry young Natives" who become involved in "criminal activities such as prostitution, assault, armed robbery, drive-by shootings, and even murder"' (2000:310). Fournier and Crey cite the current national chief of the Assembly of First Nations, Phil Fontaine, and Dave Chartrand of the Manitoba Métis, who also acknowledge the frustrations and hopelessness prevalent among many Aboriginal young people.

Appendix 3: History of Aboriginal Disputes in Canada

1 According to Wilson and Urion (1995), the Canadian reserve period began in the 1830s. Treaty policies were modified in the 1850s. By the late 1860s reserves were established in areas that had become alienated from Native control (Wilson and Urion 1995:58).

2 Position papers also were prepared by Indian associations from other provinces.

3 The MacKenzie Valley Pipeline and the James Bay and Northern Quebec agreements previously acknowledged Aboriginal ownership of traditional lands.

Appendix 7: Excerpt from RCMP (Unclassified Memo) 1 September 1995

1 For ethical reasons I have deleted the name of a second individual identified in the original RCMP memo. This deletion has no bearing on the analysis in chapter 4.

Bibliography

Agar, Michael H. 1986. *Speaking of Ethnography: Qualitative Research Methods.* Vol 2. Beverly Hills, Calif.: Sage.

Alia, Valerie, Brian Brennan, and Barry Hoffmaster, eds. 1996. *Deadlines and Diversity: Journalism Ethics in a Changing World.* Halifax, N.S.: Fernwood.

Allan, Stuart. 1999. *News Culture.* Buckingham, U.K.: Open University Press.

Allen, Irving Lewis. 1990. *Unkind Words: Ethnic Labeling from Redskin to WASP.* New York: Bergin and Garvey.

Allen, Susan L., ed. 1994. *Media Anthropology: Informing Global Citizens.* Westport, Conn.: Bergin and Garvey.

Appadurai, A. 1990. 'Disjuncture and Difference in the Global Cultural Economy.' *Public Culture* 2 (2): 1–24.

– 1991. 'Global Ethnoscapes: Notes and Queries for a Transnational Anthropology.' In *Recapturing Anthropology: Working in the Present,* edited by R.G. Fox, 191–210. Santa Fe, N.M.: School of American Research Advanced Seminar Series.

Asch, Michael. 1992. 'Errors in *Delgamuukw*: An Anthropological Perspective.' In *Aboriginal Title in British Columbia: Delgamuukw vs The Queen,* 221–43. Lantzville, B.C.: Oolichan Books.

– 1993. *Home and Native Land: Aboriginal Rights and the Canadian Constitution.* Vancouver: UBC Press.

Babbie, Earl. 1994. *The Practice of Social Research.* 7th ed. Belmont, Calif. Wadsworth.

Barthes, Roland. 1975. *The Pleasure of the Text.* Translated by Richard Miller. New York: Hill and Wang.

Bauman, Richard. 1977. 'The Nature of Performance.' In *Verbal Art as Performance,* 7–14. Rowley, Mass.: Newbury House.

Begin, Patricia, Wendy Moss, and Peter Niemczak. 1992. *The Land Claim*

Dispute at Oka. Research Branch, Library of Parliament, Catalogue No.
  YM32–2/235–1992–10E. Ottawa: Minister of Supply and Services Canada.
Bennett, Lance, and Murray Edelman. 1985. 'Toward a New Political Narra-
  tive.' *Journal of Communication* 35: 156–71.
Berger, Peter L., and Thomas Luckmann. 1966. *The Social Construction of
  Reality.* Garden City, N.J.: Doubleday.
Berkowitz, Dan. 1997. 'Non-Routine News and Newswork: Exploring a What-
  a-Story.' In *Social Meanings of News,* edited by Dan Berkowitz, 362–75.
  Thousand Oaks, Calif.: Sage.
Biagi, Shirley. 2001. *Media Impact: An Introduction to Mass Media.* 5th ed.
  Toronto: Nelson/Thomson Learning.
Bird, S. Elizabeth, and Robert W. Dardenne. 1988. 'Myth, Chronicle and Story:
  Exploring the Narrative Qualities of News.' In *Media, Myths, and Narratives
  Television and the Press,* edited by James W. Carey, 67–86. Newbury Park,
  Calif.: Sage.
Blomley, Nicholas. 1996. '"Shut the Province Down": First Nations Blockades
  British Columbia, 1984–1995.' *B.C. Studies* 3: 5–35.
Breed, Warren. 1955. 'Social Control in the Newsroom.' *Social Forces* 33: 326–35.
Canadian Broadcasting Corporation. CBC Radio. 1995. 'The Cops, the Natives
  and the CBC.' *Now the Details,* 17 September.
– CBC Television. 1995. 'Standoff at Gustafsen Lake.' *The National,* 24 Sep-
  tember.
Chan, Janet B.L. 1997. *Changing Police Culture: Policing in a Multicultural
  Society.* Cambridge: Cambridge University Press.
Chomsky, Noam. 1989. *Necessary Illusions.* Boston: South End Press.
Christians, Clifford G., Kim B. Rotzoll, and Mark Fackler. 1991. *Media Ethics:
  Cases and Moral Reasoning.* 3d ed. 128–35. White Plains, N.Y.: Longman.
Coates, Ken. 1999. 'Being Aboriginal: The Cultural Politics of Identity, Mem-
  bership and Belonging among First Nations in Canada.' In *Aboriginal
  Peoples in Canada: Futures and Identities,* edited by Michael Behiels, Montreal:
  Association for Canadian Studies Association d'études canadiennes.
Cook, Timothy E. 1998. *Governing with the News: The News Media as a Political
  Institution.* Chicago: University of Chicago Press.
Croteau, David, and William Hoynes. 2000. *Media Society: Industries, Images,
  and Audiences.* 2d ed. Thousand Oaks, Calif.: Pine Forge Press.
Cryderman, Brian K., Chris N. O'Toole, and Augie Fleras. 1992. *Police, Race
  and Ethnicity: A Guide for Police Services.* 2d ed. Toronto: Butterworths.
Darnton, Robert. 1975. 'Writing News and Telling Stories.' *Daedalus* 104: 175–94.
Day, Louis Alvin. 2000. *Ethics in Media Communications: Cases and Controver-
  sies.* 3d ed. Scarborough, Ont.: Nelson / Thomson Learning.
Doyle, Aaron, Brian Elliot, and David Tindall. 1992. 'Framing the Forests:

Corporations, The B.C. Forest Alliance and the Media.' In *Organizing Dissent: Contemporary Social Movements in Theory and Practice*. 2d ed., edited by W. Carroll, 240–68. Toronto: Garamond Press.

Duranti, Alessandro. 1994. 'The Sociocultural Dimensions of Discourse.' In *Handbook of Discourse Analysis*. Vol I, edited by T. van Dijk, 193–230. London: Academic Press.

– 1994. *From Grammar to Politics: Linguistic Anthropology in a Western Samoan Village*. Berkeley: University of California Press.

Eagleton, Terry. 1996. *The Illusions of Postmodernism*. Oxford: Blackwell.

Fairclough, Norman. 1989. *Language and Power*. London: Longman.

Fallows, James. 1996. *Breaking the News: How the Media Undermine American Democracy*. New York: Pantheon Books.

Finlay, J.L., and D.N. Sprague. 1984. *The Structure of Canadian History*. 2d ed. Scarborough, Ont.: Prentice Hall.

Fisher, Robin. 1977. *Contact and Conflict: Indian-European Relations in British Columbia, 1874–1890*. Vancouver: University of British Columbia Press.

Foucault, Michel. 1972. *The Archeology of Knowledge*. Translated by A.M. Sheridan Smith. London: Tavistock.

– 1980. *Power-Knowledge: Selected Interviews and Other Writings, 1972–1977*, edited by Colin Gordon. Brighton: Harvester.

Fournier, Susanne, and Ernie Crey. 2000. 'We Can Heal: Aboriginal Children Today.' In *Visions of the Heart: Canadian Aboriginal Issues*. 2d ed., edited by David Long and Olive Patricia Dickason, 303–30. Toronto: Harcourt Brace Canada.

Freire, Paulo. 1993. *Pedagogy of the Oppressed*. 20th Anniversary Edition. New York: Plenum.

Frideres, James S. 1988. *Native Peoples in Canada: Contemporary Conflicts*. Scarborough, Ont. Prentice Hall.

Furniss, Elizabeth. 1995. 'Resistance, Coercion, and Revitalization: The Shuswap Encounter with Roman Catholic Missionaries.' *Ethnohistory* 42(2): 231–63.

– 1999. *The Burden of History: Colonialism and the Frontier Myth in a Rural Canadian Community*. Vancouver: UBC Press.

Gamson, William, and Andre Modigliani. 1989. 'Media Discourse and Public Opinion: A Constructionist Approach.' *American Journal of Sociology* 95(1): 1–37.

Gans, Herbert. 1979. *Deciding What's News: A Study of CBC Evening News, NBC Nightly News, Newsweek, and Time*. New York: Random House.

Garbarino, Merwyn S. 1977. *Sociocultural Theory in Anthropology*. Prospect Heights, Ill.: Waveland Press.

Geertz, Clifford. 1973. *The Interpretation of Cultures*. New York: Basic Books.

– 1988. *Works and Lives: The Anthropologist as Author*. Stanford, Calif.: Stanford University Press.

Ginsburg, F. 1991. 'Indigenous Media: Faustian Contract or Global Village?' *Cultural Anthropology* 6(1): 92–112.

Ginzberg, Effie. 1985. *Power without Responsibility: The Press We Don't Deserve – A Content Analysis of the Toronto Sun*. Toronto: Urban Alliance on Race Relations.

Gitlin, Todd. 1980. *The Whole World Is Watching: Mass Media in the Making and Unmaking of the New Left*. Berkeley: University of California Press.

Glavin, Terry. 1996. 'The Circus Comes to Gustafsen Lake.' In *This Ragged Place*, 108–120. Vancouver: New Star Books.

Goffman, Erving. 1959. *Presentation of Self in Everyday Life*. Garden City, N.J.: Doubleday.

– 1961. *Encounters*. Indianapolis, Ind.: Bobbs Merrill Company.

– 1970. *Strategic Interaction*. Oxford: Basil Blackwell.

– 1974. *Frame Analysis*. New York: Harper and Row.

Goody, Jack. 1987. *The Interface between the Written and the Oral: Studies in Literacy, Family, Culture and the State*. New York: Cambridge University Press.

Gramsci, Antonio. 1971. *Selections from the Prison Notebooks of Antonio Gramsci*. Edited and translated by Quintin Hoare and Geoffrey Nowell Smith. New York: International.

Grenier, Marc. 1994. 'Native Indians in the English-Canadian Press: The Case of the "Oka Crisis."' *Media, Culture and Society* 16: 313–36.

– ed. 1992. *Critical Studies of Canadian Mass Media*. Toronto: Butterworths.

Gumperz, John, and Dell Hymes. 1964. *The Ethnography of Communication*. Washington, D.C.: American Anthropological Association.

Hackett, Robert. 1991. *News and Dissent: The Press and the Politics of Peace in Canada*. Norwood, Ont.: Ablex.

Hackett, Robert, Richard Gruneau, et al. 2000. *The Missing News: Filters and Blind Spots in Canada's Press*. Aurora, Ont.: Canadian Centre for Policy Alternatives / Garamond Press.

Hackett, Robert, and Yuezhi Zhao. 1998. *Sustaining Democracy? Journalism and the Politics of Objectivity*. Toronto: Garamond Press.

Hall, Stuart, and John O'Hara. 1984. 'The Narrative Construction of Reality: An Interview with Stuart Hall.' *Southern Review* 17(1): 3–17.

Harris, Debbie Wise. 1991. 'Colonizing Mohawk Women: Representation of Women in the Mainstream Media.' *Resources for Feminist Research* 20(1–2): 15–20.

Harris, Marvin. 1968. *The Rise of Anthropological Theory*. New York: Harper Collins.

Harris, Robert. 1983. *Gotcha! The Media, the Government and the Falklands Crisis*. London: Faber and Faber.

Hartmann, Paul, and Charles Husband. 1971. 'The Mass Media and Racial Conflict.' *Race* 12: 267–82.

Henry, Frances. 1994. *The Caribbean Diaspora in Toronto: Learning to Live with Racism*. Toronto: University of Toronto Press.

Herman, Edward S., and Noam Chomsky. 1988. *Manufacturing Consent: The Political Economy of the Mass Media*. New York: Pantheon Books.

Hymes, Dell. 1974. *Foundations in Socioliguistics: An Ethnographic Approach*. Philadelphia: University of Pennsylvania Press.

– 1980. 'Functions in Speech.' In *Language in Education*, 1–18. Washington, D.C.: Center for Applied Linguistics.

– 1981. 'Breakthrough to Performance.' In *In Vain I Tried to Tell You: Essays in Native American Ethnopoetics*. 79–141. Philadelphia: University of Pennsylvania Press.

Jamieson, Kathleen Hall, and Karlyn Kohrs Campbell. 2001. *News, Advertising, Politics and the Mass Media: The Interplay of Influence*. 5th ed. Toronto: Nelson / Thomson Learning.

Jhappan, C. Radha. 1990. 'Indian Symbolic Politics: The Double-Edged Sword of Publicity.' *Canadian Ethnic Studies* 22(3): 19–39.

Jorgensen, Joseph G. 1972. *The Sun Dance Religion: Power for the Powerless*. Chicago: University of Chicago Press.

Kallen, Evelyn. 1995. *Ethnicity and Human Rights in Canada*. 2d ed. Toronto: Oxford University Press.

Kellner, Douglas. 1992. *The Persian Gulf TV War*. Boulder, Colo.: Westview Press.

– 1995. 'Reading the Gulf War: Production/Text/Reception.' In *Culture Studies, Identity and Politics Between the Modern and the Post Modern Media Culture*, 198– 228. London: Routledge.

Kleinig, John. 1996. *The Ethics of Policing*. Melbourne, Australia: Cambridge University Press.

Kline, Susan L., and Glenn Kuper. 1994. 'Self-presentation Practices in Government Discourse: The Case of US Lt. Col. Oliver North.' *Text* 14(1): 23–43.

Knight, Rolph. 1978. *Indians at Work: An Informal History of Native Indian Labour in British Columbia, 1858–1930*. Vancouver: New Star.

Kottak, Conrad Phillip. 1990. *Prime-Time Society: An Anthropological Analysis of Television and Culture*. Belmont, Calif.: Wadsworth.

– 1996. 'The Media, Development and Social Change.' In *Transforming Societies, Transforming Anthropology*, 135–163. Ann Arbor: University of Michigan Press.

Lambertus, Sandra. 2001. 'Redressing the Rebel Indian Stereotype: Anthropology and Media Policy.' *Practicing Anthropology* 23(2) 39–43.

– 2002. 'Anthropology and Media.' In *Cultural Anthropology*, edited by William Haviland, Gary Crawford, and Shirley Fedorak, 111–12. Toronto: Harcourt Brace Canada.

– 2003. 'News Discourse and Aboriginal Resistance in Canada.' In *Discourse and Silencing*, edited by Lynn Thiesmeyer, 233–72. Philadelphia: John Benjamins.

Langford, Tom, and J. Rick Ponting. 1992. 'Canadians' Responses to Aboriginal Issues: The Roles of Prejudice, Perceived Group Conflict and Economic Conservatism.' *Canadian Review of Sociology and Anthropology* 29 (May): 140–66.

Lett, James. 1987. 'An Anthropological View of Television Journalism.' *Human Organization* 46(4): 356–359.

Lévi-Strauss, Claude. 1955. 'The Structural Study of Myth.' *Journal of American Folklore* 68: 428–44.

– 1963. *Structural Anthropology*. New York: Basic Books.

– 1973. *Structural Anthropology 2*. Translated by Monique Layton. London: Penguin Books.

– 1978. *Myth and Meaning*. 1977 Massey Lecture. Toronto: University of Toronto Press.

Linde, Charlotte. 1993. *Life Stories: The Creation of Coherence*. New York: Oxford University Press.

Lippmann, Walter. 1922. *Public Opinion*. Reprint, New York: Macmillan, 1961.

Long, David. 1992. 'Culture, Ideology, and Militancy: The Movement of Native Indians in Canada, 1969–1991.' In *Organizing Dissent: Contemporary Social Movements in Theory and Practice*, edited by W. Carroll, 118–34. Victoria, B.C.: Garamond Press.

– 1997. 'The Precarious Pursuit of Justice: Counterhegemony in the Lubicon First Nation Coalition.' In *Organizing Dissent: Contemporary Social Movements in Theory and Practice*. 2d ed., edited by W. Carroll, 151–70. Toronto: Garamond Press.

Long, David, and Olive Patricia Dickason, eds. 2000. *Visions of the Heart: Canadian Aboriginal Issues*. 2d ed. Toronto: Harcourt Brace Canada.

Lorimer, Rowland, and Jean McNulty. 1996. *Mass Communication in Canada*. 3d ed. Toronto: Oxford University Press.

Lule, Jack. 1997. 'The Rape of Mike Tyson: Race, the Press, and Symbolic Types.' In *Social Meanings of News*, edited by Dan Berkowitz, 376–95. Thousand Oaks, Calif.: Sage.

Lull, James. 1991. *China Turned On: Television, Reform, and Resistance*. New York: Routledge.

Lyons, A.P. 1990. 'The Television and the Shrine: Towards a Theoretical Model of the Study of Mass Communication in Nigeria.' *Visual Anthropology* 3(4): 429–56.

Marcus, George E., and Michael M.J. Fischer. 1986. *Anthropology as Cultural Critique*. Chicago: University of Chicago Press.

Mascia-Lees, Frances E., Patricia Sharpe, and Colleen Ballerino Cohen. 1989. 'The Postmodernist Turn in Anthropology: Cautions from a Feminist Perspective.' *Signs: Journal of Women in Culture and Society* 15(1): 7–33.

Mazingo, Sherrie. 1988. 'Minorities and Social Control in the Newsroom: Thirty Years after Breed.' *Discourse and Discrimination*, edited by Geneva-Smitherman Donaldson and Teun A. van Dijk, 93–130. Detroit: Wayne State University Press.

McKenna, Paul F. 2000. *Foundations of Community Policing in Canada*. Scarborough, Ont.: Prentice Hall Allyn and Bacon Canada.

McLuhan, Marshall. 1968. *The Medium is the Message*. New York: Columbia Records.

Miller, John. 1998. *Yesterday's News: Why Canada's Daily Newspapers Are Failing Us*. Halifax, N.S.: Fernwood.

Morris, M., and P. Patton, eds. 1979. *Michel Foucault: Power, Truth, Strategy*. Sydney, Australia: Feral.

Morrison, R. Bruce, and C. Roderick Wilson, eds. 1995. *Native Peoples: The Canadian Experience*. 2d ed. Toronto: Oxford University Press.

Norris, Christopher. 1992. *Uncritical Theory: Postmodernism, Intellectuals and the Gulf War*. Amherst: University of Massachusetts Press.

Norris, Pippa. 1997. 'News of the World.' In *Politics and the Press: The News Media and Their Influences*, edited by Pippa Norris, 275–90. Boulder, Colo.: Lynne Rienner.

Ortner, Sherry. 1984. 'Theory in Anthropology since the Sixties.' *Comparative Studies in Society and History* 26(1): 126–66.

Palango, Paul. 1998. *The Last Guardians: The Crisis in the RCMP ... and in Canada*. Toronto: McClellend and Stewart.

Palmer, Andie Diane N. 1994. 'Maps of Experience: Shuswap Narratives of Place.' PhD diss., Washington State University.

Parenti, Michael. 1993. *Inventing Reality: The Politics of News Media*. New York: St Martin's Press.

Pickering, Michael. 1995. 'The Politics and Psychology of Stereotyping.' *Media, Culture and Society*. 17: 691–700.

Ponting, J. Rick. 1987. *Profiles of Public Opinion on Canadian Natives and Native*

Issues. Calgary: Research Unit for Public Policy Studies, Faculty of Social Sciences, University of Calgary.

– 1990. 'Internationalization: Perspectives on an Emerging Direction in Aboriginal Affairs.' *Canadian Ethnic Studies* 22(3): 85–109.

Roberts, Carl W., ed. 1997. *Text Analysis for the Social Sciences*. Mahwah, N.J.: Lawrence Erlbaum.

Robinson, Gertrude J. 1998. *Constructing the Quebec Referendum: French and English Media Voices*. Toronto: University of Toronto Press.

Romano, C. 1986. 'What? The Grisly Truth about Bare Facts.' In *Reading the News*, edited by R.K. Manoff and M. Schudson, 38–78. New York: Pantheon.

Rosaldo, Renato. 1989. *Culture and Truth: The Remaking of Social Analysis*. Boston: Beacon Press.

Royal Canadian Mounted Police. 1993, 1997, 1998, 1999, 2000, 2001. *RCMP Operational Manual II.16. Media/RCMP Relations*. Ottawa: RCMP Access to Information and Privacy Branch.

– 1993. *RCMP Operational Manual II.16 Media/RCMP Relations. 'E' Division (British Columbia)*. Ottawa: RCMP Access to Information and Privacy Branch.

– 1996. *Disclosure of Personal Information in the Public Interest. RCMP Protocol*. Ottawa: Access to Information and Privacy Branch.

– 1998. *RCMP and the Media: A Spokesperson's Guide*. Ottawa: RCMP Access to Information and Privacy Branch.

– 2000. 'Community, Contract and Aboriginal Policing Services,' *Aboriginal Policing Review Final Report*. Ottawa: RCMP Access to Information and Privacy Branch.

Royal Commission on Aboriginal Peoples. 1996. 'Arts and Heritage.' *Report of the Royal Commission on Aboriginal Peoples* 3(6): 621–47.

– 1996. 'Public Education: Building Awareness and Understanding.' *Report of the Royal Commission on Aboriginal Peoples* 5(4): 91–116.

Sahlins, Marshall. 1987. *Islands of History*. Chicago: University of Chicago Press.

Said, Edward. 1979. *Orientalism*. New York: Random House.

Salzmann, Zdenek. 1993. *Language, Culture and Society: An Introduction to Linguistic Anthropology*. Boulder, Colo.: Westview Press.

Sapir, Edward. 1921. *Language: An Introduction to the Study of Speech*. San Diego: Harcourt Brace.

Silverstone, Roger. 1988. 'Television, Myth and Culture.' In *Media, Myths, and Narratives: Television and the Press*, edited by James W. Carey, 20–47. Newbury Park, Calif.: Sage.

Sinclair, Gordon, Jr. 1999. *Cowboys and Indians: The Shooting of J.J. Harper*. Toronto: McClellend and Stewart.

Speck, Dara Culhane. 1987. *An Error in Judgement: The Politics of Medical Care in an Indian/White Community*. Vancouver: Talon.

Standing Committee on Aboriginal Affairs. 1991. *Fifth Report of the Standing Committee on Aboriginal Affairs*. chair, Ken Hughes, M.P. Ottawa: House of Commons, Issue No. 59.

Steltenkamp, Michael F. 1993. *Black Elk: Holy Man of the Oglala*. Norman: University of Oklahoma Press.

Stevenson, Nick. 1995. 'The Media and the Gulf War: Hegemony, the Audience and Simulation.' In *Understanding Media Cultures: Social Theory and Mass Communication*, 186–95. London: Sage.

Straubhaar, Joseph, and Robert LaRose. 2000. *Media Now: Communications in the Information Age*. 2d ed. Scarborough, Ont.: Nelson/Thomson Learning.

Stocking, George W., Jr. 1968. *Race, Culture and Evolution: Essays in the History of Anthropology*. New York: Collier-Macmillan.

Stubbs, Michael. 1983. *Discourse Analysis: The Sociolinguistic Analysis of Natural Language*. Oxford: Basil Blackwell.

Switlo, Janice G.A.E. 1997. *Gustafsen Lake: Under Seige*. Peachland, B.C.: TIAC Communications.

Tannen, Deborah, ed. 1993. *Framing in Discourse*. New York: Oxford University Press.

Task Force to Review Comprehensive Claims Policy. 1985. *Living Treaties: Lasting Agreements Report of the Task Force to Review Comprehensive Claims Policy*. Ottawa: Department of Indian Affairs and Northern Development.

Tedlock, Dennis. 1983. 'Ethnography as Interaction: The Storyteller, the Audience, the Fieldworker and the Machine.' In *The Spoken Word and the Work of Interpretation*, 285–301. Philadelphia: University of Pennsylvania Press.

Tennant, Paul. 1990. *Aboriginal Peoples and Politics*. Vancouver: UBC Press.

Thomson, Duncan Duane. 1985. 'A History of the Okanagan: Indians and Whites in the Settlement Era.' PhD diss., University of British Columbia.

Tuchman, Gay. 1978. *Making News: A Study in the Construction of Reality*. Beverly Hills, Calif.: Sage.

Ungar, Sanford J. 1990. 'The Role of a Free Press in Strengthening Democracy.' In *Democracy and the Mass Media*, edited by Judith Lichtenberg, 368–98. New York: Cambridge University Press.

Valverde, Mariana. 1991. 'As If Subjects Existed: Analyzing Social Discourses.' *Canadian Review of Sociology and Anthropology* 28(2): 173–87.

Vancouver East Community 4. 1997. 'Gustafsen Lake.' *Nitewatch*, produced by Patrice Leslie, January. Vancouver: Vancouver East Community 4.

van Dijk, Teun. A. 1987. 'How "They" Hit the Headlines: Ethnic Minorities in the Press.' In *Discourse and Discrimination*, edited by G. Smitherman-Donaldson and T.A. van Dijk, 221–62. Detroit: Wayne State University Press.

– 1988. *News Analysis: Case Studies of International and National News in the Press*. Hillsdale, N.J.: Lawrence Erlbaum.

– 1989. 'Critical News Analysis.' *Critical Studies* 1(1): 103–26.

Van Maanen, John. 1988. *Tales of the Field: On Writing Ethnography*. Chicago: University of Chicago Press.

van Velsen, J. 1964. 'Note on the Situational Analysis.' In *The Politics of Kinship*, 23–9. Manchester: Manchester University Press.

– 1967. 'The Extended-Case Method and Situational Analysis.' In *The Craft of Social Anthropology*, edited by L.L. Epstein 129–49. Suffolk, U.K.: Chaucer Press.

Weatherford, E. 1990. 'Native Visions: The Growth of Indigenous Media.' *Aperture* 119: 58–61.

Weaver, Sally M. 1981. *Making Canadian Indian Policy: The Hidden Agenda, 1968–1970*. Toronto: University of Toronto Press.

Webster, Mike. 1996. 'Influence in Crisis Management.' In *RCMP Gazette* 58:(2) 8–14.

– 1996. 'The Use of Force and the Gustafsen Lake Barricade.' In *RCMP Gazette* 58:(2) 16–19.

White Eye, Bud. 1996. 'Journalism and First Nations.' In *Deadlines and Diversity: Journalism Ethics in a Changing World*, edited by Valerie Alia, Brian Brennan, and Barry Hoffmaster, 92–7. Halifax: Fernwood.

Wilson, Clint. C., II, and Felix Gutierrez. 1985. *Diversity and the End of Mass Communication*. London: Sage.

Wilson, C. Roderick, and Carl Urion. 1995. 'First Nations Prehistory and Canadian History.' In *Native Peoples: The Canadian Experience*. 2d ed, 22–66. Toronto: Oxford University Press.

Wimmer, Roger D., and Joseph R. Dominick. 2000. *Mass Media Research: An Introduction*. 6th ed. Scarborough, Ont.: Nelson Canada.

Winter, James. 1997. *Democracy's Oxygen: How Corporations Control the News*. Montreal: Black Rose.

Wolf, Eric R. 1990. 'Distinguished Lecture: Facing Power – Old Insights, New Questions.' *American Anthropologist* 92: 586–96.

Yin, Robert K. 1994. *Case Study Research: Design and Methods*. 2d ed. London: Sage.

York, Geoffrey. 1989. *The Dispossessed: Life and Death in Native Canada*. London: Vintage Press.

Zelizer, Barbie. 1997. 'Journalists As Interpretive Communities.' In *Social Meanings of News*, edited by Dan Berkowitz, 401–19. Thousand Oaks, Calif.: Sage.

Zwicker, Barrie, and Dick MacDonald, eds. 1982. *News: Inside the Canadian Media*. Ottawa: Deneau.

Author Index

Topic Index